The Regulation of Executive Compensation

The Regulation of Executive Compensation

Greed, Accountability and Say on Pay

Kym Maree Sheehan

Barrister and Solicitor, Supreme Court of Victoria, Melbourne, Australia

Edward Elgar

Cheltenham, UK • Northampton, MA, USA

Published by
Edward Elgar Publishing Limited
The Lypiatts
15 Lansdown Road
Cheltenham
Glos GL50 2JA
UK

Edward Elgar Publishing, Inc.
William Pratt House
9 Dewey Court
Northampton
Massachusetts 01060
USA

A catalogue record for this book
is available from the British Library

Library of Congress Control Number: 2012939103

ISBN 978 0 85793 832 9

Typeset by Servis Filmsetting Ltd, Stockport, Cheshire
Printed and bound by MPG Books Group, UK

Contents

Figures

Tables

Abbreviations

AASB	Australian Accounting Standards Board
ABI	Association of British Insurers
ACSI	Australian Council of Superannuation Investors Inc
AGM	annual general meeting
AICD	Australian Institute of Company Directors
AIMA	Australian Investment Managers' Association
ALP	Australian Labor Party
APRA	Australian Prudential Regulatory Authority
ASB	Accounting Standards Board (UK)
ASIC	Australian Securities and Investments Commission
ASX	Australian Securities Exchange Ltd
ASX CG Council	Australian Securities Exchanges Corporate Governance Council
BERR	Department for Business Enterprise and Regulatory Reform (UK)
BIS	Department for Business Innovation and Skills (UK)
CAMAC	Corporations and Markets Advisory Committee
CASAC	Companies and Securities Advisory Committee
CEO	chief executive officer
CFO	chief financial officer
CGI	Corporate Governance International (proxy advisor, Australia)
CLERP	Corporate Law Economic Reform Program (Australia)
DTI	Department of Trade and Industry (UK)
EPS	earnings per share
FRC	Financial Reporting Council (UK)
FRS	Financial Reporting Statements (UK)
FSA	Financial Services Authority (UK)
FSC	Financial Services Council (Australia) – formerly IFSA
GFC	Global financial crisis of 2008–2009
GM	general manager
HR	human resources

ICAEW	Institute of Chartered Accountants of England and Wales
ICGN	International Corporate Governance Network
ICSA	Institute of Chartered Secretaries and Administrators (largely UK)
IFRS	International Financial Reporting Statements
IFSA	Investment and Financial Services Association (Australia)
IMA	Investment Management Association
ISC	Institutional Shareholders Committee
ISS	Institutional Shareholder Services
IVIS	Institutional Voting Information Service
KPI	key performance indicator
LSE	London Stock Exchange
LTI	long term incentive
LTIP	long term incentive plan
NAPF	National Association of Pension Funds
PIRC	Pensions Investment Research Consultancy (UK)
PRI	Principles of Responsible Investment
Remco	Remuneration Committee
RiskMetrics	RiskMetrics Group Inc
RREV	Research Recommendations and Electronic Voting Ltd
SEC	Securities and Exchange Commission (USA)
STI	short term incentive
Treasury	Department of Treasury (Australia)
TSR	total shareholder return
UNEP FI	United Nations Environment Programme Finance Initiative

Preface

Say on pay is the latest in a series of regulatory techniques introduced by governments to regulate executive remuneration. This book focuses on say on pay as introduced by the UK government in 2002 and by the Australian government in 2004: mandatory disclosure of remuneration in a 'remuneration report' plus a mandatory annual advisory shareholder vote on that report. To say the vote is only advisory in status is important: the shareholders in general meetings are not making a decision that binds the company to action. This book is based on eight years of researching and thinking on these issues.

As my primary interest is government policy and law reform, I examine the claims made about say on pay: what policy goals are behind its introduction and why it is a better solution than the traditional response of mandatory disclosures. Chapter 1 presents a potted history of these policy debates around four recurring themes: curbing executive greed; improving board accountability for executive remuneration; increasing the level of engagement or dialogue between shareholders and company boards on executive remuneration; and ensuring pay is aligned with performance. Anyone familiar with the debates in 2011–12 in both the UK and Australia would immediately see that these issues still lie at the heart of policy debates on regulating executive remuneration.

To analyse say on pay, I draw upon some concepts from regulatory theory to devise a map of the regulatory space within which say on pay happens. I call this space the regulated remuneration cycle (chapter 2). I then use empirical evidence from the first three years of its operation in the UK and Australia to critically analyse the operation of say on pay in practice. In chapters 3 to 8, I draw extensively upon interview evidence to look behind the rhetoric of say on pay and government policy goals to the reality of making decisions about the 'pay' and the 'say'. My methodology for selecting participants and the interview formats are outlined in the methodology appendix at the end of the book. I am grateful to all the participants in these interviews for their insights, candour and humour.

The regulated remuneration cycle can be deployed to analyse the system of rules surrounding executive remuneration in other jurisdictions and how a 'say on pay' (particularly an advisory-only vote) might be supported or challenged by other rules and practices with the cycle. It may indicate some more extensive reform of existing executive remuneration laws is required before introducing a say on pay.

At times in the book, I refer to the guidance as it stood during the period I studied the practices (the first three years of operation of say on pay in each jurisdiction), while at other times I use the current guidance. I also do not refer to any of the EU initiatives specifically for the UK, as I take the local adoption of these as the pertinent 'rule' for my analysis.

Acknowledgements

I would like to thank my colleagues, Professor Geof Stapledon, Dr Chander Shekhar and Professor Christine Parker for their support over the course of this study.

I would also like to thank my friends who sustained me on this journey, in particular, Alasdair Murrie-West, Isabel Parsons, John Roberts, Joellen Riley, Susan Shearing, Dominique Allen and Carrie McDougall. I also acknowledge the warm support from colleagues at the Melbourne Law School and the Sydney Law School.

Finally, a thank you to my family for their unfailing support and encouragement: Beverley and Kevin, Terry, Allison, Tristan, Brendan and Kieran Sheehan.

1. Greed, accountability and say on pay

Regulations introduced by the UK government in 2002[1] and legislation introduced by the Australian government in 2004[2] aimed to improve board accountability for executive remuneration practices within listed companies, in an effort to curb excessive remuneration payments. Both jurisdictions adopted the same regulatory solution: a mandatory *remuneration report* within the annual report and a mandatory annual *advisory vote* at the annual general meeting (AGM) of the company to 'adopt' the report.[3] The initiatives of 2002 and 2004 did not occur in a vacuum, but were a natural progression from earlier attempts to address the same challenges. These new legislative initiatives were promulgated into a 'regulatory space'[4] that was already rich with attempts to influence executive remuneration accountability and practice. They would only 'work' to the extent that they mobilised and held accountable the existing players in that space to change remuneration practices: institutional shareholders, remuneration consultants, boards of directors of listed (quoted) companies and their remuneration committees. In making laws on executive remuneration, governments in liberal economies such as the UK and Australia walk a policy tightrope: whether to allow company boards to exercise their powers of management free from government constraint, or to choose to regulate this conduct to address the general public's concern with executive greed.

Evidence of this policy tightrope is found in government reform approaches since the early 1990s. The Modern Company Law Review (UK) found a need to strengthen the best practice framework for executive remuneration developed from the Cadbury,[5] Greenbury[6] and Hampel[7] reports. The spirit of Greenbury, of a *de minimis* framework of listing rules and best practice, was designed to give companies flexibility to adopt and adapt practices to suit the company's specific circumstances. The government was content to support this 'spirit' provided best practice was seen to be working.[8] It became increasingly frustrated with the prominent attention given to the quantum of directors' remuneration in the press, not to mention the failure of some companies to adopt the *Combined Code*'s guidance.[9] A 1999 report for the Department of Trade and Industry (DTI) recommended new rules to ensure remuneration committees explained their remuneration policies and made full disclosure of all elements of individual directors' remuneration:[10] a departure from Cadbury's approach of limited named disclosure for the chairman and highest paid UK director only.[11] Legislation to underpin best practice guidance was necessary to achieve what best practice guidance alone could not – 'increased transparency, strengthened accountability and more effective linkage between pay and performance and the competitiveness benefits this brings'.[12] The UK government was not willing to dismantle the largely principles-based framework for regulating remuneration practice even though there was evidence to suggest companies were non-compliant.

Of these initiatives, it is the Greenbury Committee that considered the factors and techniques necessary to regulate executive remuneration. The two important factors that combined to regulate executive remuneration were board responsibility (the membership and tasks of the remuneration committee) and shareholder monitoring; with two regulatory techniques needed: disclosure, to improve the transparency of remuneration practices (the obligations to disclose all elements of remuneration) and, secondly, giving shareholders voting rights for remuneration decisions. It considered, and rejected, a vote on the committee's report on remuneration as a standard AGM item of business. Instead the committee endorsed shareholder approval of policy when circumstances warranted that approval should be sought.[13] This vote was only in relation to remuneration policy, not the policy and outcomes now disclosed in the directors' remuneration report. A shareholder vote to approve all share-based incentive plans (irrespective of whether new shares were issued or not) was recommended,[14] with the London Stock Exchange (LSE) amending its listing rules to this effect from 1 July 1996.

Many of the same elements seen in the current regulation of executive remuneration in the UK existed from 1996: best practice guidance in a code, listing rules that mandated disclosure of compliance with that code and shareholder guidance on share plans all contributed to a regulatory framework within which remuneration practices happened, but within which authority for ensuring the rules were followed by companies was shared. Greenbury recognised that the plethora of rules, especially multiple sources of shareholder guidance with incompatible positions on the best remuneration practices,[15] created difficulties for companies.

Australia too considered how to improve executive remuneration practices in a series of corporate governance initiatives in the 1990s. Yet successive federal governments were tentative in using their legislative powers to improve remuneration disclosure. Up until the 1998 reforms, the Corporations Law only required banded disclosure of income received by the directors in excess of $100,000 for the financial period in the notes to the accounts;[16] although it was possible to link remuneration levels with particular directors by a series of guesstimates.[17] Consideration of these provisions by the Parliamentary Joint Committee on Corporations and Securities in 1996 and 1998 led to new mandatory disclosure of remuneration for each director and each of five 'named officers'.[18] Within three weeks of the bill passing in both houses, the provisions were referred to the Parliamentary Joint Committee on Corporations and Financial Services for review.[19]

While Australia has demonstrated a willingness to adopt what it perceives as international best practice,[20] the policy goals underpinning legislative initiatives respond to local frustrations and pressures. The change of government position from 2002 (no need for reform of executive remuneration disclosure rules)[21] to 2003 (remuneration disclosure needed urgent reform) cannot be solely explained by the findings of the HIH Royal Commission in 2003, although the findings were significant. Justice Owen noted several failures in corporate governance at HIH, including capture of the human resources (HR) committee by the chief executive;[22] and questionable remuneration practices including the absence of criteria to award bonus payments, retrospective salary adjustments,[23] plus sizeable golden hellos (sign-on bonuses) and termination payments.[24] His recommendations surrounding remuneration practices[25] prompted the formation of the ASX Corporate Governance Council and the release of the principles of corporate governance and best practice.[26]

Another corporate insolvency drew a quicker legislative response from the government, as it responded to the outrage created by the payments of million dollar bonuses to the directors of One.Tel Limited just prior to the company's insolvency.[27] The additional factor prompting a coalition government to act was the political pressure exerted by the opposition parties – the Australian Labor Party, assisted by the Australian Democrats and the Greens – which generated the moral pressure for a change to remuneration norms. The stated objectives of the reform to introduce say on pay (the Corporate Law Economic Reform Program No. 9 – or CLERP 9 as it is known) were to promote transparency, accountability and shareholder activism,[28] with the remuneration report and advisory vote 'designed to enhance transparency and accountability in relation to decisions surrounding director and executive remuneration'.[29] Achieving the framework principles of remunerating responsibly and fairly[30] through these legislative measures[31] requires shareholders to have sufficient information to monitor company remuneration and engage with remuneration committees to translate this broad principle into appropriate, company-specific practices.

The events that trigger public outrage and the policy goals behind government responses leading to the introduction of say on pay in the UK and Australia illustrate how challenging it is for governments to achieve the correct tension on the policy tightrope. The event triggering public angst is media reporting of executive greed. What is not so clear is how further transparency through disclosures in a remuneration report and an advisory vote on that report reduce executive greed and hence public outrage.

1.1   CURBING EXECUTIVE GREED

Greed: it's one of the seven deadly sins. And one of the most cited reasons by governments to justify meddling in company affairs by regulating executive remuneration. The political rhetoric of the global financial crisis (GFC) elevated this sin from the kind of garden-variety greed that you or I might indulge in occasionally to Extreme Greed, [32] practised by bankers in an unrestrained manner. Yet many inquiries and academics seemed to excuse such behaviour by focusing on the structure of the financial institution incentive schemes[33] rather than blaming the individuals who, being 'rational economic actors', adjusted their behaviour to maximise their returns.

The wrong performance incentives can create significant problems, as the findings of Lord Turner in 2009 on the causes of the global financial crisis as they relate to banks and bank-like institutions note:

> It is nevertheless likely that past remuneration policies, acting in combination with capital requirements and accounting rules, have created incentives for some executives and traders to take excessive risks and have resulted in large payments in reward for activities which seemed profit making at the time but subsequently proved harmful to the institution and in some cases, the entire system.[34]

Politicians were more critical of the individuals but blamed non-executive directors on remuneration committees, 'all too willing to sanction the ratcheting up of remuneration levels for senior managers whilst setting relatively undemanding performance targets'.[35]

This contemporary rhetoric of executive greed did not begin with the global financial crisis. Part of the recent moral panic surrounding executive remuneration in the UK can be traced to the 1990s when high amounts of remuneration were paid despite poor company or individual executive performance. The archetypal 'fat cat' in the early 1990s was Cedric Brown, CEO of the newly privatised British Gas, who received a substantial pay rise in 1994, just one year after privatisation had occurred.[36] Large scale job losses that marked his period in management fuelled public ire at the increases.[37] He was not alone: payments made to executives in other privatised utilities were also flagged by Sir Richard Greenbury as problematic.[38] However, fat cats were to be found in other listed companies: Tim Holley as CEO of Camelot plc[39] and the directors of Glaxo Wellcome plc[40] were among other directors whose pay was seen to be excessive. The Labour Party's platform for the 1 May 1997 general election in the UK included a policy against fat cats,[41] although the government did nothing concrete towards implementing this policy once elected to office. It is therefore unsurprising to read contemporary newspaper reports noting some company boards continued to reward senior executives with excessive remuneration.[42] Share options started to appreciate in value because of market sentiment surrounding the shares, rather than any evidence of improved performance.[43]

Around the time of the DTI's policy pronouncements in the new millennium, the size of remuneration payments was still attracting media attention.[44] The second consultative document released in 2001 noted that the regulations would 'underpin a framework in which there is more effective *dialogue* between companies and investors'.[45] Thus the new disclosure and voting requirements were directed at improving shareholders' capacity to engage in meaningful micro-level 'regulatory conversations'[46] with remuneration committees. It seems the government expected shareholders to address the issue of fat cats or excessive remuneration quantum as part of this regulatory conversation. In the first year of the new regime shareholders appeared willing to do so[47] by targeting companies with contracts that would pay out over two years' base salary and bonus (the performance conditions being effectively waived), supported by the DTI's 'Rewards for failure' inquiry.[48]

The Australian version of this policy goal is found in two distinct policy goals. As noted above, the CLERP 9 reforms adopted the principle espoused by the ASX Corporate Governance Council: remunerate responsibly and fairly. Remunerating responsibly and remunerating fairly are two separate principles that take issue with the quantum of remuneration. As high level principles, however, they provide little concrete guidance to remuneration committees or investors on absolute levels of pay. Instead they focus on relativities and cost–benefit analyses. Responsible remuneration can be determined by assessing the costs and benefits of the remuneration, 'the sensitivities of significant payments to key executives',[49] and the structure of remuneration payments and termination payments. Responsible remuneration balances fixed and incentive pay and does not focus too much on short term performance; while termination

payments are to be agreed in advance with 'a clear articulation of performance expectations'.[50]

A principle of remunerating fairly begs the question: to whom should
the remuneration be fair? Should this be fair to the executive, fair to the
company or fair to the shareholders? By what criterion should fairness
be assessed? Is 'fair' an absolute or a relative term? If it is a relative term,
how should such relativities be assessed: by reference to externalities (the
labour market for similar senior executives), intra-firm (the rate of senior
executive remuneration relative to the level of wages and salaries paid
to the ordinary rank and file employees),[51] or both?[52] Is this criterion of
fairness referenced to company performance rather than other remuneration, so that pay for performance should be construed not only in terms
of a linkage but a *fair* link? In other words, give a fair year's pay for a fair
year's performance?

High levels of remuneration can readily satisfy the need to be 'responsible' if the benefit to the company is that a skilled senior executive stays
(retention payment) or that the company can hire the best executive
talent in a tight labour market (golden hello). Paying a higher bonus
in a year with a higher profit than the previous year would probably
satisfy the need for fairness. Thus as norms of remuneration practice
remunerating responsibly and fairly appear to be management friendly,
or at least so vaguely worded as to be capable of multiple meanings and
interpretations.

A further policy goal noted in the CLERP 9 documentation was that
there should be no excess payments. This policy goal is linked with the
principle of 'remunerate fairly' – in other words, there is an upper bound
on remuneration that should be attached to particular company and
executive performance outcomes.[53] Australian courts have traditionally
been reluctant to define 'excessive' remuneration.[54] In part, this reluctance
reflects the view that the courts take in relation to breaches of the director's duty of care: namely that courts should not try to 'second-guess' the
directors' decisions, nor should there be an appeal on the merits of directors' decisions to the courts.[55] In a similar vein, it has been noted that the
court's duty is not to punish 'unsuccessful entrepreneurial activity'.[56] The
courts are more likely to focus on the decision-making process in terms of
whether the directors have exercised the requisite standard of care rather
than whether they made the *right* decision or whether they should have
reached a different decision.[57]

Definitions of 'reasonable' remuneration appear similarly imprecise,
although the payments which can be labelled 'reasonable' seem generous.[58] The definition of 'reasonable remuneration' in respect of related
party transactions under Chapter 2E of the *Corporations Act 2001* (Cth)

requires an assessment of reasonableness of the quantum of remuneration by reference not only to the circumstances of the public company but also to the circumstances of the related party recipient (including the responsibilities involved in the office or employment).[59] Reasonable remuneration is therefore context specific by company and by the individual manager. If the boundary between reasonable and excessive remuneration cannot be defined with precision because it is context specific, a policy goal of curbing excess remuneration is difficult to satisfy system-wide because it can only be assessed at the level of the individual executive within the individual firm.

While there have been many instances of remuneration excesses over the last ten years to which politicians have responded, passing many new laws on executive remuneration, none of the rules go so far as to say in effect, 'Don't pay $x to your executives: that's too much money.' Is this pragmatic law making? Or does it reflect the influence of companies over the form and content of these laws? As Julia Black notes, 'Rules are bargained over and they are built.'[60]

1.2   IMPROVING ACCOUNTABILITY FOR EXECUTIVE REMUNERATION DECISIONS

Improving director accountability is the other most cited reason for regulating executive remuneration, with a focus on the role of the remuneration committee. Various reform committees convened during the 1990s in the UK emphasised board accountability for executive director remuneration.[61] Through a combination of high level principles on the overall aims of executive remuneration, together with more detailed guidance on the aims and tasks of the remuneration committee and guidance on the terms of executive service contracts, the Cadbury Committee initially,[62] and subsequently the Greenbury Committee[63] and the Hampel Committee,[64] all sought to improve board policy- and decision-making processes. Alongside these industry-led initiatives, the two major shareholder representative bodies in the UK, the Association of British Insurers (ABI) and the National Association of Pension Funds (NAPF), released guidelines on best practice executive remuneration, having done so since the 1960s.[65] Yet collectively these self-regulatory and shareholder initiatives ultimately failed to achieve the better remuneration practices in listed companies that they described, prompting the UK government to impose a legislative solution to address these failures.[66]

Australian attempts in the early 1990s to improve board accountability for remuneration practices also focused on remuneration committees.[67] The ASX consulted on corporate governance practices endorsed by the Working Group on Corporate Practices and Conduct, chaired by Henry Bosch (the Bosch Committee) in 1994, some two to three years after their introduction. Concerned at the poor response by companies to the Bosch Committee's guidelines,[68] the ASX promulgated a new listing rule requiring companies to report on a list of corporate governance practices, including remuneration.[69] One year later, the ASX claimed that listed companies had 'broadly adopted' the board committee structures endorsed in the listing rules. This was soon contradicted by widely reported empirical evidence.[70]

Institutional shareholders were also active in releasing relevant guidance, with the Australian Investment Managers' Association (AIMA) releasing guidance on remuneration committees, the aims of remuneration policy and disclosure in 1995.[71] Soon after, the AIMA and the Australian Institute of Company Directors (AICD) produced a set of guidelines for executive share option schemes; albeit with the disclaimer that the existence of the guidelines was not to be taken as a representation that members of either organisation 'are bound to act in accordance with it'.[72] This need to rule-make was to fill a void in the regulatory framework that mandatory remuneration disclosures simply did not address. Despite the efforts of the Bosch Working Group, AIMA and even the AICD, self-regulatory initiatives were unable to deliver better remuneration practices. The government interpreted evidence of poor practices as an absence of proper accountability by boards of directors, justifying the government acting to do so via legislative means.

1.3   INCREASING THE LEVEL OF SHAREHOLDER ENGAGEMENT

The particular resolution in both jurisdictions is to 'adopt' the remuneration report, not to approve particular remuneration policies or practices, or the remuneration decisions made in light of these policies. A substantial vote against the remuneration report does not reveal any clear area of concern by shareholders. As with accountability, more engagement was seen as an end in and of itself. Both governments were for most of the first decade of the new millennium content to allow the funds management, superannuation and pension industries to self-regulate on the issue of engagement and voting. Listed companies are clearly not the only parties bargaining keenly with governments over the rules that should govern their activities.

1.3.1 UK Debate on Shareholder Engagement

Shareholder engagement was the focus of a separate line of inquiry begun in 1995 with the release of *Developing a Winning Partnership*[73] and the Myners Review of Institutional Investment over the period 1999 to 2001.[74] Although occupational pension funds are the predominant institutional investors in the UK,[75] most engagement is undertaken by their external fund managers. Myners noted that fund managers were generally reluctant to actively engage with underperforming investee companies.[76] He thought they should take an active role in engagement: if fund managers justified receiving high fees because of their skill in reviewing company strategy and operations as part of the investment decision, Myners believed they were also capable of making judgments about whether to intervene in these matters and how best to do so.[77] Furthermore, he found no evidence that the prohibitions on parties acting in concert in the *Takeover Code*[78] had ever been invoked during the course of an intervention to prevent fund managers combining their efforts to collectively engage with company management.[79] Thus a small individual shareholding was not a reason not to engage: it was a reason to collaborate with other institutional investors to do so.

Other factors explain this apathy: if the key performance indicator for clients is the last quarter's performance figures, the basis for selecting fund managers and their fee structures offers little incentive to intervene in companies to make changes on a longer time scale.[80] With a culture that seeks to avoid conflict,[81] and numerous real potential conflicts of interest,[82] many fund managers chose not to pursue active engagement and intervention policies.[83] They could, but there was no obvious financial gain from doing so. Myners believed that engaging with investee companies is to further the client's best interests, not to fulfil a public interest obligation.[84] This means that a regulatory design that relies on shareholders to fulfil public interest obligations such as curbing executive greed depends upon fund managers agreeing that this would further their clients' interests. While Myners did not see the overriding requirement to act in the client's best interests as curtailing engagement, it is arguably a real constraint upon any role institutional investors can play within the regulated remuneration cycle to achieve policy goals that are not linked with the financial performance of the investment. If engagement with a company could potentially culminate in a decline in that company's share price (because the engagement becomes public and undermines market confidence, or else executive dissatisfaction results in poor performance), institutional investors will choose either not to engage or may sell their shares instead.[85]

Separately, a further barrier to institutional investor voting was said to be the problems with the mechanics needed to vote by proxy.[86] *The Modern Company Law for a Competitive Economy* initiative was well aware of the issues surrounding vote execution, especially where beneficial owners could not exercise voting rights.[87] A behavioural shift by institutional investors to embracing voting as a fiduciary responsibility was needed and noted at the time.[88] The main focus, however, of the various voting inquiries beginning with the Newbold Inquiry and continuing with the reviews commissioned by the Shareholders' Working Group was on the complex chain of voting instructions between the beneficial owner and the fund manager. This chain evidently worked efficiently when corporate decisions relating to the investment were made, such as the decision to take up entitlements in a rights issue.[89] Clearly some other measure was needed to encourage institutional investors to exercise their voting rights.

The perceived need to strengthen shareholder engagement was due to the failure of the regulatory framework to deliver remuneration that matched Greenbury's fundamental principles of accountability, transparency and a clear link between pay received and performance.[90] Shareholders were to play an important role in putting into practice the government's proposed reforms on transparency and shareholder powers of control.[91] Yet the government, fully aware of a number of shortcomings with shareholders' records on engagement and voting, was persuaded to maintain the self-regulatory nature of these crucial activities.

1.3.2   Australian Debates on Shareholder Engagement

CLERP 9 reforms adopting such a non-binding advisory resolution on pay reflect an expectation that shareholders want to become involved in remuneration issues and more shareholder involvement will improve the accountability of directors.[92] Parliament contemplated the role of institutional shareholders in company affairs as part of the 1998 reforms to remuneration disclosure noted above, in the process rejecting a move to introduce compulsory voting by institutional investors.[93] The Companies and Securities Advisory Committee, CASAC, inquiring into shareholder participation one year later considered, but rejected, non-binding advisory resolutions on company management as blurring the 'fundamental' distinction between the roles of the board of directors in company management and that of shareholders.[94]

Weighing against the prospects of improving director accountability via engagement were the historically low levels of proxy voting in Australia. A study based on proxy-voting levels in a sample of 59 major Australian listed companies in the year 1999, including 40 widely held companies,[95] reported that proxy instructions represented an average 35 per cent of total voting capital.[96] The authors noted that this compared less favourably with the UK (50 per cent for a sample from the FTSE 350 in 1999)[97] and the USA (around 80 per cent).[98] Data presented to the Parliamentary Joint Committee on Corporations and Financial Services reported that the level of proxy voting among 161 widely held ASX companies in 2003 was 44 per cent of all equity with voting rights.[99] However, a 2003 study of shareholder activism by the Investment and Financial Services Association (IFSA) showed that 91 per cent of the fund managers surveyed reported they were routine voters, who voted on at least 90 per cent of all resolutions put forward by investee companies.[100]

If fund managers were largely complying with their voting obligations as this latter evidence suggests, the presence of large numbers of retail and foreign shareholders on the share register might explain the low voting rates reported in the first mentioned study. Mandating institutional investor voting was debated in Australia as part of the reforms to the company legislation in 2004 without any changes being made to mandate either voting, disclosure of voting policy or disclosure of voting practice.[101]

1.4 WHY SAY ON PAY APPEARS AN IDEAL ANSWER

Say on pay as introduced in 2002 in the UK and 2004 in Australia achieves the right tension on the policy tightrope: it satisfies the need for governments to be seen to be acting to address executive greed and poor remuneration practices, while respecting the integrity of the board of directors' decision-making processes: the mandatory annual vote by shareholders is only advisory. Indeed mandated disclosure and advisory votes strengthened the measures taken by institutional investors and market exchange operators to address executive remuneration in the 1990s, rather than presenting a radical departure from such approaches. Corporate governance codes in the 1990s emphasised the role of the remuneration committee, while offering some high level principles for remuneration practices. Institutional shareholder guidance supplemented these codes by describing in detail best practice remuneration. That new regulatory tools in the form of a mandatory remuneration report and advisory vote were deployed in 2002 and 2004 indicate that these earlier strategies, which were supposed to facilitate the principals' exercise of control over their agents, were not sufficient to ensure 'good' remuneration practices. What role would these earlier strategies and regulatory actors play with the introduction of say on pay?

The stated rationale for legislative intervention in both jurisdictions was to improve board accountability for remuneration practices. Shareholders could diligently monitor remuneration practices if governments mandated particular remuneration disclosures that made both the remuneration policy and payments transparent. Shareholders could then engage with those remuneration committees making bad remuneration decisions, voting against the remuneration report to send an unequivocal signal when private engagement failed to secure a commitment to change practices. Governments further expected that these legislative measures would make the pay for performance alignment stronger and that there would be no further remuneration excesses or examples of irresponsible remuneration payments (such as termination payments that rewarded failure). *Thus the underlying rationale for government intervention is better executive remuneration practices in listed companies.* Remuneration payments that are clearly aligned with performance would confirm this policy goal had been achieved. High levels of remuneration were acceptable provided performance warranted that level of payment.

With its 'feedback loop' of the advisory vote, say on pay improves upon previous disclosure-only initiatives: any lack of credibility in the remuneration and performance disclosed provides the occasion for shareholder engagement in the period leading up to the AGM. Creating the conditions for shareholder action is an important aim of these reforms, but relies on shareholders responding to the opportunities created. The advisory vote preserves the sanctity of the board of directors within listed companies. It also fits with institutional shareholder reluctance to undertake actions that may negatively impact on their investment: the legislation clearly states that the outcome of the vote does not affect the remuneration of any director.[102] Rather than strengthening shareholder engagement (and thus the practices that listed companies adopt), the advisory vote could undermine these policy goals if institutional investors treat engagement and voting as alternatives in practice, and prefer voting on an advisory vote to engagement and voting.

The advisory vote might also make no difference to practices – the ultimate outcome that say on pay seeks to achieve – if shareholders' tolerance for ever increasing levels of executive remuneration in investee companies is high, or if their resolve to tackle poor practices wanes in the glare of strong corporate performances, a bull market and high dividend yields.

NOTES

1. *Directors' Remuneration Report Regulations 2002* (UK) SI 2002/1986.
2. *Corporate Law Economic Reform Program (Audit Reform and Corporate Disclosure)*

Act 2004 (Cth), schedule 5, item 14 (disclosure) and schedule 5, item 7 (advisory vote).

3. In this way, the advisory vote differs from shareholder proposals studied in Ertimur, Ferri and Muslu 2010; Renneboog and Szilagyi 2011; Cziraki, Renneboog and Szilagyi 2010; Ertimur, Ferri and Stubben 2010. See Cheffins and Thomas 2001 for a preliminary discussion on these differences.
4. Scott 2001, p. 329.
5. Committee on the Financial Aspects of Corporate Governance 1992a and 1992b.
6. Study Group on Directors' Remuneration 1995.
7. Committee on Corporate Governance 1998.
8. Department of Trade and Industry 1998 [3.7].
9. Department of Trade and Industry 2001a, pp. 4, 13.
10. PricewaterhouseCoopers and the Department of Trade and Industry 1999, para. [ii].
11. Committee on the Financial Aspects of Corporate Governance 1992b, p. 7.
12. Department of Trade and Industry 2001b, para. [11].
13. Study Group on Directors' Remuneration 1995, pp. 15, 32.
14. Study Group on Directors' Remuneration 1995, pp. 16, 42. The previous listing rules only required shareholder approval if the share plan involved the issue of new shares.
15. Study Group on Directors' Remuneration 1995, p. 42.
16. *Corporations Regulations 1990* (Cth), schedule 5, cl 25(2).
17. Defina, Harris and Ramsay 1994, p. 349.
18. *Company Law Review Act 1998* (Cth) amended s 300 and inserted s 300A into the *Corporations Law*.
19. Joint Committee on Corporations and Securities 1999, pp. 1–3; Hudson and Shield 1998; Henderson 1998.
20. Joint Committee on Corporations and Financial Services 2004, p. 86.
21. Department of Treasury, Commonwealth of Australia 2002.
22. Owen 2003, pp. 282–3.
23. Owen 2003, pp. 283–96.
24. Owen 2003, pp. 301–8.
25. Owen 2003, p. lxv.
26. ASX Corporate Governance Council 2003.
27. *Corporations Amendment (Repayment of Directors' Bonuses) Act 2003* (Cth) inserted a new voidable transaction into the insolvency provisions in the *Corporations Act 2001* (Cth). These provisions allow a liquidator to apply to the court to declare void a director-related transaction entered into within four years of the day on which the winding up of the company commenced.
28. Joint Committee on Corporations and Financial Services 2004.
29. Corporations Law Economic Reform Program (Audit Reform and Corporate Disclosure) Bill 2003 (Cth), Explanatory Memorandum, p. 166.
30. ASX Corporate Governance Council 2003, p. 51.
31. Joint Committee on Corporations and Financial Services 2004, p. 33.
32. Rudd 2008.
33. Congressional Oversight Panel 2009, pp. 38–9; Institute of International Finance 2009, pp. 1–2; Organisation for Economic Cooperation and Development 2009b, pp. 16–18; Financial Services Authority 2009, pp. 79–80; Braithwaite 2009, p. 444; Crotty 2009, p. 565; Ciro and Longo 2010, pp. 16–17; Bebchuk and Spamman 2010, pp. 255–68; Committee on Oversight and Government Reform 2008, pp. 74–7.
34. Financial Services Authority 2009, p. 80.
35. Treasury Committee, House of Commons 2009, p. 3.
36. Nelson, Calvert and Woolf 1995; Dickson 1995.
37. Sweeney 1995.
38. Study Group on Directors' Remuneration 1995, pp. 9, 49–52; Department of Trade and Industry 2000a, p. 61; Lewis 1996; Cragg and Dyck 2003, pp. 187–91.
39. Cassell 1996; Chancellor 1997.

40. Donovan and Whitebloom 1997.
41. Unknown 1996; Barnett 1997; Labour Party 1996.
42. Unknown 1997a; Elliott 1998.
43. Laurance 1997; Barnett 1998; Parker 1998; Jackson 1998a, 1998b.
44. Most notable of these was Sir Christopher Gent as CEO of Vodafone plc who received a £10 million transaction bonus on the acquisition of Mannesmann AG: Dickson 2000.
45. Department of Trade and Industry 2001a, p. 13.
46. Black 2002.
47. Sheehan 2007.
48. Department of Trade and Industry 2003.
49. Department of Trade and Industry 2003, p. 53.
50. Department of Trade and Industry 2003, pp. 55–6.
51. Shields, O'Donnell and O'Brien 2003, pp 1–2.
52. ASX Corporate Governance Council 2003, p. 55. Fixed remuneration is recommended to be set at a level that is 'reasonable and fair, taking into account the company's legal and industrial obligations and labour market conditions, and should be relative to the scale of the business. . . [reflecting] core performance requirements and expectations'.
53. Joint Committee on Corporations and Financial Services 2004, p. 42.
54. Hill 1996, p. 233; Hill 2006, pp. 71–4.
55. *Harlowe's Nominees Pty Ltd v Woodside (Lakes Entrance) Oil Co NL* (1968) 121 CLR 483 at p. 493; *Howard Smith Ltd v Ampol Petroleum Ltd* [1974] AC 821 at p. 823. The authors of *Ford's Principles of Corporations Law* note that this principle is subject to statutory provisions that permit the court to review directors' decisions on the merits: Austin and Ramsay 2010, pp. 377–8.
56. *Australian Securities and Investments Commission v Rich* (2009) 75 ACSR 1 at pp. 611–12. For an example of a completion bonus payment to the director approved by that director in breach of his duties as a director, see *Diakyne Pty Ltd (ACN 099 168 402) v Ralph and Another* (2009) 72 ACSR 450 at pp. 467–79 (upheld on appeal: *Ralph v Diakyne Pty Ltd (ACN 099 168 402)* [2010] FCAFC 18, at [27]–[32]).
57. *Australian Securities and Investments Commission v Rich* (2009) 75 ACSR 1 at p. 623.
58. Defina, Harris and Ramsay 1994, pp. 342–45.
59. *Corporations Act 2001* (Cth), s 211(1)(b).
60. Black 1995, p. 96.
61. Filatotchev et al 2006, p. 55; Cheffins 1997, pp. 374–6.
62. Committee on the Financial Aspects of Corporate Governance 1992b, pp. 7, 10 (especially note 9 on membership of the remuneration committee). Adoption of the *Code* was seen not only to establish best practice but also to encourage shareholder pressure so as to ensure its principles would be quickly adopted: Committee on the Financial Aspects of Corporate Governance 1992a, p. 52; Department of Trade and Industry 2000a, p. 66 (especially note 85).
63. Study Group on Directors' Remuneration 1995.
64. Committee on Corporate Governance 1998.
65. Stapledon 1996, p. 74.
66. Seidl 2007, pp. 707–9; Dine 2006, pp. 76–8.
67. Working Group on Corporate Practices and Conduct 1991, p. 14; Working Group on Corporate Practices and Conduct 1992, pp. 14, 26. Working Group on Corporate Practices and Conduct 1995.
68. Australian Stock Exchange 1994, pp. 4, 6.
69. Australian Stock Exchange, *Listing Rules*, r 3C(3)(j). An indicative list of practices was set out in Appendix 33 and included disclosure of 'the main procedures for establishing and reviewing the compensation arrangements for the Chief Executive Officer and other senior executives', as well as the remuneration of the board of directors.

Companies were required to report on this for annual reporting periods ending on or after 30 June 1996.

70. Ramsay and Hoad 1997, pp. 454–5, 457, 465; Gluyas 1997a, 1997b; Unknown 1997b; Blue 1998.

71. Australian Investment Managers' Association 1995, p. 6 (guideline 11, disclosure of quantum and components of each director's remuneration together with the same information for each of the five highest paid executives, including the details of the CEO's service contract); p. 22 (recommended practice on board and executive remuneration policy and on disclosure). Since its inception in 1995 to the present day, this publication has been known as the Blue Book.

72. Australian Investment Managers' Association and the Australian Institute of Company Directors 1994, [3].

73. Myners 1995.

74. Myners Review of Institutional Investment for HM Treasury 2001.

75. Myners Review of Institutional Investment for HM Treasury 2001, p. 5.

76. Myners Review of Institutional Investment for HM Treasury 2001, p. 11.

77. Myners Review of Institutional Investment for HM Treasury 2001, p. 90.

78. *City Code on Takeovers and Mergers* (UK), Rules 9.1(a) and (b).

79. In 2009, the Panel released guidance on its interpretation of the *Code* rules which stated that the prohibitions on acting in concert will not preclude the kind of activity Myners envisaged: Panel on Takeovers and Mergers 2009, paras [1.2], [1.4]. There are several other problems with forming a coalition, including the risk of the engagement becoming public knowledge (which can lead to a share price decline): Keay 2007, pp. 660–1.

80. Myners Review of Institutional Investment for HM Treasury 2001, p. 91.

81. This explains why engagement activities such as interventions start out as covert activities: Stapledon 1996, p. 127; Lamming et al 2004, p. 30.

82. Myners Review of Institutional Investment for HM Treasury 2001, p. 91. The main type of institutional investor prone to such conflicts of interest is fund management firms within banking or insurance groups which have commercial relationships with FTSE 100 companies. For suggestions on reform, see Ingley and van der Walt 2004, pp. 545–6; Short and Keasey 1997, pp. 35–8.

83. Department of Trade and Industry 2000b, pp. 71–3.

84. Department of Trade and Industry 2000b, pp. 11, 90; Institutional Shareholders' Committee 2002, p. 2.

85. Stapledon 1996, p. 128.

86. National Association of Pension Funds 1999.

87. Department of Trade and Industry 2000a, pp. 85–9.

88. Department of Trade and Industry 1999c, p. 19.

89. Myners 2004, p. 12.

90. Department of Trade and Industry 1999a.

91. Department of Trade and Industry 2001c, pp. 55–6, 58–9. Trade and Industry Committee, House of Commons (UK) 2003, paras [111]–[19].

92. Corporations Law Economic Reform Program (Audit Reform and Corporate Disclosure) Bill 2003 (Cth), Explanatory Memorandum, p. 170.

93. Companies and Securities Advisory Committee 2000, pp. 63–6.

94. Companies and Securities Advisory Committee 2000, p. 38.

95. The study's authors defined a company as widely held if no shareholder held more than 20 per cent of the issued ordinary share capital: Stapledon, Ramsay and Easterbrook 1999, p. 19.

96. Stapledon, Ramsay and Easterbrook 1999, p. 20.

97. Pension Investment Research Consultants Ltd, *Proxy Voting Trends 1999*, cited in Stapledon, Ramsay and Easterbrook 1999, p. 21.

98. Stapledon, Ramsay and Easterbrook 1999, pp. 26–7.

99. Joint Parliamentary Committee on Corporations and Financial Services, Commonwealth of Australia, *Committee Hansard*, Canberra, 9 March 2004, p. 16

(Sandy Easterbook, Corporate Governance International, CGI, a proxy advisory firm).

100.   Investment and Financial Services Association and KPMG 2003, p. 2. At that time IFSA members held around 25 per cent of the ASX by market capitalisation: p. 8.

101.   Chapple and Cheung 2005, p. 81.

102.   *Companies Act 2006* (UK), c 46, s 439(5), formerly *Companies Act 1985* (UK), c 6, s 241A(8).

2. The regulated remuneration cycle

There are many presentations of the legal framework for executive remuneration, such as that devised by the Productivity Commission during its 2009 inquiry into executive remuneration in Australia.[1] These presentations may fail to effectively link the disparate elements of legislation, regulations, accounting standards and best practice statements that we have already seen have been an integral part of the regulation of executive remuneration. A more holistic model is required if we are to fully appreciate how say on pay as a regulatory technique fits in with other techniques. Drawing on the concepts of regulatory space,[2] the enforcement pyramid,[3] and Julia Black's writings on rule dimension and regulatory conversations,[4] this chapter presents the regulated remuneration cycle as a device that is valuable in analysing the regulation of executive remuneration via say on pay.

2.1 REGULATORY SPACE

A regulatory space within which executive remuneration 'happens' would take into account the evidence we have already seen in chapter 1 of bodies such as the Cadbury Committee, the Association of British Insurers and, in Australia, the ASX Corporate Governance Council, the Investment and Financial Services Association all of which were issuing guidance about executive remuneration practices. It would also take into account the further evidence of institutional investors monitoring remuneration practices within listed companies, not to mention the evidence of behind-the-scenes attempts to seek to influence board decisions on these practices. In other words, mandating a remuneration report (a disclosure vehicle for the 'pay') together with an annual non-binding vote on that report (the 'say') in the UK and Australia did not replace these existing activities.

More critically, regulatory space as an analytical tool acknowledges that government with its legal authority is only one regulator among many regulators[5] who seek to influence conduct by listed companies with respect to their pay practices, if not the conduct of the other regulators within the regulatory space, such as pension and superannuation fund

17

trustees. It looks beyond the layers of rules[6] and the silos of rule-making authority,[7] to the interactions between the various parties who seek to influence conduct, in what Colin Scott describes as 'a complex of interests and actions'.[8] Crucially, regulatory space is interested in how norms are made (whether by way of legal rules or non-legal rules, standards or conventions), the monitoring of the levels of compliance and the mechanisms by which '[r]egulated actors are held within the acceptable limits of the regime (whether through formal enforcement or through other mechanisms by which deviating from the norm is corrected)'.[9] Regulatory space is explicitly interested in the nature of regulatory capacity, which is based on a wide range of resources potentially held by various actors. It does not presume a hierarchical relationship between the regulator and the regulated: that is, it does not presume that law will invariably trump other sources of authority.

Scott identifies four limits with regulatory space as a framing device;[10] although only three of these are pertinent to the regulation of executive remuneration in Australia and the UK. First, as regulatory space analysis adopts a non-hierarchical conception of regulation, it may not authentically represent 'the space' if regulation is actually experienced as hierarchical. If much of the regulation is actually in the form of non-legal rules, with little or no overlap with legal rules, the regulation will not be hierarchical and thus this limit offers no obstacle to deploying regulatory space analysis for our current purposes.

The second limit in the regulatory space perspective is that 'it risks creating a neo-liberal normative agenda which is sceptical of the capacity of the state to steer market actors'.[11] Such an agenda already exists for executive remuneration and yes: there is much scepticism about the ability of government to steer boards of directors towards making better remuneration decisions; not to mention steering institutional investors towards active engagement and monitoring of remuneration practices. The risk in paying more attention to indirect regulation and, in the process, 'questioning instrumental conceptions of direct governance' is the third limit in the regulatory space perspective that we need to consider. 'Governance' is used in its political science connotation of steering by the state, rather than the state directly controlling, producing and delivering.[12] This limit is linked with the first limit: ignoring obvious hierarchical regulatory structures in a search of 'more complex control processes within which no identifiable controller exercises the control function'.[13] The state would be directly controlling remuneration decisions if it made these subject to review by a government agency.[14] This has not yet occurred in the UK and Australia. Scott's third limit thus presents few issues for the UK and Australia.

2.2 THE REGULATED REMUNERATION CYCLE

Executive remuneration can be conceived as a cycle of four activities:

- Remuneration practice: the actual practices of firms and individual executives in relation to remuneration. Remuneration practice includes setting remuneration policy, writing the remuneration contract, execution of the contract (namely the executive performs and the company makes payments according to the contract) and termination of the contract.
- Remuneration disclosure: the disclosure of remuneration annually via the remuneration report together with ad hoc disclosures related to remuneration, such as share transactions, margin loans and company loans.
- Engagement on remuneration: the engagement between the company and shareholders on remuneration, both proactive and reactive.
- Voting on remuneration: the annual advisory vote on the remuneration report and any other remuneration-related resolutions.

This is illustrated in Figure 2.1: the regulated remuneration cycle, which shows the regulators and key advisors (remuneration consultants and

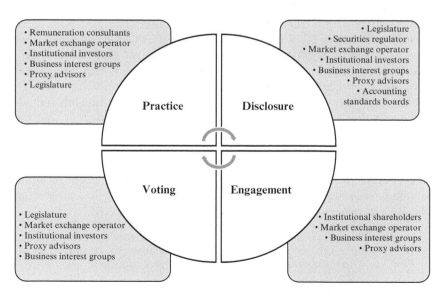

Figure 2.1   The regulated remuneration cycle

proxy advisors) involved in each of the four activities. This figure explicitly illustrates two important aspects of the regulatory framework for executive remuneration. First, there are four distinct activities in the remuneration cycle: practice, disclosure, engagement and voting. Secondly, a variety of organisations act as regulator. There is an iterative process in the regulation of executive remuneration practice, with developments in its regulation influenced by evolutionary developments in the activities of disclosure, engagement and voting. A requirement to disclose a particular aspect of remuneration practice (for example, hedging of unvested share-based remuneration payments) is likely to lead to evolutions within individual firms of practice related to such payments. A requirement for boards to disclose how they take into account shareholder criticisms of the firm's remuneration practices[15] is likely to lead to a change in remuneration practice: boards will seek out shareholders after the remuneration report vote to discover the reasons behind the lack of support for the report. Ideally, individual regulators will consider the other regulators, the whole cycle and the time lags implicit within the cycle when making new rules or amending existing rules.

2.3   PATTERN OF REGULATION ACROSS THE FOUR ACTIVITIES

Our analysis of the regulation of executive remuneration must delve further into each of the four activities so that we can appreciate the extent to which each is regulated. Clearly there are 'rules' and 'rules' within executive remuneration. A tool to analyse rule forms is therefore necessary, although the tripartite classification of rules (mandatory, default, permissory)[16] found in much academic literature on corporate law is inadequate for this task. The primary reason for this inadequacy is that the tripartite classification focuses upon legal rules, using verbal clues such as 'shall have', 'must have' and 'may have' to determine the classification to which the rule belongs. This will be inadequate to explain the rules found in corporate governance codes or the statements of expectations found in shareholder guidance. For example, look at the following statement from the 2011 statement of remuneration principles from the ABI:

> Pension related payments *should not be used* as a mechanism for increasing total remuneration. The pension provision for the executives *should where possible be* in line with the general approach to the employees as a whole. (My italics)[17]

The tripartite classification can make little sense of this particular rule as the verbal clues in italics cannot readily fit into one of the three categories

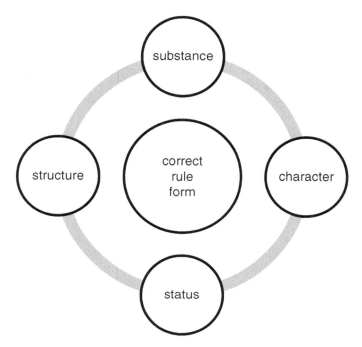

Figure 2.2   Black's four dimensions of rules

noted above. While pension-related payments should not be used to increase total remuneration, they may well do so. Does this mean that shareholders applying the ABI guidelines will invariably vote against any company's remuneration report disclosing this practice? Or can the company explain why it does not comply with this rule, such that non-compliance will be tolerated?

Julia Black provides an alternative framework for analysing the form of a rule. According to Black, the form of the rule can be characterised along four dimensions: the substance of the rule (what the rule says); its character (permissive or mandatory);[18] its status (whether the rule has legal force and what sanctions are attached); and its structure. This framework is summarised in Figure 2.2: the four dimensions of rules.

The final dimension of structure consists of a further four dimensions:

- the scope of the rule (for example, should all companies be required to have a remuneration committee or only listed companies; from our earlier example, a rule about 'pension-related payments' and their relationship to the overall quantum of remuneration);

Rule applies only exceptionally	Very precise rule	Simple rule	Clear rule
SCOPE	**PRECISION**	**SIMPLICITY**	**CLARITY**
Rule applies generally	Vague rule	Complex rule	Opaque rule

Figure 2.3   Further dimensions of rule structure

- the degree of precision of the rule (compare, for example, 'every listed company must have a remuneration committee made up of independent directors only', with 'a company should have a remuneration committee', with 'a company should have a process for setting executive remuneration' – the degree of precision of the rule moves from being very precise to being less precise, even vague);
- the simplicity or complexity of the rule ('a listed company should have a remuneration committee', compared with 'every listed company should have a remuneration committee consisting only of directors who comply with the definition of independence set out in the code'); and
- the clarity or opacity of the rule ('a listed company must have a remuneration committee', compared with 'a listed company must remunerate responsibly and fairly').

These dimensions are summarised in Figure 2.3: the further dimensions of rule structure.

Black's framework for selecting the correct 'arrow' involves multiple choices and a series of decisions to translate a 'norm' of executive remuneration into a set of words with rule-like characteristics, either as part of a principles-based approach to regulation, or a more detailed and highly specific set of requirements. While Black's model suggests that four binary choices inform a decision on rule structure, there is an interrelationship between these elements. The choice within each dimension of structure lies on a continuum and depends on the choices made in the other three dimensions of structure, as well as the choices made in the other dimensions of substance, character and status. With this framework in mind, we now turn to the pattern of rules in each of the four activities in the regulated remuneration cycle.

2.3.1   Remuneration Practice

The pattern of rules for the UK and Australia is set out at the end of this chapter in Tables 2.1 (UK) and 2.2 (Australia). The first row in each of the tables identifies the regulators involved in making the rules, with the broad substance of the rule summarised in the first column. Closer analysis reveals two broad areas of regulation: rules that govern the content of the remuneration contract, and rules that govern the process of writing the contract. Optimal contract theory and the managerial power thesis of Bebchuk and Fried provide the necessary rationale for rules about structures and forms of remuneration (for example, cash, shares, options, superannuation/pension). The managerial power thesis justifies rules to allow owners (shareholders) to write part of the contract because their agents (the board of directors) cannot be relied upon to negotiate terms that work in the owners' favour.[19] It justifies rules to prohibit some forms of payment because these allow managers to extract rents (payments) unrelated to performance.[20] The managerial power thesis would also punish non-performance by making termination of employment more likely,[21] in the process reducing the size of any payments made on termination.[22] However, it also allows for a contract with a high potential payoff via performance-related remuneration, balanced by low fixed remuneration.[23] As the theory suggests, the managerial power thesis is particularly concerned with how the contract is written and will seek to reduce the degree of influence managers exert over the board of directors by requirements for independence.[24]

Optimal contract theory too seeks rules that describe the relationship between pay and performance to write a contract in which risk is allocated efficiently between the owners and managers, while meeting the different utilities of owners and managers. It pays the manager a reservation wage as a guaranteed or fixed sum, so that the manager, being a rational economic actor, will stay with the firm and not choose to work for another firm.[25] It shares the profits and the risks of non-performance efficiently between owners and managers. Setting performance measures in this contract is not easy: it is difficult to tease out the individual manager's contribution to the observed performance of the firm.[26] Relative performance evaluation metrics may be preferred to absolute metrics because a relative performance metric takes out industry-wide shocks and is less 'noisy' than an absolute measure.[27] As an alternative, owners may select a rank order tournament measure that makes payments to whoever comes first, second, third, and so on, irrespective of their actual performance.[28] It is the best contract in the circumstances, not necessarily the perfect contract.[29] As it is a contract written to align the managers' interests with the owners' interests, some 'skin in the game' in the form of share-based payments, especially those that are subject to holding locks over a performance period, is likely.

A second feature of regulation of remuneration practice is that it consists largely of non-legal rules. This reflects the actors who are regulating in this area, in particular institutional investors. Legislatures are careful to avoid being seen to regulate the quantum and structure of remuneration[30] as this would interfere with this market. Furthermore, the actors who do regulate are largely seeking to do so via what they describe as principles to be applied flexibly.[31] According to Joseph Raz, principles 'prescribe highly unspecific actions . . . [that] can be performed on different occasions by the performance of a great many heterogeneous generic acts'.[32] If this is so, then 'compliance with the principle will, at least in theory, be achievable by a number of alternative routes'.[33] In other words, it should be possible to have a variety of remuneration practices that comply with the principle 'to remunerate fairly and responsibly' or the principle 'board accountability for executive remuneration'.

2.3.2   Disclosure

Disclosure laws are an explicit feature of corporate law,[34] and the transparency they promote has been regarded as the triumphant principle in the globalisation of companies and securities regulation.[35] Information is also crucial to the operation of markets;[36] and incorporates both information released by the company itself and information on the company released by infomediaries such as analysts, proxy advisors and the media, as well as information gleaned through informal networks.[37] It is therefore unsurprising that a different pattern of rules and regulators is evident in this activity when compared with remuneration practice. Table 2.3 (UK) and Table 2.4 (Australia) at the end of this chapter show the pattern of regulation for this activity.

The first feature of note is the prominence of legal rules across both jurisdictions. Mandated disclosures seek to ensure a uniformly informed market:[38] any information asymmetries are likely to result in inefficient prices. It forces companies to disclose information they would not normally disclose to enable parties to make better contracts with companies.[39] It can also legitimise 'an inherently conflicted process'.[40] That said, mandated disclosure of individual executive pay is not universally welcomed, being frequently cited as the reason behind the increases in the levels of pay[41] (based on the 'me too' syndrome) and credited with driving executives away from the listed company sector into the private sector.[42]

Secondly, an additional 'regulator', the accounting standards bodies established under statute,[43] is also involved in making detailed rules about how to report and value items of remuneration. Accounting standards are underpinned by principles,[44] with some more 'principle-ish' (that is, more general and less rule like) than others. A principles-based approach to accounting relies on interpretation of the standards: any accounting treatment that accords with the principles is compliant with the standards and thus the law.[45] One challenge is deciding where to draw the boundary between legislation and accounting standards to avoid overlapping content.[46]

2.3.3 Engagement

Executive remuneration is a social practice governed largely by statements of good practice ostensibly in the form of broad principles that allow for flexible application. Key to this social practice are the conversations about how the principles should apply to a particular company or to a particular executive. These interpretations or negotiations, as regulatory conversations,[47] occur at the micro level, as conversations between a remuneration consultant and a remuneration committee; or between a remuneration committee and an institutional investor. They can also occur at a more formal level, as discussions about the formulation of rules and policies (for example, in law reform, or by way of consultations on policy updates by a proxy advisory firm). These regulatory conversations can be one-on-one (remuneration committee and chief executive, remuneration committee and shareholder), or occur in two- or three-way conversations: for example, remuneration committee with remuneration consultants and the chief executive, remuneration committee with a number of institutional investors, proxy advisors and perhaps even the media if the firm's remuneration practices attract sufficient notoriety.

Understanding the micro level at which this regulation 'happens' is crucial to appreciating how say on pay works in practice. The quality of these conversations is crucial. Poor conversations are likely to result in suboptimal application where principles, standards or guidance surrounding executive remuneration are narrowly interpreted as rules to be followed to the letter, irrespective of the outcome. The regulatory conversations are also sources of ongoing rule making, because defining what is 'good' practice looks not only at established practices, but also at emerging practices. There is an iterative process of market practice, firm practice and statements of good practice that functions as an 'observational schema'.[48] Firms watch how the market responds to practices in other companies before adopting the same practice. When the market response to a new practice is positive (expressed as a good outcome on the advisory vote), other companies adopt this practice and report via disclosures in the remuneration report that they have done so. This, in turn, encourages other firms to consider adopting the practice. However, by the time 'the follower' firms consider the practice, the statement of good practice has evolved further. Figure 2.4 illustrates this process.

Company
discloses
new practice

That statement
reviewed by outsiders
using Code as observational
schema (OS)

Company amends its practice
to take into account what other
companies are doing and investors
responses, based on use of Code OS

Other companies and analysts
realise Code is being used
for comparisons, so also
adopt Code to analyse company

Company directors
observe what other companies are
doing with regards to Code and
how their investors are responding
to that, using Code as OS

*Figure 2.4   Iterative rule making using Code of best practice as an
            observational schema*

In the regulated remuneration cycle, the activity of engagement formally captures the micro-level conversations between remuneration committees and institutional investors, driven by the disclosures in the remuneration report. Shareholders seek to establish whether the company is complying with various requirements (in particular shareholders' own requirements for executive remuneration) as well as eliciting any further information that might explain company performance and thus pay. However, this pattern of regulation for this activity in the UK and Australia, illustrated in Tables 2.5 and 2.6 respectively, at the end of this chapter, shows how governments have avoided mandating engagement. Most of the rules about engagement come from institutional investor groups both nationally and internationally. Statements of principles from the International Corporate Governance Network (ICGN), the Institutional Shareholders' Committee, the Australian Council of Super Investors and the Financial Services Council (FSC) all emphasise the importance of engagement. On a transnational level, the United Nations' *Principles of Responsible Investment* were developed for institutional investors, with 'active ownership' incorporating engagement as a routine activity. Yet the adoption of the principles via paid subscription, with ongoing reporting activities and the threat of 'expulsion' for non-reporting, represents a form of market regulation, or perhaps merely certification.

2.3.4 Voting

Shareholder voting, in the anatomy of corporate law,[49] is regarded as a key corporate governance mechanism.[50] Yet voting can also be seen as a form of private enforcement;[51] that is, a different type of regulatory technique. This regulatory context of vote as enforcement is one in which an advisory vote makes sense, as the relevant laws expressly state that the decision of the shareholders on the advisory vote does not bind the company.[52] Table 2.7 (UK) and Table 2.8 (Australia) at the end of the chapter show the pattern of regulation for this activity.

As with disclosure, legal rules dominate. The nature of the legal rules can be further categorised as content rules giving specific voting rights (such as the rule that requires listed companies to conduct a resolution to adopt the remuneration report at the company's AGM), together with facilitative rules that enable shareholder voting to happen (for example, a legal rule that allows a shareholder to appoint a proxy to vote at the AGM).[53] The intervention by governments into the internal decision-making affairs of the company via content rules reflects the government's role in allowing a certain amount of tension between shareholders and boards of directors to exist, stepping in to adjust this balance of power when necessary to further its own policy objectives.[54] The facilitative rules are very important components of a say on pay by providing mechanisms to enable greater participation by shareholders in general meetings.[55]

Tables 2.7 and 2.8 also show that there are many rules on voting to be found in institutional investor practice guidance and business interest group practice statements. Many exist side by side with legal rules on the same topic, yet adopt a different rule form, with the substance of the rule directed towards how the legal rule can operate in practice.

2.4 THE ENFORCEMENT PYRAMID FOR GOOD REMUNERATION PRACTICES

Enforcement of the rules for good remuneration practices relies on something other than legal sanction alone. Influencing board behaviours are market exchange operators and institutional shareholders through rules about remuneration processes and practices. If those with the greatest incentives to monitor and detect breaches of the rules are the preferred enforcers,[56] then ultimately shareholders alone enforce these rules about remuneration practices that lie at the heart of government policy goals. The enforcement pyramid devised by Ayres and Braithwaite explains how responsive regulation works by showing that having a variety of strategies allows the regulator to respond to the level of compliance or non-compliance exhibited by the regulated. It is a useful visual tool to appreciate how compliance is achieved in the regulatory space for executive remuneration, with suitable modifications to reflect the range of sanctions in the regulatory space for executive remuneration imposed by more than one regulator.[57] This is presented in Figure 2.5.

If 'accountability' is to be improved via the introduction of the advisory vote, this pyramid indicates a lack of a specific sanction or tool for it to occur. The advisory vote could impose a 'name and shame' sanction or a 'social norm sanction' by imposing moral costs,[58] or 'outrage costs'[59] on directors, who want to avoid such naming.[60] However, the social norms encapsulated in corporate governance guidelines or institutional investor guidelines might not be 'obligational norms' where departure attracts self-censure, even if it attracts criticism by others.[61] A norm of 'remunerating

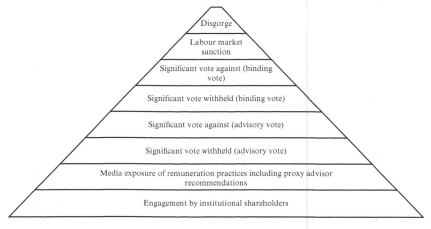

Figure 2.5   Enforcement pyramid for remuneration practices

fairly' or 'do not pay excessive remuneration' may be interpreted very differently by a CEO, the chair of the remuneration committee, a remuneration consultant, a proxy advisor, a fund manager or a superannuation/pension fund trustee. Engagement as a regulatory conversation is the opportunity to influence views on such norms. While shareholders and directors benefit from cooperation, because their relationship is ongoing with no planned end,[62] it is also clear that shareholders must be prepared to exercise the advisory vote right to signal publicly the failure to reach agreement privately.

The only legal sanctions that will prevent a particular practice occurring are those associated with termination payments[63] or disguised returns of capital,[64] related party transactions,[65] issues of securities to a director,[66] and approval of an employee incentive scheme.[67] Such sanctions all relate to payments made by the company without first obtaining shareholder approval as required by the legislation/listing rules. To design effective sanctions, however, we must consider two matters: what sanction is imposed on the board making the decision in breach of the legislation, and what sanction, if any, is imposed on the executive (including an executive director) receiving the payment in such circumstances. Both are needed to create a disincentive for boards and executives to breach these practice rules.

Take related party transactions in Australia as an example: any person involved in the company failing to obtain shareholder approval[68] breaches the Act. This breach attracts a civil penalty[69] or a criminal offence if the involvement is dishonest.[70] The actual payment is not invalid and the transaction is not unwound merely because it breaches this requirement.[71] The second category of sanctions might include a specific rule requiring the executive to disgorge the payment.[72] A different type of sanction might be necessary if the policy goal is to use law to improve the accountability of directors for their executive remuneration decisions. What happens when the advisory vote fails to achieve the desired changes in practice? Both the UK and Australia allow shareholders to call a meeting of members and to pass a resolution to remove a director.[73] The threat of removal exists: is it used?

2.5 CONCLUSION

To successfully introduce a say on pay, governments, regulators and the regulated must understand how it fits within the existing framework of rules surrounding executive remuneration. The regulated remuneration cycle as a map of the regulatory space for executive remuneration clearly places the disclosure via the remuneration report and the voting on that report within a context of four separate activities, each exhibiting its own pattern of regulation and regulators. This device makes it clear that the rules for remuneration practice are an important place to begin any examination of how say on pay works in practice.

NOTES

1. Productivity Commission of Australia 2009, p. 127.
2. Hancher and Moran 1989; Scott 2001.
3. Ayres and Braithwaite 1992, p. 39; Gunningham and Grabosky 1998, p. 396.
4. Black 2002; Black 1995.
5. Corbett and Bottomley 2004, p. 63.
6. Villiers 2006, pp. 37–9; Farrar 2008, p. 275.
7. Productivity Commission of Australia 2009, p. 127.
8. Scott 2001, p. 331.
9. Scott 2001, pp. 330–1.
10. Scott 2001, pp. 352–3.
11. Scott 2001, p. 352.
12. King 2007, p. 19.
13. Scott 2001, p. 330.
14. Unlike the US government's response to the global financial crisis with appointing a remuneration 'tsar' to review the remuneration practices of recipients of government funding under the Troubled Asset Relief Program.
15. The so-called 'first strike' of the two-strikes legislation introduced in Australia in 2011, discussed further below in chapter 10.
16. Eisenberg 1989, p. 1461; Cheffins 1997, p. 217.
17. Association of British Insurers 2011, p. 6.
18. In this way, Black's classification incorporates aspects of the tripartite classification, but character is only one of four dimensions.
19. Bebchuk and Fried 2004, p. 17.
20. Bebchuk and Fried 2004, pp. 189–92.
21. Bebchuk and Fried 2004, pp. 88–9.
22. Bebchuk and Fried 2004, p. 191.
23. Bebchuk and Fried 2004, p. 190.
24. Bebchuk and Fried 2004, p. 195.
25. Diamond and Verrechia 1982, p. 276.
26. Holmström 1982, p. 325.
27. Aggarwal and Samwick 1999, pp. 2000, 2023–4; Bizjak, Lemmon and Naveen 2008, pp. 154–5; Ezzamel and Watson 2002, pp. 208–13.
28. Lazear and Rosen 1981; Conyon and Sadler 2001, pp. 153–6.
29. Core, Guay and Larcker 2003, pp. 27–8, 39–40.
30. Joint Committee on Corporations and Financial Services 2004, p. 37.
31. See further chapter 3.
32. Raz 1972, p. 838.
33. Oxera 2006, p. 29.
34. Villiers 2006, pp. 15–16.
35. Braithwaite and Drahos 2000, p. 162.
36. Chiu 2006a, p. 744.
37. The strength of such networks should not be underestimated: Braithwaite and Drahos 2000, pp. 121–74.
38. Coffee 1994, p. 725.
39. Ogus 2006, p. 81.
40. Bebchuk and Fried 2004, p. 192.
41. Joint Committee on Corporations and Financial Services 2004, pp. 43–4.
42. Filatotchev et al 2006, p. 104.

43. In the UK the Accounting Standards Board (ASB) has authority under *The Accounting Standards (Prescribed Body) Regulations 2005* (UK) SI 2005/697 reg 2 to make accounting standards recognised as such by the *Companies Act 2006* (UK), c 46, s 464(1). In Australia the Australian Accounting Standards Board (AASB) has authority under the *Corporations Act 2001* (Cth), s 334(1) to make accounting standards.
44. Psaros 2007, p. 528; Bennett, Bradbury and Prangnell 2006, p. 196.
45. In the UK, quoted companies are required to prepare annual financial statements which comply with the accounting standards: *Companies Act 2006* (UK), c 46, s 403(1). For Australia, see *Corporations Act 2001* (Cth), s 296(1).
46. Department of Trade and Industry 1999b, paras [6.7]–[6.9].
47. Black 2002.
48. Seidl 2007, pp. 711–15, 721.
49. Armour, Hansmann and Kraakman 2009, pp. 35, 39.
50. Filatotchev et al 2006, p. 122.
51. Armour 2008, pp. 6–7.
52. *Companies Act 2006* (UK), c 46, s 439(5); *Corporations Act 2001* (Cth), s 250R(3).
53. *Companies Act 2006* (UK), c 46, ss 324–30. The right to appoint a proxy in s 324 cannot be overridden by a company's articles, although the articles may provide for additional rights: s 331. In Australia, see *Corporations Act 2001* (Cth), s 249X.
54. Kirkbride and Letza 2004, pp. 89–90.
55. Companies and Securities Advisory Committee 2000.
56. Stigler 1975, p. 176.
57. Gunningham and Grabosky 1998, p. 396.
58. Ogus 2006, p. 106.
59. Bebchuk and Fried 2004, pp. 64–6.
60. Tirole 2006, pp. 16–17; Ogus 2006, p. 130.
61. Eisenberg 1999, p. 1257.
62. Meidinger 1987, p. 366.
63. *Corporations Act 2001* (Cth), s 200B(1) prohibits payments made in connection with retirement from office unless prior shareholder approval is obtained under s 200E(1) for payments falling outside the exceptions in ss 200F, 200G and 200H. In the UK, *Companies Act 2006* (UK), c 46, ss 217–19, with exceptions to this requirement for prior approval in ss 220–21.
64. *Companies Act 2006* (UK), c 46, ss 847(2),(3).
65. *Corporations Act 2001* (Cth), s 208(1); *Companies Act 2006* (UK), c 46, ss 197(1), 198(1), 200(2), 201(2), 203(1).
66. ASX *Listing Rules*, rule 10.14.
67. ASX *Listing Rules*, rule 7.2, exception 5; FSA Handbook, *Listing Rules*, LR 9.4.1(2)R.
68. *Corporations Act 2001* (Cth), s 79 defines 'involved'.
69. *Corporations Act 2001* (Cth), s 1317E(1)(b). The civil penalty options are a pecuniary penalty of $200,000 for an individual and $1 million for a body corporate: s 1317G; and compensation (including an account of profits) could also be sought: s 1317H. ASIC could also apply to the Court under s 206C(1) for the person to be disqualified from managing a corporation.
70. *Corporations Act 2001* (Cth), s 209(3). Conviction would also result in automatic disqualification from managing a corporation as a breach of s 209(3) is punishable by imprisonment for a period of up to five years.
71. *Corporations Act 2001* (Cth), s 209(1).
72. An example of this can be found in the termination payment provisions in Australia: *Corporations Act 2001* (Cth), s 200J(1)(b).
73. *Corporations Act 2001* (Cth), s 249D (members' right to request directors call a general meeting of members) and s 203D (company may remove a director by ordinary resolution); *Companies Act 2006* (UK), c 46, s 303(1) (members' right to request directors call a general meeting of members) and s 168(1) (company may remove a director by ordinary resolution).

Table 2.1 Remuneration practice (UK)

Aspect of practice		Legislature	Securities regulator (FSA)	Financial Reporting Council (FRC)	Regulator		
					Business interest groups	Institutional investors	Proxy advisors
REMUNERATION DECISION PROCESS RULES							
Remuneration committee				CG Code (C/E)	Practice statement (V)	Practice guidance (V) Voting guidance (V)	
Structure				CG Code (C/E)		Practice guidance (V) Voting guidance (V)	
Tasks or activities				CG Code (C/E)		Practice guidance (V)	
Use of remuneration consultants				CG Code (C/E)		Practice guidance (V)	
Remuneration policy				CG Code (C/E)		Practice guidance (V)	Voting guidance (V)
REMUNERATION CONTRACT CONTENT RULES							
Remuneration contract	Common law[i]				Practice statement (V)	Practice guidance (V) Voting guidance (V)	
Base pay						Practice guidance (V) Voting guidance (V)	
Annual bonus/short term incentives				CG Code (C/E)		Practice guidance (V) Voting guidance (V)	

32

Long term incentive schemes		CG Code (C/E)		Practice guidance (V) Voting guidance (V)
Share-based remuneration	Listing rules (M)	CG Code (C/E)		Practice guidance (V) Voting guidance (V)
Performance criteria		CG Code (C/E)		Practice guidance (V) Voting guidance (V)
Pension	Pension laws (M) Taxation laws (M)	CG Code (C/E)		Practice guidance (V)
Termination provisions	Company law (M)			Practice guidance (V) Voting guidance (V)
Shareholdings				Practice guidance (V)
Share transactions	Listing rules (M)	CG Code (C/E)	Practice statement (V)	
Loans	Company law (M)			

Notes:

i   The remuneration contract is regulated by the private law of contract and common law principles in respect of the interpretation of that contract, the implication of terms into the contract, as well as the enforceability of gardening leave clauses and restraints of trade. Statutory modifications to particular terms of the employment contract (for example, in relation to any payments that require prior shareholder approval, are reported against the relevant aspect of practice).

ii See Table 2.9 for key to abbreviations.

Table 2.2   Remuneration practice (Australia)

Aspect of practice	Legislature	Regulator				
		Securities regulator (ASIC)	Market exchange operator (ASX and ASX CG Council)	Business interest groups	Institutional investors	Proxy advisors
REMUNERATION DECISION PROCESS RULES						
Remuneration committee			CG Code (INWN)	Practice statement (V)	Practice guidance (V)	
Structure			CG Code (INWN)	Practice statement (V)	Practice guidance (V)	Voting guidance (V)
Tasks or activities			CG Code (INWN)	Practice statement (V)	Practice guidance (V)	
Use of remuneration consultants			CG Code (INWN)	Practice statement (V)	Practice guidance (V)	
Remuneration policy			CG Code (INWN)	Practice statement (V)	Practice guidance (V)	Voting guidance (V)
REMUNERATION CONTRACT CONTENT RULES						
Remuneration contract	Common law			Practice statement (V)	Practice guidance (V)	
Base pay			CG Code (INWN)		Practice guidance (V)	
Annual bonus/short term incentives			CG Code (INWN)		Practice guidance (V)	

Item	Legislation / Code source	Practice statement	Practice guidance	Further guidance
Long term incentive schemes	CG Code (INWN)		Practice guidance (V)	Voting guidance (V)
Share-based remuneration	CG Code (INWN); Listing rules (M)	Practice statement (V)	Practice guidance (V)	Practice guidance (V)
Performance criteria	CG Code (INWN)	Practice statement (V)	Practice guidance (V)	Voting guidance (V)
Superannuation	Superannuation laws (M); Taxation laws (M)		Practice guidance (V)	Practice guidance (V)
Termination provisions	CG Code (INWN); Listing rules (M); Company law (M)	Practice statement (V)	Practice guidance (V)	Practice guidance (V)
Shareholdings			Practice guidance (V)	
Share transactions	CG Code (INWN)		Practice guidance (V)	
Loans	Company law (M)	Practice statement (V)	Practice guidance (V)	
Margin loans	CG Code (INWN)		Practice guidance (V)	Practice guidance (V)
Hedging positions	CG Code (INWN)		Practice guidance (V)	

Note: See Table 2.10 for key to abbreviations.

Table 2.3   Disclosure of remuneration (UK)

Aspect of disclosure	Legislature	Securities regulator (FSA)	Other government department (DTI/BERR/BIS)	Regulator			
				Market exchange operator (FSA) or Financial Reporting Council (FRC)	Accounting standards setter	Institutional investors	Proxy advisors
Definition of remuneration			Regulations (M)				
Whose pay to be disclosed	Company law (M)		Regulations (M)				
Frequency of disclosure	Company law (M)						
Disclose via a discreet remuneration report	Company law (M)			Listing rules (M)			
Remuneration policy			Regulations (M)	Listing rules (M)			
Remuneration committee membership		DTR (M)	Regulations (M)	Listing rules (M)			

	Company law	DTR	Regulations	Listing rules / CG Code	Accounting standards	Practice guidance
Remuneration committee activities		DTR (M)		Listing rules (M) CG Code (C/E)		Practice guidance (V)
Material advisors to remuneration committee			Regulations (M)	CG Code (C/E)		Practice guidance (V)
Service contracts	Company law (M)		Regulations (M)	Listing rules (M)		Practice guidance (V)
Remuneration payments			Regulations (M)	Listing rules (M)	Accounting standards (M)	Practice guidance (V)
Pensions			Regulations (M)	Listing rules (M)		Practice guidance (V)
Loans	Company law (M)	DTR (M)	Regulations (M)		Accounting standards (M)	
Options and other SBPs			Regulations (M)	Listing rules (M)	Accounting standards (M)	Practice guidance (V)
Shareholdings				Listing rules (M)		
Share trading		DTR (M)				
Termination payments			Regulations (M)			Practice guidance (V)
Tabular disclosure format			Regulations (M)			

Table 2.3 (continued)

Aspect of disclosure	Legislature	Securities regulator (FSA)	Other government department (DTI/BERR/BIS)	Regulator		Institutional investors	Proxy advisors
				Market exchange operator (FSA) or Financial Reporting Council (FRC)	Accounting standards setter		
Performance graph			Regulations (M)				
Performance criteria			Regulations (M)			Practice guidance (V) Voting guidance (V)	
Valuations					Accounting standards (M)		
Sign-off within company	Company law (M)						
Audit certification	Company law (M)		Regulations (M)		Accounting standards (M)		
Other directorships				Listing rules (M) CG Code (C/E)			
Compliance with CG Codes		DTR (M)		Listing rules (M)		Practice guidance (V)	

Note: See Table 2.9 for key to abbreviations.

Table 2.4 Disclosure of remuneration (Australia)

Aspect of disclosure	Regulator						
	Legislature	Securities regulator (ASIC)	Market exchange operator (ASX)	Accounting standards setter (AASB) Auditing standards setter (AuSB)	Business interest group	Institutional investors	Proxy advisors
Definition of remuneration	Corporations law (M)			Accounting standards (M)			
Whose pay to be disclosed	Corporations law (M)			Accounting standards (M)		Practice guidance (V)	
Frequency of disclosure	Corporations law (M)		Listing rules (M) CG Code (INWN)				
Remuneration report	Corporations law (M)						
Remuneration policy	Corporations law (M)		Listing rules (M) CG Code (INWN)			Practice guidance (V)	
Remuneration committee membership	Corporations law (M)		Listing rules (M) CG Code (INWN)			Practice guidance (V)	
Remuneration committee activities	Corporations law (M)		Listing rules (M) CG Code (INWN)			Practice guidance (V)	

Table 2.4 (continued)

Aspect of disclosure	Regulator						
	Legislature	Securities regulator (ASIC)	Market exchange operator (ASX)	Accounting standards setter (AASB) Auditing standards setter (AuSB)	Business interest group	Institutional investors	Proxy advisors
Material advisors to remuneration committee							
Contractual terms	Corporations law (M)	Regulations (M)				Practice guidance (V)	
Remuneration payments	Corporations law (M)	Regulations (M)		Accounting standards (M)		Practice guidance (V)	
Superannuation		Regulations (M)		Accounting standards (M)			
Loans							
Options and other SBPs	Corporations law (M)	Regulations (M)		Accounting standards (M)		Practice guidance (V)	Voting guidance (V)
Shareholdings	Corporations law (M)		Listing rules (M)	Accounting standards (M)			
Share trading	Corporations law (M)	SR guidance (V) class order (M)	Listing rules (M) Guidance (V)				

	Corporations law (M)	Regulations (M)	Listing rules (M) / CG Code (1NWN)	Accounting / Auditing standards (M)	Practice guidance (V)	Practice / Voting guidance (V)
Termination payments		Regulations (M)		Accounting standards (M)	Practice guidance (V)	Practice guidance (V)
Tabular disclosure format					Practice guidance (V)	Practice guidance (V)
Performance graph					Practice guidance (V)	
Performance criteria	Corporations law (M)	Regulations (M)			Practice guidance (V)	Voting guidance (V), Practice guidance (V)
Valuations	Corporations law (M)	Regulations (M)		Accounting standards (M)	Practice guidance (V)	Voting guidance (V), Practice guidance (V)
Sign-off within company	Corporations law (M)				Practice guidance (V)	
Audit certification	Corporations law (M)			Accounting standards (M), Auditing standards (M)	Practice guidance (V)	
Other directorships	Corporations law (M)					
Compliance with CG Codes			Listing rules (M), CG Code (1NWN)		Practice guidance (V)	Practice guidance (V)

Note: See Table 2.10 for key to abbreviations.

Table 2.5 *Engagement (UK)*

Aspect of engagement	Regulator						
	Legislature	Securities regulator (FSA)	Other government agency	Takeovers panel	Market exchange operator (FSA)	Institutional investors	Business interest groups
What companies should do to facilitate engagement					CG Code (C/E)		Practice statement (V)
Policy on engagement			PT guidance		CG Code (C/E)	Practice guidance (V)	
Monitoring companies					CG Code (C/E)	Practice guidance (V)	
Intervention					CG Code (C/E)	Practice guidance (V)	
Reporting on engagement						Practice guidance (V)	
Acting in concert	Securities law (M)	MAR (V)		Takeover Code (M)		Practice guidance (V)	

Note: See Table 2.9 for key to abbreviations.

Table 2.6 Engagement (Australia)

Aspect of engagement		Regulator					
	Legislature	Securities regulator (ASIC)	Market exchange operator (ASX) or ASX CG Council	Takeovers panel	Institutional investors	Proxy advisors	Business interest groups
What companies should do to facilitate engagement			CG Code (INWN)			Voting guidance (V)	Practice statement (V)
Policy on engagement					Practice guidance (V)		
Monitoring companies					Practice guidance (V)		
Intervention					Practice guidance (V)		
Reporting on engagement					Practice guidance (V)		
Acting in concert	Company law (M)	SR guidance		Takeovers panel Guidance (V)			

Note: See Table 2.10 for key to abbreviations.

43

Table 2.7 *Voting (UK)*

Aspect of voting	Regulator							
	Legislature	Securities regulator & market exchange operator (FSA)	Takeovers panel	Other government agency	Financial Reporting Council	Business interest groups	Institutional investors	Proxy advisors
Advisory vote on remuneration report (C)	Company law (M)						Voting guidance (V)	Voting guidance (V)
Binding vote on share plan (C)		Listing rules (M)			CG Code (C/E)		Practice guidance (V)	Voting guidance (V)
Binding vote on termination payment (C)	Company law (M)							
Binding vote on related party transaction payment (C)	Company law (M)	Listing rules (M)						
Notice of meeting requirements (F)	Company law (M)	DTR (M)			CG Code (C/E)	Practice statement (V)		
Proxy appointments (F)	Company law (M)	DTR (M)			CG Code (C/E)	Practice statement (V)	Practice guidance (V)	
Corporate representative appointments (F)	Company law (M)					Practice statement (V)		
Voting procedures (F)	Company law (M)				CG Code (C/E)	Practice statement (V)	Practice guidance (V)	

	Company law	DTR / Takeover	PT guidance / Regulations / CG Code	Practice statement	Practice guidance
Disclosure of voting outcomes (F)	Company law (M)				Practice guidance (V)
Disclosure of voting practice by institutional investors (F)	Company law (M)		PT guidance (V) CG Code (C/E)	Practice statement (V)	Practice guidance (V)
Share capital (F)	Company law (M)	DTR (M)			Practice guidance (V)
Voting rights disclosure (F)		DTR (M)			Practice guidance (V)
Major shareholder notifications (F)		DTR (M)			
Company to disclose major shareholders (F)			Regulations (M)		
Institutional investors should exercise voting rights (C)			PT guidance (V) CG Code (C/E)		Practice guidance (V)
Institutional investors have a strategy for proxy voting (C)			PT guidance (V)		
Member's right to direct company to appoint an independent assessor to prepare a report on a poll result (M)	Company law (M)				
Acting in concert (C)		DTR (M) Takeover Code (M)			

Note: See Table 2.9 for key to abbreviations.

Table 2.8 Voting (Australia)

Aspect of voting	Regulator						
	Legislature	Securities regulator (ASIC)	Takeovers panel	Market exchange operator (ASX)	Business interest groups	Institutional investors	Proxy advisors
Advisory vote on remuneration report (C)	Corporations law (M)				Practice statement (V)	Practice guidance (V)	Voting guidance (V)
Binding vote on share plan (C)				Listing rules (M) CG Code (INWN)		Practice guidance (V)	Voting guidance (V)
Binding vote on issue of securities to a director (C)				Listing rules (M)		Practice guidance (V)	
Binding vote on termination payment (C)	Corporations law (M)			Listing rules (M)		Practice guidance (V)	
Binding vote on related party transaction payment (C)	Corporations law (M)	SR guidance		Listing rules (M)		Practice guidance (V)	
Notice of meeting requirements (F)	Corporations law (M)			Listing rules (M)	Practice statement (V)	Practice guidance (V)	

	Law (M)	SR guidance	Takeovers panel guidance (V)	Listing rules (M)	Practice statement (V)	Practice guidance (V)
Proxy appointments (F)	Corporations law (M)				Practice statement (V)	Practice guidance (V)
Voting procedures (F)	Corporations law (M)				Practice statement (V)	Practice guidance (V)
Disclosure of voting outcomes (F)	Corporations law (M)			Listing rules (M)	Practice statement (V)	Practice guidance (V)
Disclosure of voting practice by institutional investors (F)						Practice guidance (V)
Share capital disclosure (F)	Corporations law (M)			Listing rules (M)		
Major shareholder notifications (F)	Corporations law (M)			Listing rules (M)		
Institutional investors should exercise voting rights (C)						Practice guidance
Institutional investors have a strategy for proxy voting (C)						Practice guidance
Acting in concert (F)	Company law (M)	SR guidance	Takeovers panel guidance (V)			Practice guidance (V)

Note: See Table 2.10 for key to abbreviations.

47

Table 2.9   Key to UK tables

C	Content rule
C/E	Comply or explain non-compliance (compliance with the guideline is voluntary but the company must disclose whether it complies or else explain in its disclosure why it does not comply with the guideline)
CG Code	*The Combined Code*
DTR	Disclosure and Transparency Rules found in the *FSA Handbook*
F	Facilitative rule
M	Mandatory
MAR	*Market Conduct Handbook*, found within the *FSA Handbook*
Practice guidance	Shareholder practice guidance
Practice statement	Business interest group practice statement
PT guidance	Pension trustee guidance (guidance developed by an expert group convened by a government department and aimed at pension trustees)
SBPs	Share-based payments
V	Voluntary
Voting guidance	Guidance to shareholders on what voting response particular remuneration practices will attract. It can be issued either by a proxy advisor (the main source) or by an institutional investor

Table 2.10   Key to Australian tables

AASB	Australian Accounting Standards Board
ASIC	Australian Investments and Securities Commission
ASX	Australian Securities Exchange
ASX CG Council	Australian Corporate Governance Council
AuSB	Auditing and Assurance Standards Board
C	Content rule
CG Code	ASX Corporate Governance Council, *Corporate Governance Principles and Recommendations*, 2nd edition (2007)
F	Facilitative rule
INWN	If not, why not (compliance with the guideline is voluntary but the company must disclose whether it complies or else explain why it does not comply)
M	Mandatory
Practice guidance	Shareholder practice guidance (for example, that issued by the Australian Council of Super Investors Inc, or by the Investment and Financial Services Association)
Practice statement	Business interest group practice statement (issued by the Australian Institute of Company Directors, the Business Council of Australia or the Chartered Secretaries Association)
SBPs	Share-based payments
SR guidance	Securities regulator guidance (guidance on how the securities regulator interprets the relevant laws and regulations, together with information on enforcement)
V	Voluntary
Voting guidance	Proxy advisor voting guidance (for example, that issued by Risk Metrics (Australia) Pty Ltd)

3. Institutional investor rule making

The patterns of regulation for remuneration practice outlined in the previous chapter in Tables 2.1 and 2.2 confirm that the primary rules for regulating practice within companies are not 'laws' found on the statute books, but 'rules' in the form of statements of remuneration practices from institutional shareholders, corporate governance councils and business interest groups. Of course, not all of these statements are clearly labelled as 'best practice'. For example, the ABI calls its set of rules *guidelines*[1] and the Financial Reporting Council (FRC) presents its statements of practice as a *code*, while the Australian equivalent is *principles and practice*.[2] For the Institute of Chartered Secretaries and Administrators (ICSA), their statement is *guidance*;[3] while the proxy advisor Riskmetrics or Institutional Shareholder Services (Australia) presents its statements on practice as *policy*.[4] Given these descriptions (aside from code, which indicates an all-encompassing statement of the rules), all suggest a degree of flexibility in application. Is this how the rules work in practice? What makes the practices described in these documents 'best'? Are they best because they are preferred by shareholders, so signal what shareholders will actively monitor? Or are they best because they truly are the practices that successful companies adopt and thus should be emulated by any company seeking similar success? In the field of corporate law, 'best practice' is seen as a form of 'soft law' that sets aspirational standards rather than the minimum standards and rule-like forms typical of 'hard' law.[5] From the perspective of the regulated remuneration cycle, best practice standards or principles are treated as another set of rules that apply to shape remuneration practices within companies.

To understand how certain remuneration practices come to be designated as best, we can first look to genesis of the corporate governance 'codes'. Take what is now known as the *UK Corporate Governance Code*, formerly the *Combined Code* of three previous sets of guidance, from the Cadbury Committee, the Greenbury Committee and the Hampel Committee, supplemented by the Higgs Committee on non-executive directors. In many ways it looks like a law reform process conducted by a government department or agency. First, an inquiry is called in response to a crisis and terms of reference are settled. A prominent business person is appointed to form a committee to investigate and make recommendations on the terms of reference. Then invited persons and the public at large are invited to submit evidence and/or comments. Public hearings to supplement written evidence may be conducted. From this a report identifying problems and proposing solutions is developed. The final outcome is undoubtedly influenced by the fact that business people are in charge of the process. Are the practices these reports endorse merely what business likes (that is, known and preferred practices)? Alternatively, are they practices most businesses already do or can readily adopt without much effort and without upsetting the internal power relationships within the company: in other words? The reports themselves provide no indication as to why these practices were considered 'best'. It is, however, quite clear to these committees that this regulatory approach avoids further legal intrusions into company management:

> The report represents a shared view of the action which needs to be taken in the field of financial reporting and accountability . . . we believe that our approach, based on compliance with a voluntary code coupled with disclosure, will prove more effective than a statutory code.[6]

> The way forward as we see it lies not in statutory controls, which would be at best unnecessary and at worst harmful, but in action to strengthen accountability and encourage enhanced performance . . . in our view, these fundamental principles of accountability, transparency and performance, and the related arrangements and procedures need to be encapsulated in a new Code of best practice on Directors' remuneration which companies will observe and implement.[7]

3.1 INSTITUTIONAL INVESTORS AND BEST PRACTICE

While the *Combined Code* has been studied by scholars,[8] shareholder guidance is less well studied. Before I examine remuneration practices in the UK and Australia as shaped by say on pay, I first examine institutional investor rule making in both of these jurisdictions, and its perceived influence on remuneration practices.

3.1.1 Institutional Investor Rule Making in the UK

The two major UK shareholder representative bodies and many individual fund managers in the UK release guidance on executive remuneration.[9] Both the ABI and the NAPF issue guidelines on what constitutes best practice or good practice executive remuneration,[10] including a joint position statement on executive service contracts.[11] The stated purpose for such rule making is to guide the design of individual company remuneration policy and to provide a benchmark for voting decisions.[12] It can also reflect members' interest in investee company performance,[13] and assumes a link between remuneration and individual executive performance as it contributes to company performance.[14]

Both the ABI and NAPF use specialist committees to develop the executive remuneration rules,[15] consistent with Seidl's view that codes of practice must be developed by experts to have credibility.[16] In this instance, the relevant 'experts' are investment experts, not remuneration experts. The guidance informs the analysis of company practice undertaken by the proxy voting services offered by the ABI and the NAPF to their members. These activities could still occur without publicly disclosing the guidance to companies. Disclosing the guidance and using engagement to encourage its voluntary adoption by remuneration committees reduces the likelihood that shareholders will have to confront large numbers of recalcitrant boards.

The affiliated proxy advisory services benchmark company practices against the guidance developed by the specialist committees, but take slightly different approaches to this task. The ABI's Institutional Voting Information Service (IVIS) rates company practices against the ABI's guidelines in the proxy report (for the remuneration report resolution, as well as any resolution to approve or amend a share plan) as well as the company's compliance with the *Combined Code* using a colour-coded scheme to signal the level of compliance, not an explicit voting recommendation.[17] By way of contrast, Research Recommendations and Electronic Voting Ltd (RREV) makes voting recommendations based on compliance with NAPF policy.

The influence of ABI and NAPF guidance on remuneration practices might be linked to a perception that it drives proxy advisor recommendations which, in turn, largely drive institutional investor voting behaviour. Companies believe that adopting their stated practices will produce a vote in favour of the remuneration report. For one institutional investor representative I interviewed, the statement serves a couple of purposes:

> I think that first up, it makes sense for investors to have a common statement . . . Also for the companies, it allows them to know what to expect of their shareholders and to hold them to account if we don't live up to our obligations. And for the authorities: it's all directed towards them to say, 'We are living up to our responsibilities as responsible shareholders and we can prove that to you by showing you the standards that we've set out . . . And although there are lots of guidelines out there . . . we don't think that there is a duplication, we think that they build upon what is already in existence.

When I asked what makes this practice 'best', two other representatives noted:

> It's developed in the greatest traditions – it's an evolutionary thing. These have come about not from 10, but 20 to 30 years of practice . . . they evolve into best practice, they aren't just 'This is the way to do things'. It's 'this is the way that things have been done. This is the way things have progressively got better.'

> What our guidelines seek to do is explain very much the up-to-the-minute thinking of investors, and a considered thinking of investors, who want to see companies in which they've invested succeed and don't want to stand in the way of success.

Individual institutional shareholders are unlikely to exert the same level of influence. Many fund managers who release their own guidance justify their interest using agency theory principles of alignment of interests between shareholders and owners;[18] to fulfil the duties of a responsible investor;[19] to ensure companies are managed in the long term interests of shareholders;[20] or a combination of these.[21] The interviews confirmed most fund managers will have detailed internal policies but will typically only disclose these to clients to avoid problems with companies which deal with another side of the financial services company:

> We have pretty detailed guidelines, but they are only internal . . . the only reason they're not on the website is that it causes us too many problems in terms of conflict of interest on the corporate side. Particularly with a company who has its corporate business with us, calling up and saying 'What do you mean I can't combine the role of chairman and chief exec.?' . . . We make them available only to clients. (Corporate Governance Manager, UK Fund Manager)

The pressure to make a public statement is to attract pension fund clients, with the statement providing 'an anchor point' for discussions with clients. A version of the guidelines may also be given to investee companies:

> We wanted to publish our own policy . . . Our mandated pension funds were the drivers for our policy being published . . . [It] is an aid to the trustees and it's also a way that the investee companies can identify our approach on corporate governance. (Corporate Governance Manager, UK Fund Manager)

> I think it's probably our beneficiaries [that are the intended audience of this statement], to the wider world in terms of the approach we take and the engaged stance we have on corporate governance. (Corporate Governance Manager, UK Pension Fund)

> [having our own guidelines] is a criticism we get a lot from company chairmen and remuneration consultants: how are they supposed to keep up

with everybody's sets of code? . . . We know what we are setting out to do. We have some client constituents who want a copy of our policy. We have American clients where the governance function is driven by compliance with the regulations – 'oh, there's a policy in the filing cabinet' – which I find a bit depressing but I have to live with it. They're my clients. I respond to what they require. (Corporate Governance Manager, UK Fund Manager)

3.1.2   Institutional Investor Rule Making in Australia

The purpose of rule making is to set out the principles members should adopt when determining their approach to corporate governance issues,[22] or to allow members to manage governance risk as well as ensuring companies adopt practices that 'reinforce the accountability of boards and management teams to shareholders'.[23] As with their UK counterparts, both the Australian Council of Superannuation Investors Inc (ACSI) and IFSA (now known as the Financial Services Council) rely on committees to develop their statements of best practice. A difference emerges in the make-up of these committees. ACSI's Guideline Review Sub-Committee of seven members is heavily weighted towards the full-time staff of ACSI, with, at that time, RiskMetrics, as the outsourced provider of the proxy voting advisory service for ACSI members, also contributing to the development of the guidelines.[24] By way of contrast, IFSA's rule-making process for remuneration mirrors that of the ABI and NAPF. It is undertaken by its Investment Board Committee of 18 individuals from the Australian funds management and asset consulting industries, supported by two full-time staff members of IFSA. As with all IFSA committees, the Investment Board Committee is responsible for overseeing the development of policy, seeking member input and recommending a final form of the policy for IFSA board approval.[25]

These different committee configurations mean the ACSI proposals are made by individuals separated from the investment decision, either as full-time members of ACSI's staff, representatives from the proxy advisory firm or representatives of super funds. One representative I interviewed talked me through the process:

> There is quite a rigorous process to developing a standard and it really starts with identifying the issue; that can happen through various sources. It can happen through the media and through the industry. It can happen internally here at [organisation] . . . We would go away and convene a steering group or a working committee which would include senior representatives from the industry who go away and are charged with actually developing the guidelines. Typically you are talking about a medium term process here . . . once we have a draft it goes out to all members, the CEOs, and interested stakeholders, external and internal for a formal consultation period which varies between four

to six weeks. Then we take on feedback from there and that goes back to the working group to work through and they put a recommendation to the relevant board committee.

Like the codes of best practice discussed above, the above process is drawing upon the knowledge within the industry body's own 'group', rather than seeking expert remuneration advice from remuneration consultants as an input into this process. So, what makes the guidance 'best practice'?

> It isn't something I could sit away for a couple of days and put together and that's it, it's launched. It's the actual rigour behind the process and actually consulting widely, ensuring that we cover a broad section of the industry and industry generally and get agreement on various positions and ultimately that is what we see as best practice.

Aside from the guidance prepared by the institutional investor groups, relatively few individual institutional investors publicly issued their own guidance on remuneration practices. Of the 35 fund managers I included in this study,[26] seven had remuneration guidance or proxy voting guidance (including remuneration issues) available from their website. Only one of the 23 superannuation funds studied issued remuneration guidance publicly in the period to 2009, although three other funds had guidance that was available for members. A further four super funds are affiliated with Regnan, a governance research and engagement service owned by eight institutional investors, including industry funds and fund managers. Regnan has its own policy position on executive remuneration:[27] funds that retain Regnan to engage on their behalf can be said to adopt its position on remuneration.

The fund managers justified their interest in executive remuneration as a way to align interests to maximise shareholder returns[28] or to mitigate conflicts of interest.[29] For superannuation funds, assessing governance risk forms part of the fiduciary duty to beneficiaries to deliver the highest possible return on investments and assess and manage all foreseeable risks.[30] Those institutional investors who develop their own statement on corporate governance (including remuneration) do so as part of the risk management compliance manual or the investment guidelines. Most of the fund managers interviewed also relied upon some combination of the ACSI and IFSA principles, in addition to the ASX Corporate Governance Principles. The combination covers any deficiencies within the individual guidance being, in the words of one fund manager, 'a little bit motherhood and apple pie', providing greater leverage with companies:

ACSI's guidelines are a bit soft on non-executive directors' options, whereas the stock exchange has a policy against it and so do we . . . the guidelines are just useful in a sense that they give us an out with our companies. If they're feeling aggrieved that we've voted against something we will say 'Look, it breaks ACSI guidelines, RiskMetrics has recommended against it and so on and so forth and we think it's pretty poor practice too.'

Superannuation funds were largely guided by ACSI's guidelines, with one fund relying on a combination including IFSA and the proxy advisory firm's guidance because 'They all chip away at different parts and they contribute to a base level of what's acceptable and what's not.'

Where individual superannuation funds devised policies it was in part to direct fund managers on the issues:

We have asset consultants who advise us on the selection and the ongoing per-formance of managers. So the asset consultants use the ESG [environmental, social and governance] policy in the selection and ongoing management of man-agers. We correspond directly with our managers, to advise them of the policy and ask them how do they comply with (a) the policy and (b) our requirements as a signatory to the United Nations *Principles of Responsible Investment.*

Such policies could also form part of the super fund's overall investment policy:

We just want to make sure that the companies we invest in . . . to ensure that the boards are accountable for the decisions they made and also to ensure that we know corporate governance should enhance investment performance or add shareholder value in the longer term.

A different aim is to inform members on the fund's approach to environ-mental, social and governance issues, as these two superannuation fund representatives explain:

It's to articulate to our members the approach that we're adopting. That's probably the key purpose because internally, corporate governance has been a consideration for a long time. So it's just publicly articulating that it's something that we look at.

The bulk of it talks about the proxy voting process we're going to follow. But also it broadly outlines to our members how we are trying to take into consideration broader ESG issues.

There are some different rationales underlying these statements: a stated voting policy is very different in its form, use and thus potential impact, from a statement that is 'motherhood and apple pie'. Different audiences are catered for in these statements: companies, asset managers, fund managers and members of superannuation funds. Some pay homage to the ACSI and IFSA guidelines and gap fill where these are silent, whereas others develop their own guidelines that replace these sets of guidance. Such guidance may not actually be intended for a company director audience, but for a superannuation fund trustee audience.

Yet other fund managers serving the same industry superannuation funds do not see any need to develop their own statement of principles, even as a set of voting guidelines. Three of the fund managers interviewed did not have a formal policy on corporate governance or remuneration. Two fund managers explain why:

> There's no hard and fast rule on these things . . . say someone who has built up a business and has no equity ownership in the business and he's done a phenomenal job, you might have a bit more flexibility there to approve something . . . [the ACSI and IFSA guidelines are] probably 50 per cent of the decision. Every situation needs to be taken on its circumstances.

> Corporate governance in and of itself is not the most important thing. It's one of the things that aligns with what you are trying to do in order for a company to make it into our investment universe.

3.2 DOES SHAREHOLDER GUIDANCE TRULY REPRESENT BEST PRACTICES?

Do companies respond to new guidance from shareholders? Several different views emerge from the UK interviews I conducted. One corporate governance manager noted that sending out copies of guidance to the remuneration committee is valuable:

> It does lead to a dialogue. We will get several letters back in response, saying 'Thank you. Can you please elaborate on this point because we want to consider this internally.'

Remuneration consultants also find aspects of the guidance good, although some guidelines are 'more aspirational than others'. The influence of individual fund manager guidance is less certain. If each corporate governance person across the various institutions has individual preferences for particular remuneration practices – what one remuneration consultant described as 'different quirks' – companies will 'cherry pick' the relevant guidance if it is not possible to comply with conflicting requirements:

> Some institutions say 'We like this performance measure' and others say 'No, we don't like that one, we like this one' and others say 'No, we don't like those two over there, this is what we like'. And you get to the point where you say 'What on earth is going on?'. (FTSE 100 company secretary)

Remuneration committees believe 'best practice' is firm specific, with the following description typical of those provided in the interviews:

> It is a set of remuneration policies which reflect the nature of the company, the business it's in, the challenges that it's facing and the need to incentivise and retain the executive directors within that field.

This contrasts with the views of at least one institutional investor representative:

> Best practice is not our invention that we are imposing on people. It works because we actually take to heart what the practitioners think. We then translate that into a set of guidelines that informs the community about where and how the judgments are set to fall.

Given the guidelines' attempt to cover all industries, but that they 'plainly are not applicable to every sector', there has to be, according to one company secretary, 'a compromise as to how we can have our best practice'. Compromise is by no means certain:

> [T]here are certain pillars of UK corporate governance best practice that you breach at your peril . . . when companies try and put their head above the parapet and do something different, they get a bit of a hard time. (Remuneration consultant)

The committee representatives were divided on whether it was possible to deviate from the guidance. Most investors had some tolerance for departures from the guidelines, or at least, 'they were willing to discuss it'. One company representative noted, 'Individual institutional investors have their own views. They don't blindly follow the lobby groups.' In part this tactic by institutional investors may be to avoid criticisms of adopting 'too formulaic an approach' to remuneration practices. Indeed one of the institutional representatives affirmed the statements are 'guidelines, not rules', while individual investors say they are 'open to bespoke arrangements' and 'welcome variation'. That too can be problematic for remuneration committees:

> I think the problem is the remuneration system comes out with guidelines which they then try and apply to every sector . . . So then I think you should go to

them and say 'For our sector this is the sort of thing we need'. But that depends upon the effort that you're prepared to put into it, it depends a bit upon your ability to dress the thing up a bit in line with the guidelines.

A different view is that 'comply and explain' are not in practice equally acceptable alternatives,[31] if institutional investors 'pretty much box tick'. Some institutional investors note they are 'a bit guilty' of this:

> When they see a plan [that conforms with the guidance] they'll sign it off, but when they see something with a return on capital employed target or something else, they'll start to scrutinise it in a bit more detail which I suppose is natural human behaviour . . . [T]he result is a situation whereby the performance targets that are in place are not actually aligned with the performance targets used to drive the business.

3.2.1 Australian Views of Best Practice

That fund managers rely on a combination of the ACSI, IFSA and ASX Corporate Governance Council guidance to arrive at a core set of good practices indicates that no one set of guidance is authoritative or comprehensive. This may impact on its influence on remuneration practice. Remuneration consultants were divided on the influence of the guidance issued by ACSI and IFSA, with one consultant claiming the guidelines were

> not very influential at all.[32] Boards and directors are mindful [of them], as are executives. In part they reflect what practice is, and in part they reflect those elements of practice that institutional investors are broadly at ease with, or accept they can't change.

Two remuneration committee chairs regard the proxy advisors' guidance as more influential on practice than the institutional investor guidelines. Most of the remuneration committee chairpersons interviewed noted that it was possible to deviate from these 'best practice' guidelines. Fund managers were seen as flexible:

> The fund managers are generally out there all the time, they know what's going on. They're practical people . . . It's the trustees and the corporate governance people that are the problem.

The general consensus was that deviations from the guidelines were accepted 'if you explained why and you are generally within their framework'. In other words,

> I think that they are still recognising that we have to make up our minds. And when people lose that, it will be the end of business.

However, whether deviation is possible varies

> from institution to institution. Some unquestionably adopt a box-ticking approach, so it's the line of least resistance . . . Others will reflect on what you tell them, but with varying degrees of sophistication, analysis and understanding.

For remuneration committee chairpersons, best practice is 'fit for purpose', even if

> it is a fine line that rewards success but does not pay for failure, is aligned with the owners, appears fair and reasonable to stakeholders, and retains outstanding executives, and promotes alignment of executive interests with shareholder interests.

For remuneration consultants, best practice, 'as a multi-dimensional concept' is adaptable to individual company circumstances including 'industry sector and the relevant stage in the business cycle', and 'balances superior performance with risk mitigation'. These views of best practice reflect a view that the guidance can be adopted if suitable. If it is not suitable, it will only be adopted if it can be modified to suit the company. Otherwise it will be rejected. In terms of specific practices, the guidance has had 'virtually no impact on short term incentives'. The situation for long term incentives (LTIs) is different, where 'a lot of follow-the-leader behaviour [is] observed in the market'. There is also a problem with some of the guidance around performance criteria being 'not particularly well thought out' with 'a danger sometimes that they might not necessarily lead to the best outcomes for the company or for the shareholders'.

3.3   RULE MAKING IN THE REGULATED REMUNERATION CYCLE

Three differences between the UK and Australia are evident from the evidence: the level of experience of institutional investors as rule makers, the development of remuneration policies by individual institutional investors, and the acceptance of the guidance by remuneration committees and their consultants.

3.3.1 Experience as Rule Makers

The UK institutional investor groups have long histories of rule making and respond to emerging remuneration practices by releasing guidance to coincide with the remuneration committee's decision-making process. The ABI and the NAPF have been promulgating guidance on remuneration since the late 1980s and, in the case of the ABI, frequently update the guidance (2002, 2004, 2005 and 2008). Combined with the proxy advisory services based on these guidelines, I expect a clear link between institutional investor rule making and voting recommendations.

In Australia, changes to these groups in the late 1990s/early 2000s impacted on the development of, and acceptance of, remuneration guidelines by investors and companies alike. The ACSI is a relatively young association (2001) with a narrow membership base of industry super funds, not retail funds.[33] Its first set of corporate governance guidelines in 2003 were the extant guidelines for the first year of the advisory vote in Australia. The major update to the executive remuneration principles in August 2005 was too late in the regulated remuneration cycle, coming after decisions about remuneration had been made for the financial year 2005–06. While IFSA has a longer history both as an association (since 1997) and as a rule maker for executive remuneration, a fifth edition of the Blue Book released around the time of the CLERP 9 reforms in October 2004 was not revised until June 2009, thus missing the first four years of the advisory vote and the opportunity to influence practice.

3.3.2 Individual Institutional Investor Rule Making

UK fund managers are more likely than their Australian counterparts to have developed their own remuneration guidelines, either as a separate corporate governance policy or as part of a proxy voting policy. This may reflect a different competitive environment within the funds management industry in the UK compared with Australia and the influence of initiatives such as Myners' *Principles* upon pension trustee decisions when awarding mandates to fund managers. Where Australian institutional investors did issue individual guidance, it largely endorsed the guidance issued by the ACSI, IFSA and ASX Corporate Governance Council rather than provide any additional rules for remuneration. This may indicate that Australian institutional investors do not see any particular advantage in promulgating different rules, whereas their UK counterparts, based on the interview evidence, appear to take pride in their detailed views on remuneration issues.

3.3.3   Influence on Practices

The evidence above shows a clear difference of opinion as to the importance of shareholder guidance between UK remuneration committee
chairs and their remuneration consultants and their Australian counterparts. Remuneration consultants and remuneration committees in the UK
are more accepting of the guidance made by groups such as the ABI and
NAPF than their Australian counterparts, because deviations from best
practice are not tolerated by shareholders. Australian remuneration committees and consultants appear more ambivalent about the influence of the
investor guidance.

I begin my examination of the influence of shareholder guidance on
remuneration practices by examining the remuneration committee in
chapter 4, before considering how it undertakes its key tasks and meets its
performance obligations in chapters 5 (UK) and 6 (Australia).

NOTES

1. Association of British Insurers 2009.
2. ASX Corporate Governance Council 2007; cf. ASX Corporate Governance Council
    2003.
3. Institute of Chartered Secretaries and Administrators 2003.
4. RiskMetrics 2008.
5. Enriques, Hansmann and Kraakman, 2009, p. 67; Armour, Hansmann and Kraakman
    2009, p. 39.
6. Committee on the Financial Aspects of Corporate Governance 1992a, pp. 9, 12.
7. Study Group on Directors' Remuneration 1995, pp. 11–12.
8. Clarke 2007, pp. 133–44; Solomon and Solomon 2004, pp. 45–64; Armour, Deakin and
    Konzelmann 2003, pp. 538–40.
9. Stapledon 1996, p. 74. Twenty-three of the 32 fund managers in the UK study (see
    methodology appendix for further details) publicly released corporate governance guid-
    ance or voting policies with a stated position on executive remuneration.
10. For example, see Association of British Insurers 2002 and 2004a; National Association
    of Pension Funds 2004 and 2005.
11. Association of British Insurers and the National Association of Pension Funds 2002
    and 2008.
12. Association of British Insurers 2002, p. 1.
13. National Association of Pension Funds 2003, p. 2. A more detailed statement of the
    NAPF policy on various remuneration issues is contained in National Association of
    Pension Funds 2005, pp. 27–48.
14. This link is expected under optimal contract theory, see chapter 2 above, 23–4.
15. The ABI's Share Scheme Committee in 2004 consisted of 19 fund managers and cor-
    porate governance personnel: Association of British Insurers 2004b, p. 25. The NAPF
    committee consists of fund managers, company pension scheme representatives and
    service providers such as actuaries: National Association of Pension Funds 2008, p. 14.
16. Seidl 2007, p. 708.
17. See http://www.ivis.co.uk/UsingIVIS_ReportColourCoding.aspx for a description of
    these codes (accessed 8 March 2012).

18. Baillie Gifford & Co 2008, p. 18; Barclays Global Investors 2008, p. 5; JP Morgan Asset Management (UK) Limited 2007, p. 2.
19. Newtown Asset Management 2008, p. 4.
20. BlackRock Investment Management (UK) Limited 2007, p. 3; F&C Management Limited 2008, p. 2; Jupiter Asset Management Limited 2008, p. 2.
21. Insight Investment 2007, p. 2.
22. Investment and Financial Services Association Limited 2009, p. 5.
23. Australian Council of Superannuation Investors Inc 2009, pp. 1, 3.
24. Australian Council of Superannuation Investors Inc 2009, p. 35.
25. Investment and Financial Services Association Board Committee Charter (2005); Investment and Financial Services Association Limited 2007b, pp. 8–10. The Code of Ethics notes that final approval is to be given by the Standards Oversight and Disciplinary Committee of IFSA, comprising three board members, rather than ratified by the whole board.
26. The methodology appendix explains the process of selecting fund managers.
27. Regnan Governance Research & Engagement Limited 2009.
28. Barclays Global Investors Australia Limited 2007, p. 4.
29. AMP Capital Investors 2007, p. 3.
30. Statewide Superannuation Trust 2008, p. 2.
31. MacNeil and Li 2006.
32. Cf. McConvill and Bingham 2004.
33. Australian Prudential Regulatory Authority 2007.

4. Remuneration committees

One important device that regulates the directors' remuneration decision-making powers is the company's constitution or articles of association. In the UK, the constitution operates as a contract binding the company and its members.[1] Under Australian law, the constitution operates as a contract between the company and each director and company secretary, the company and each member, and a member and each other member.[2] In this way, the constitution presents a form of private ordering.[3] This may be supplemented by 'policy' documents such as a Remuneration Committee Charter or terms of reference. The classification as policy documents is to distinguish these 'leadership tools'[4] from constitutional documents that may only be amended by shareholders passing a special resolution.[5] The company's constitutional documents may not necessarily identify the remuneration committee by name, instead containing a provision allowing the directors to delegate any of their powers to a committee of directors (with some procedural rules supplementing this decision making).[6] The constitution may also specifically allocate decisions on remuneration to 'the board' or to 'the directors'. As the case of *Guinness plc v Saunders* illustrates, a failure to follow these requirements can mean that the committee's decision to pay the remuneration decided upon is not a valid decision of the company.[7]

It has taken a while for remuneration committees to be elevated to the status of a 'compulsory' committee, akin to the audit committee, and one that can only consist of non-executive directors who must satisfy the definition of being 'independent' of management. The *Combined Code* in the UK only ever recommended that companies have a remuneration committee.[8] The company law statute does not prescribe that the board of directors must have committees charged with particular tasks, only that the board of directors may delegate any or all of its powers to a sub-committee of directors.[9] While changes made by the FSA in response to the global financial crisis create an obligation on a bank or other financial institution to have a remuneration committee,[10] the recently revised *UK Corporate Governance Code* has not changed the pre-GFC position in relation to other companies.[11]

The position in Australia is similar but not identical. Until 2011,

Australian listed companies were only encouraged to have a remuneration committee (unless they were also regulated by the Australian Prudential Regulatory Authority (APRA) and thus required, post-GFC, to have a remuneration committee).[12] Even with the reforms introduced by the government in response to the recommendations of the Productivity Commission,[13] the rule mandating remuneration committees for constituents of the S&P/ASX 300 index is found in the ASX *Listing Rules*,[14] not in the *Corporations Act 2001* (Cth).[15] Committee members must be non-executive directors, not specifically 'independent' directors. In other words, a rule that the remuneration committee must be independent, a seemingly obvious rule from the perspective of the managerial power thesis of Bebchuk and Fried,[16] is not a 'given'. Both jurisdictions have rules that emphasise no individual should be *directly* involved in deciding his or her own remuneration,[17] although the fiduciary obligations imposed on directors would arguably lead to the same result so as to avoid an actual or potential conflict of interest.

These rules reflect the belief that an appropriate process will deliver an appropriate outcome.[18] Board structure is seen as an appropriate proxy for board success.[19] Some scholars cast doubt on just how independent of management the remuneration committee can be.[20] As Ella Mae Matsumura and Jae Yong Shin note:

> Independence is inherently virtually impossible to observe, and its surrogate definition is a rules-based list of conditions that cannot hold if a director is to be deemed independent. Consequently, firms may focus on satisfying the rules for independent directors rather than the broader concept of independence, similar to situations where people focus on rules to specify ethical behavior instead of evaluating whether particular behavior is ethical.[21]

That independence might be a chimera is supported by evidence suggesting a correlation exists between the level of CEO pay and the number of outside directors on the remuneration committee who were appointed by the CEO (because the CEO was a member of the nomination committee).[22]

It is also difficult to maintain strict independence in practice. The UK guidance is practical in acknowledging that consulting with individuals on their own remuneration is appropriate.[23] Such an approach is also consistent with human resource management theories that suggest remuneration should be tailored to the individual executive if it is to provide an incentive and thus motivate performance to achieve the defined goals.[24] It also reflects the beliefs of remuneration committee members:

> I think it's up to the chief executive – I feel very strongly that it's management – that should be recommending to the remuneration committee how they think

and in particular how the chief executive thinks the company should best be run in terms of reward. (FTSE 100 remuneration committee chair)

So the rem one's a challenging one because of the vested interests. Normally this comes up through the HR Group and, in my experience, they attempt to do a very professional job. But what are you going to do: are you going to rely solely on their input? Or are you going to use your own gut feel? Either of those I suspect would be dud decisions. (S&P/ASX 200 remuneration committee chair)

4.1   ADVISORS TO THE REMUNERATION COMMITTEE

To undertake its tasks, the remuneration committee relies on external and internal advisors because

Unlike the audit committee that gets a relatively well-worn path and sets of rules driven essentially by the accounting profession and the auditors . . . the remuneration committee's challenge is far more difficult because it's one of the few situations where we board members are required to provide a level of creative decision making of our own. (Remuneration committee chair, ASX 200 company)

Table 4.1 summarises the key advisors to the remuneration committee and the types of information they provide to the committee. The key external advisors are remuneration consultants, lawyers, accountants, actuaries and analysts/stockbrokers. There are also several internal advisors: the CEO, HR Director, company secretary and the chief financial officer. The information provided by these advisors can be distinguished as either general information about practices and trends, or specific information about what practices should exist in the particular company. CEOs will seek to influence decisions on executive remuneration[25] because of this link with strategy:

We have a new chief executive . . . I wouldn't be surprised if [CEO] asks us to slow down [a review of remuneration policies] because he might well want to feel that he has got a better, a more clearly formulated view about strategy and the future before we do anything to change our remuneration policies in case there is a need to change them again. (FTSE 100 company secretary)

By influencing the remuneration policies for subordinates, CEOs influence how that policy will be applied to them. Structural separation *is* important.[26] Yet, while the CEO is not a member of the committee, he or she will typically attend remuneration committee meetings. The CEO can provide

Table 4.1   The remuneration committee's information sources and advisors

Advisor	External	Internal	General information	Specific information
Remuneration consultants	✓		Market updates Trends One-on-one education of directors	Benchmarking of executives' remuneration Comparator group Salary recommendations Long term incentive schemes – vehicles, valuations Scenario modelling
Lawyers	✓		Legal updates, including bills, legislation and recent cases from the courts	Advice on contracts Tax structuring Share plan terms Terminations Advice on disclosures
Accountants	✓		Updates on tax and trends in reporting	Advice on tax structuring Advice on disclosure, reporting and valuations Advice on actual performance measures (calculation of TSR performance)
Actuaries	✓			Superannuation and pension modelling Modelling for share plans (e.g. binomial, Black Scholes)
Analysts/ stockbrokers	✓		Market information	Reports on company's prospects (EPS forecasts, profit targets)
CEO		✓	Routine briefings on company matters	Strategy proposals Remuneration proposals for direct reports Reports on delivery against targets Performance appraisals of direct reports (to inform succession planning)
CFO		✓	Routine briefings on company matters Financial reports	Budgets Forecasts Performance against budget

Table 4.1   (continued)

Advisor	External	Internal	General information	Specific information
HR manager		✓	Routine briefings on human resource matters Updates on company policies and procedures	Executive remuneration policy proposals Information on current remuneration arrangements Advice on company procedures Advice on broader remuneration arrangements Performance management information
Company secretary		✓	General information on meeting procedures and committee procedures	Continuous disclosure Director share dealings Notices of meeting and accompanying documents Proxy voting forms Proxy voting records (48 hour deadline) Meeting procedures

perspectives and insights on his or her direct reports, their career track records and their core skills, according to one S&P/ASX 200 remuneration committee chair interviewed. The most senior human resources manager is also a frequent invitee to the committee's meetings,[27] although one FTSE 100 company secretary noted that his company specifically excluded them and other company executives to ensure 'complete independence'. The range of general advice and information provided by these executives about company strategy, progress on delivery of that strategy, financial information, relevant company policies and procedures is part of the 'universe' within which the remuneration committee sets the remuneration strategy.[28]

Executives preparing these reports can influence the committee directly by advising on a specific decision, or indirectly, for example by providing organisational history or background and context (Australian remuneration consultant). Boards of directors are used to relying on reports from management to make decisions:

Boards work by papers coming up with decisions and recommendations, and the board says 'yay', 'nay', or 'we'll have a think about it'. [With] the rem committee, a lot of that still happens, but given the vested interest of the executives, this is not a totally arm's-length presentation. (S&P/ASX 200 remuneration committee chair)

Even outside the meetings, executives will seek to influence their remuneration. The following two quotes illustrate how this might occur:

We usually leave this very room with him being unhappy and me not being happy because I didn't get exactly what I wanted, but it's a negotiation, a meeting of minds, and when we get to a meeting of minds, I then recommend it to the remuneration committee. (S&P/ASX 200 remuneration committee chair)

For the chief executive here, and I'm aware of the pressure, there are some pressures from his colleagues who want to get paid more . . . Some of the pressure comes from greedy executives, to be frank about it, because they are greedy. (FTSE 100 remuneration committee chair)

4.2 REMUNERATION CONSULTANTS

Of the external advisors, remuneration consultants are almost universally engaged by companies in the UK.[29] The *Combined Code* (now the UK *Corporate Governance Code*) recommends that companies make available a statement as to the independence of the remuneration consultants.[30] A company might go to some lengths to monitor the independence of its remuneration consultants[31]

[b]ecause we don't want them believing they're going to be earning large amounts from the company and therefore they could be swayed in the advice that they give to the committee. (FTSE 100 company secretary)

There is no consensus among remuneration consultants on whether they should be briefed by management or by the remuneration committee directly. According to one UK consultant, 'the worst possible environment is one in which the non-executive directors design the compensation without the involvement of the executive directors'. Or, as another UK consultant noted, 'a bad remuneration committee . . . is fed by management and takes instructions from management'. However, even where the remuneration consultants are engaged directly by the committee, 'it's important to keep them in the box and not let them run the business' (FTSE 100 remuneration committee chair). A company secretary agreed that even while remuneration consultants are an essential advisor to the committee,

I don't think that advice should be accepted without challenge. I think it is very much incumbent upon the committee to use advisors as just what they are – advisors. They are not decision makers. And there remains a very large responsibility on the committee to spend the time to understand the issues that are around and to challenge or be innovative themselves. And to perhaps ensure that the instructions to the advisors are to produce what the committee wants, rather than what the advisors want to produce.

Yet remuneration committees can also use the remuneration consultants in different ways: 'to take a particular stance with management' (FTSE 100 remuneration committee chair); to show that 'this is right or management are smoking something' (FTSE 100 human resource director). There may be further reason for retaining consultants:

[t]he main reason remuneration consultants are there is because corporate governance box tickers like the remuneration consultants [to be] there to give [their] independent blessing to the arrangements. But it's not an independent blessing at all. (FTSE 100 remuneration committee chair)

This striving for independent advice can lead to different remuneration consultants being retained by company management and by the remuneration committee, although one UK remuneration consultant noted that 'The impact of that type of approach on board harmony is neutral at best. And it's double fees.'

4.2.1 Australian Use of Remuneration Consultants

Up until 2011, Australian listed companies were not required to disclose their use of remuneration consultants.[32] However, they appear to be commonly retained.[33] All the Australian-based remuneration consultants I interviewed noted that it was important to understand that there are two sources of instructions from a company: instructions from management and instructions directly from the board. This is despite the ACSI guidelines which mirror the NAPF requirements in requiring the remuneration committee to directly appoint the remuneration consultants and for those consultants to report exclusively to the remuneration committee and to the board.[34] Even where retained by the remuneration committee, practice to date has been in some instances for the CEO to actually suggest the remuneration consultants to be engaged (S&P/ASX 200 remuneration committee chair). While one consultant suggested the reports prepared for management and the remuneration committee are the same, another consultant suggested there were 'subtle little differences': the remuneration committee wants a genuine arm's-length view, while some management teams or the CEO might attempt to 'cherry pick' the comparator group (Australian remuneration consultant).

Most remuneration committee chairs I spoke to noted they would not feel comfortable 'going it alone' without the information supplied by remuneration consultants. As one Australian remuneration committee chair noted, 'I think they are [essential] in the sense that it gives you another dimension in a broader market context.' In other words, despite the fact that other listed companies are disclosing their remuneration practices in remuneration reports, directors still believe remuneration consultants are essential. Another remuneration committee chair explained:

> You go and have a look at other rem reports. But as you've seen if you've studied any, deciphering the reports requires not an inconsiderable amount of skill. Even simple things like, you'll see a dollar value against long term incentives. I can guarantee those figures are never right. Never ever right.

They also offer a form of protection for directors when dealing with shareholders:

> Because these days there are many questions about whether the board has done everything it had to do. So that does not mean that we shouldn't make our own decisions, that we shouldn't do our own work. But they are an extra check on what we are doing. (S&P/ASX 200 remuneration committee chair)

One remuneration committee chair I spoke to had a different approach to retaining consultants:

> We have developed our own systems which the company has traditionally used and we don't need external advice in applying those systems. Having said that, it doesn't preclude us from time to time seeking advice, but as a general rule, we don't feel we need to go to them every time we want to do something.

4.2.2 Data Produced by Remuneration Consultants

Nearly all the remuneration committee chairs, company secretaries and remuneration consultants I spoke to agreed that remuneration consultants had been blamed for the ratcheting of executive remuneration, although academic studies suggest this blame is misplaced.[35] However, as an Australian remuneration committee chair (who engages remuneration consultants) noted, '[t]he remuneration consultants will play a role, not by promoting it, but by not criticising it. They'll say, "It's alright because everyone is doing it."' Some remuneration consultants even conceded there was some truth to the allegations; that some remuneration consultants had presented data 'with more of a leaning to the upper quartiles, saying [to their clients], "if you want to have the best talent, you should be paying up above the median."'

With remuneration consultant data being an important but widely criticised input into remuneration committee decisions, how do directors confirm the information with which they have been provided? One approach is to engage another firm of remuneration consultants to simply review the work of the other:

> We'd come up with something and then we would run it in front of the other lot for an opinion. Now we said, 'You don't do any other work for us: what do you think of this?'. (FTSE 100 remuneration committee chair)

However, the following quotes are more typical of the views expressed by the other interviewees:

> We don't do any scientific validation of it. The members of the committee, and I as the servant of the committee, will all have views from what we've read about pay trends. There is usually a disparity I've found between what the press is reporting and what the consultants are reporting. Not necessarily in the same direction each time, but there does seem to be a sizeable gap each time. (FTSE 100 company secretary)

> We don't investigate it very carefully. We see a copy of their report but their report comes to us from the company on the recommendations of the CEO, so he's been through it with his immediate contacts and they have obviously 'made it work' so that it works . . . I have never seen a remuneration consultant put the salaries down. (S&P/ASX 200 remuneration committee chair)

For those who do some type of check, various methods are used to verify the data. Aside from the reports provided at the client's request, remuneration consultants also play an important role by providing market overviews. Typically these documents cover the constituents of a particular index,[36] or they may target a particular industry.[37] Many consulting firms run informal seminars where a small number of remuneration committee chairs meet to discuss remuneration trends and issues.[38] Remuneration committees use this information during their deliberations to validate the data provided by their own remuneration consultants.

The broad industry/index overview may also be part of remuneration consultants' presentation to the remuneration committee, prior to beginning work on the annual review of remuneration (Australian remuneration consultant). Additionally, members of remuneration committees will typically sit on more than one board committee within the company and will also sit on the board of other companies, either as executive or non-executive directors. Remuneration committee members who are only in non-executive roles bring information on practices from other companies. This information is also used to verify the information from remuneration consultants:

> A number of the members of our remuneration committee are on the boards of other companies so they have information which, although not directly comparable [to that provided by remuneration consultants], is indicative. (FTSE 100 company secretary)

> How do I validate the information they provide to you? Only one way – and that is most of us sit on other boards.[39] Is it the only way we can do it? Do we know if the top 25 per cent quartile is correct? No. And I don't think we've got any chance of doing that. But they have given us quite good insights into hurdles for example; quite good insights into the mixture between shares and cash. And I can validate quite a lot of that from the other boards I am on. And don't forget: there are other directors in a big public company that are also on other boards. (S&P/ASX 200 remuneration committee chair)

Of course, the risk with such an approach is that the directors are working from 'common reference points',[40] rather than from an objectively different perspective gained from involvement in making remuneration decisions at other listed companies.

Being on other committees within the *same* company gives directors additional information not only about the company, but also about the senior executives whose remuneration the committee must decide on.[41] It also provides an opportunity for the non-executives to build relationships with these executives, adding social and psychological factors into the remuneration decision-making process.[42] More neutrally, it can provide additional information about the firm's accounting processes:

> You know, in terms of ratcheting up the [remuneration] figures: I sit on the audit committee as well . . . if you are measuring something like return on invested capital [as part of your incentive schemes] there are myriad ways to measure it in a company and I think it's jolly useful to understand how the company actually measures it and what the various assumptions are that go into it. (FTSE 100 remuneration committee chair)[43]

Much of the above evidence is troubling. If directors do not check the validity of the information at all but simply rely on it without question, they risk being in breach of their duty to exercise reasonable care and diligence.[44] While using their own contemporaneous experiences on other boards to validate the information is an improvement, the other boards have been advised by remuneration consultants who draw upon the same sources of information – disclosed remuneration practices (if not the same

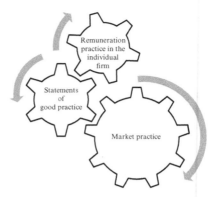

Figure 4.1   Iterative rule making

comparator groups). The remuneration surveys are helpful,[45] but report historical data at a time when the directors need data to make decisions about next year's payments.

4.3   CONCLUSION

If institutional investor guidelines are less influential in Australia than in the UK, remuneration consultants may exert more influence over practice in Australia than in the UK. While practice is changing in Australia, most recently to reflect new amendments to the *Corporations Act 2001* (Cth),[46] for the period examined in this book, management routinely engaged remuneration consultants. Even allowing for guidance to influence practices, it remains unclear whether best practice as described in the various pieces of guidance is truly 'best'. Three separate forms of practice – best practice (in guidelines), market practice (aggregated practices in the market) and firm-specific practices (bespoke practices) interact in a manner that does not readily allow us to identify what exactly drives innovation in remuneration practices. (This is set out in Figure 4.1.) As one remuneration consultant said:

> There are two questions which I think are very very common when you're meeting with a new client or even perhaps if you haven't seen the client for a while, even if it's the annual review time: number one, not necessarily in sequence: number one – 'What's the right answer?' To which my stock answer is 'There is no right answer, that's why you're here in a committee and you've got to make a decision on some stuff I'm going to talk over with you.' The other question is 'What's best practice?'

How shareholders monitor and enforce their own guidance, together with the failure of many boards of directors to stand up to shareholders and insist on the firm's bespoke arrangements, may result in the emergence of particular practices even though no consensus exists to say they are truly the best practices:

> I think [shareholder guidance] has been influential because directors have been scared if they don't comply . . . some like the Australian Shareholders Association have the most prescriptive guidelines . . . some of the larger shareholder institutions . . . have a much more open approach and will be willing to listen. (Australian remuneration consultant)

> They're actually laying out the groundwork for what they see as acceptable community norms and I think, given this current environment now, that it will play out to a tension between the struggle between the non-executive director roles and their fiduciary duty to the entity versus the superannuation trustees promoting the community norm. (Australian remuneration consultant)

I examine shareholder guidance and its influence on remuneration practices in more detail in the next two chapters as I examine the evidence of the remuneration committee at work undertaking the annual review of remuneration and the major review of remuneration.

NOTES

1. *Companies Act 2006* (UK), c 46, s 33(1), formerly *Companies Act 1985* (UK), c 6, s 14(1).
2. *Corporations Act 2001* (Cth), s 140(1).
3. Collins 2004, pp. 12–17.
4. Carver 2006, pp. 41–51.
5. *Corporations Act 2001* (Cth), s 136(2); *Companies Act 2006* (UK), c 46, s 21(1), formerly *Companies Act 1985* (UK), c 6, s 9(1). These requirements may be supplemented by additional requirements prescribed by the company's constitution: *Corporations Act 2001* (Cth), s 136(3); *Companies Act 2006* (UK), c 46, s 22(1).
6. For example, see the default provisions in Table A, regulation 72: *Companies (Tables A to F) Regulations 1985* (UK) SI 1985/805. I note Paul Davies' caution that the model articles are not necessarily appropriate to use as a generalised statement of practice in companies: Davies 2008, pp. 366–7.
7. [1990] 2 AC 663 at pp. 686–9 (Lord Templeman); pp. 698–700 (Lord Goff of Chieveley). In this particular case, article 91 of Guinness plc's articles of association allowed *the board* (not the remuneration committee) to grant special remuneration to a director in particular circumstances.
8. The *Combined Code* (2008), main principle B.2.
9. This rule is typically found in the company's articles of association.
10. Financial Services Authority, *Senior Management Arrangements, Systems and Controls* (2012), SYSC 19A.3.12R(1),(3).
11. *UK Corporate Governance Code* (2010), code provision D.2.1.
12. Australian Prudential Standard *APS 510 Governance* (2009), para. 47.

13. Australian Government 2010.
14. *ASX Listing Rules*, rule 12.8 applies from 1 July 2011 to companies listed in the S&P/ASX 300 at the beginning of its financial year.
15. The *Corporations Act 2001* (Cth), s 198D states that the board can delegate any of its powers to a sub-committee of directors, with s 190 attaching consequences to the delegation for the purposes of the duty to exercise reasonable care and diligence in s 180(1).
16. Bebchuk and Fried 2004, pp. 28–9.
17. *UK Corporate Governance Code* (2010), main principle D.2; ASX Corporate Governance Council 2007, p. 35.
18. Conyon 1997, pp. 103–4, 115; Lawrence and Stapledon 1999; Huse 2005, p. 66.
19. Roberts, McNulty and Stiles 2005, p. 19.
20. Bebchuk and Fried 2004, pp. 77, 82; Main et al 2008, pp. 228–9.
21. Matsumura and Shin 2005, p. 109.
22. Chalmers, Koh and Stapledon 2006, p. 268 (based on Australian data). This is consistent with US evidence: Shivdsani and Yermack 1999; Perry and Zenner 2001. For a study of board structure and pay for performance, see Carpezio, Shields and O'Donnell 2011 (Australia) and Gregory-Smith 2011 (FTSE 350).
23. *UK Corporate Governance Code* (2010), p. 23.
24. Vroom 1964, p. 195.
25. Maitlis 2004. See Adams 2009 for a discussion of the impact of the dual role of monitor and advisor upon information exchange.
26. Roberts and Stiles 1999, p. 47.
27. Main and Johnston 1992, p. 16; Conyon 1997, p. 188; Main et al 2008, p. 229.
28. Australian Institute of Company Directors 2004, p. 15.
29. Conyon, Peck and Sadler 2009, p. 49.
30. The *Combined Code* 2008, B.2.1.
31. United States House of Representatives Committee on Oversight and Government Reform, Majority Staff 2007, pp. 8–9; Cadman, Carver and Hillegeist 2010.
32. In June 2011, the federal parliament passed the *Corporations Amendment (Improving Accountability on Director and Executive Remuneration) Act 2011* (Cth) requiring companies to disclose the name of their remuneration consultants in the remuneration report.
33. Productivity Commission of Australia 2009, p. 181.
34. This is a long-standing principle for ACSI: Australian Council of Superannuation Investors Inc 2005 p. 12 (principle 12.2); Australian Council of Superannuation Investors Inc 2007, p. 10 (principle 12.3(f)); Australian Council of Superannuation Investors Inc 2009, p. 17 (principle 10.3(f)); Australian Council of Superannuation Investors Inc 2011a, p. 17 (principle 10.3(f)).
35. Murphy and Sandino 2010; cf. Voulgaris, Stathopoulos and Walker 2010.
36. For example, see Deloitte & Touche LLP 2003.
37. For example, Halliwell Consulting (UK) 2004.
38. For example, the Remuneration Committee Chair forum conducted by Ernst and Young in Australia.
39. Bebchuk and Fried 2004, pp. 33–4.
40. Perkins and Hendry 2005, p. 1457.
41. This information will redress the information asymmetry between the executives and the board on the executives' talent: Dewartripont, Jewitt and Tirole 1999.
42. Bebchuk and Fried 2004, pp. 31–2; O'Reilly III and Main 2005, pp. 21–3; O'Reilly III and Main 2007, pp. 8–9.
43. Jackson et al 2006, p. 33, report Watson Wyatt data which note that 36 per cent of FTSE 100 companies in the financial year 2003–04 had non-executive directors serving on both the remuneration and audit committees.
44. Under Australian law, this duty is found in the *Corporations Act 2001* (Cth), s 180 and in common law and in equity: *Permanent Building Society (in liq) v Wheeler* (1994) 11

WAR 187. For the UK, the duty is now found in the *Companies Act 2006* (UK), ss 46, 174.

45. Ogden and Watson 2011.
46. *Corporations Amendment (Improving Accountability on Director and Executive Remuneration) Act 2011* (Cth), schedule 1, s 206K.

5.   UK remuneration practice – best practice?

To understand more about the relationship between guidance on practice and actual practices, I now examine two processes undertaken by remuneration committees: the annual review of remuneration and the major review of remuneration practice.

5.1   THE ANNUAL REVIEW OF REMUNERATION

The annual review encompasses a series of decisions about remuneration: the annual fixed salary, the STI targets and potential payouts, the LTI grants of share-based payments, and decisions about the previous year's bonus. Figure 5.1 presents a 'typical' annual review, based on interviews with UK remuneration committee representatives and remuneration consultants. The light text boxes represent remuneration consultant input, with the dark boxes representing decisions made by the remuneration committee. As one FTSE100 remuneration committee chair I interviewed noted:

> the thing I have done . . . is just insisted all of these decisions have got to be made at the start of the financial year. Because you do get an awful lot of drift on remuneration committees and people put off difficult decisions.

While the remuneration committee's process has been described by Main et al as validating, calibrating and conforming,[1] it is difficult to fit the committee's process within the typical description of the board role as one of 'performance and conformance'.[2]

5.1.1   Remuneration Strategy

Remuneration strategy is identified in various sources of guidance available to directors.[3] The following list collates those sources into a set of guiding principles or statements of the aims of remuneration policy:

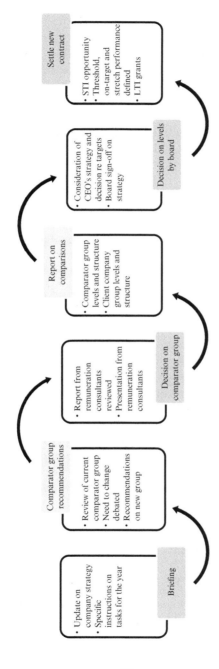

Figure 5.1   The annual review of remuneration

- Remuneration practices promote corporate success which translates into value creation for shareholders.
- Remuneration practices allow companies to retain key executives and motivate all executives.
- Remuneration practices use appropriate benchmarks to set the levels of remuneration.
- There is a link between remuneration outcomes and individual and corporate performance as measured on a sliding scale.
- Performance targets (and thus remuneration outcomes) align the interests of executives with those of shareholders.
- An appropriate balance is set between fixed and variable pay.

These principles are then translated into rules for different remuneration practices with varying degrees of specificity. These principles do not establish any quantum targets to tackle remuneration excesses. In equating corporate success with value creation and with references to 'appropriate benchmarks', 'appropriate balance' and pay linked to performance on a sliding scale, no amount of remuneration can be determined from these principles alone. They offer no substantive guidance on what amount of remuneration is too much, or too little, or even 'just right'.[4]

5.1.2   Benchmarking

An important task in the annual review is the compilation of market data on remuneration. Capturing the 'market' involves a strategic selection of a comparator group of companies.[5] Management, remuneration committees and remuneration consultants will all have a view on the constituents of this group. It is a critical stage because peer groups can be used to justify pay rises divorced from actual company performance,[6] identified in some empirical studies as 'pay for luck'.[7] The comparator group that the board chooses may be different from the group investors would choose. According to one UK remuneration consultant, directors ask, 'Does this company do what we do?' Investors are typically interested in a sector so want to see the company comparing its performance and remuneration practices with other companies in the sector. One FTSE 100 remuneration committee chair commented:

> My perspective is that there is no perfect comparator group. It's as simple as that. Whereas it would be quite easy to get a comparator group if you are a smallish company, when you are a large company and [my company] is the largest by far in its sector. Who really then is a comparator group? . . . You've also got the problem when other companies get taken over as there is a takeover premium of maybe 30–40 per cent of share price. And that can make quite a big

difference to the comparator group. That doesn't mean the company was doing wonders for its shareholders. It may mean that the management sort of gave up. They weren't able to do things well and the company hoisted a 'for sale' sign or whatever. And yet, it makes this comparator group measurement adverse for [my company].[8]

Once the comparator group is selected, the remuneration consultants compile data on the remuneration quantum and structure of the payments made to executives in the comparator group of companies. This includes total compensation and the balance of fixed pay and variable pay, with variable pay further disaggregated into STIs and LTIs. The data on incentives will also indicate which particular vehicles (cash, options, other forms of share-based payments) are used. Statistical analysis allows for medians and quartiles to be determined, with the client company's executives and their payments fitted within these data, so as to identify where the company's executives sit 'in the market'.

5.1.3   Fixed Remuneration

Fixed remuneration consists of two components: base salary and pension. Base salaries are set by reference to the market rate for executives and need to be justified when salaries are set at the market median or higher;[9] and a satisfactory explanation is needed for base salary increases in excess of the rate of inflation.[10] Contrary to the guidance, nearly all the sample companies disclosed that individual performance is taken into consideration when settling the amount of base salary. The following disclosure is typical:

> The Committee's objective is that executive director basic salaries should be paid at an appropriate level to take account of both *personal performance* and of salaries within a comparator group of financial institutions. The Committee considers that *exceptional performance*, whether corporate or individual, should be rewarded through bonus and incentive schemes rather than base salary.[11]

Table 5.1 provides evidence from remuneration consultant surveys of the rate of increase in base salaries for FTSE 100 companies for the period 2003–07. The most dramatic increase is in 2004 (the second year of the advisory vote) in the upper quartile.[12] An element of this increase can be 'me tooism':

> Ooh, I do a job that's much more important than that, our company is much better, therefore I'm underpaid. (Remuneration committee chair, FTSE 100 company)

Inevitably, there is a comparison often seen by the executives with their colleagues and peers in other industries and that can create a source of pressure. (Company secretary, FTSE 100 company)

Table 5.1   FTSE 100 percentage increases in base salary: 2003–07

Year reviewed	Upper quartile (%)	Median (%)	Lower quartile (%)
2003	12.22	7.92	4.75
2004	16	8	4
2005	10	8	3
2006	10	6	4
2007	10	7	4

Boards should be able to respond to such pressures, but remuneration committee chairs cited 'weak boards' and 'greedy executives' as the source of the problem. Taken together, they are a heady combination. Constraining base salary is particularly important in the UK market because

Everything tends to get hung off base salary . . . so if you tweak the base, you've got multiple leverages. So that puts strong pressure on base salaries . . . what you might think is neither here nor there, the odd per cent, is really serious. (Remuneration committee chair, FTSE 100 company)

5.1.4   Pensions

The *UK Corporate Governance Code*, the ABI guidelines and the NAPF guidance all recommend that pensionable salary should not include annual bonus payments.[13] The ABI guidance further recommends that remuneration committees balance pension against the other elements of the remuneration package, including the performance-based components; implying that smaller pension payments as a percentage of total remuneration are preferred. The observed practice of annual increases to base salary noted above has a flow-on increase to the percentage of pension contribution.

Table 5.2 presents evidence of the size of pension payments in FTSE 100 companies over the period 2003–07, based on information reported by Deloitte in its annual surveys.[14] The left hand side of the table reports the data for defined benefit pension schemes and draws upon actuarial calculations. The right hand side of the table reports the data for defined contribution pension schemes. Both sides of the table confirm that pensions form a significant part of fixed remuneration expenses in any given year, lying anywhere in the range from an additional 15 per cent of base salary to a

Table 5.2   *FTSE 100 contributions to pension schemes as a percentage of base salary: 2003–07*

	Defined benefit pension schemes – value of contribution as a percentage of base salary (%)			Defined contribution pension schemes – value of contribution as a percentage of base salary (%)		
	Lower quartile	Median	Upper quartile	Lower quartile	Median	Upper quartile
2003	27	42	63	15	28	40
2004	18	30	40	15	31	40
2005	30	43	70	15	29	39
2006	30	43	67	20	25	39
2007	37	51	70	20	26	35

Sources: Deloitte & Touche 2003, p. 86; Deloitte & Touche 2004, pp. 74–8; Deloitte & Touche 2005, pp. 79–91; Deloitte & Touche 2006, pp. 83–96; Deloitte & Touche 2007, pp. 77–82.

massive 70 per cent of base salary for defined benefit schemes in the upper quartile. Given pensions will be paid out irrespective of performance, the reputation risk to the remuneration committee and the company is real, as is evident in the scandal in 2009 surrounding the pension payment to the former chairman of the Royal Bank of Scotland, Fred Goodwin.[15]

5.1.5   Variable Remuneration

There are two components to variable pay: the annual bonus or short term incentive and the long term incentive. Annual bonus payments are designed to 'encourage and reward an aspect of performance that is different from that encouraged by long-term incentive schemes but still relevant and important [based on] what individuals can influence and what is important for the company'.[16] Annual bonus performance measures are linked with company strategy and are linked with the company's budgeting process.[17] Thus research findings of no evidence of relative performance evaluation for annual bonus payments are unsurprising.[18]

Remuneration consultants are typically not involved in this process: they do not advise on what measures the company should use, nor do they measure the performance actually achieved. In other words, management recommends the relevant performance metrics to the committee. One remuneration consultant went so far as to suggest that the mark of a CEO was how well he or she undertook this task of selling the budget to the board. However, this consultant also noted that it is easier to project what good performance looks like over the period of an STI than it is with an LTI. He also noted that where the balance between these two forms of incentive payments should lie will take into account the relevant industry sector. A pharmaceutical company has a long lead time for products and thus a longer time horizon for performance than a retailer where performance is churning out year after year of grocery sales.

Another remuneration consultant observed that whether the budget is or is not challenging is an internal company decision, and this is not something remuneration consultants can decide or advise on. Whatever measures the company chooses for its STI, the more difficult issue is deciding what level of performance represents 'challenging' or 'stretch' performance and what percentage of STI should pay out for achieving budget targets. A third remuneration consultant noted this quest for the perfect measure: 'If I knew the answer to that, I'd be lying on a beach somewhere.' A different remuneration consultant was sceptical about the performance measures chosen, especially the softer performance measures such as customer service or culture change initiatives, which can form around 15 per cent of the annual bonus payment. Customer service[19] is 'hardly something a senior executive is engaged in', while changing culture 'is not something that can happen in one year. It takes longer to do that well.'

Yet for remuneration committees, this act of setting targets and the ensuing discussions define success within the company and are important to executives;[20] and some of the measures derided by remuneration consultants are important to remuneration committees,[21] as the following three quotes illustrate:

> This [strategy plan] was a kind of one-off that we put in place at the suggestion of the new CEO. He was particularly keen of getting throughout [company] improved customer relations and customer satisfaction . . . The idea was to help him in doing the things which he considered were absolutely necessary.

> The customer service measure: we moved away from an old externally benchmarked customer satisfaction which was a research survey which we felt was subject to too many externalities . . . The new measures are more robust.

> The strategic focus of the business was reviewed with the help of external management consultants. That resulted in management adopting [strategy programme] . . . we would budget on a riskier basis . . . the thing with the short term incentive is to have senior managers as focused as possible on things they can influence directly, personally and moving these days really from quarter to quarter . . . the weighting of the elements for the top team has varied over the last few years. We don't go into detail on that in the report, but the balance between corporate profit, divisional profit, corporate cash generation, divisional cash generation and personal objectives, has fluctuated quite a lot.

Long term incentives are managed very differently from short term incentives. Aside from deciding the proportion of total remuneration that should be based on long term performance, the critical decisions are what performance criteria to adopt and what link should exist between performance and reward. The ABI guidelines for share-based incentives specifically identify total shareholder return (TSR) relative to an index or peer group as a generally acceptable performance measure.[22] Aside from offering guidance on how to calculate TSR, the ABI also expresses a clear preference for performance periods of three years or longer, with shares that vest subject to a further period of deferral until finally released to the executive. The guidance endorses regular annual phased shares awards, with vesting conditional on satisfaction of 'challenging' performance conditions,[23] and no re-testing of performance in subsequent performance periods. It also recommends remuneration committees set threshold vesting amounts based on a multiple of base salary, with a staggered or sliding scale for vesting (where a minimum hurdle is set and attracts a level of vesting, with higher vesting for achievement of progressively higher performance hurdles) preferred to 'cliff-edge' vesting (which is binary in nature – achieve the hurdle and all vests). The guidance for LTIs is detailed and highly prescriptive.

This guidance is reflected in company disclosures, as most companies adopt a standard approach combining two measures: relative TSR and earnings per share (EPS) growth over the rate of inflation (proxied by the retail price index).[24] Relative TSR was not a popular measure with the remuneration committee representatives I spoke to, although one representative described it as the 'least worst' measure because 'It's stable. It's robust. Everyone understands it. You can't manipulate it.' Problems cited by remuneration committees with TSR include the lack of a perfect comparator group,[25] the lack of control executives have over the outcome (which also reduces its effect as a performance motivator)[26] and being 'a bit random' in delivering awards:[27]

Nobody wanted there to be any TSR in the performance share plan. The management and the remuneration committee were absolutely at one in not wanting it. One member of our remuneration committee . . . was very keen that we should make a point of having no TSR because we all believe it to be a hopeless motivator, and [instead attempt to] persuade the external investor community that we were right and they were wrong . . . We've been criticised for having only one-third TSR. The institutions would like us to have anywhere from one-half to 100 per cent. I think it is fair to say that the people who are in the plan here discount that third . . . clearly for investors, if their total return on capital growth and income is better from one investment than another, then they would prefer the one that got them the better return. And they would like that to be the fixation of management. From our side of course, we argue that there are things over which we have control or at least influence, and the earnings is in that category. Our control over how the market views what we do is slim.

I think it's very difficult to say you don't want any TSR or any TSR-like element in your long term incentive. So we kept it. The question is what comparator group . . . should we have it absolute or relative, or relative to an index?

The performance share plan is not working . . . and that's one of the reasons why we're looking at it because it's not incentivising the executives. It's not incentivising the executives because they have no control over it.

Remuneration consultants agreed with the comments noted above. TSR had its problems: while it reflected the way that fund managers' own performance is measured, it did not necessarily represent a good measure of corporate performance. Selecting the right comparator group was difficult, although a sector-based group was identified by remuneration consultants as a better choice than an index. However, one remuneration consultant noted that some comparator groups within sectors were small; as a result potentially large payments are being based on 'wafer-thin decisions'. Contrary to the assertion noted above, it is possible to manipulate TSR outcomes by shifting the dates from which the share prices is measured (with one remuneration consultant commenting that this can dramatically alter the result), and TSR approaches can include weighted averaging of the share price over three months at the beginning and end of the nominated performance period. It was also incorrect to suggest that outstanding performance was rewarded by relative TSRs, as such schemes begin to pay out for achieving performance at the median of the comparator group and pay out in full at the 75th percentile. Academic research indicates some evidence of income smoothing to mitigate earnings and share price volatility.[28] While these findings were based on US data for the period 1992–2005, replicating the study using UK data may well reveal similar results.

5.1.6   Ad Hoc Remuneration Decisions

Outside the annual cycle of meetings that forms the annual review described above, the remuneration committee can be called upon to make decisions when a senior executive is hired, promoted, resigns or is terminated.

On hiring a new executive, companies will frequently have to pay an amount equivalent to the value of surrendered equity incentives at the executive's previous employer. One FTSE 100 HR director spoke of the internal verification undertaken prior to making an offer:

We will do extensive research into the value, one to validate that they actually have it, two: we'll go down into the financial department and drill into Reuters 3000 Extra and we'll get everything from the analysts' reports, the financials. If it's a US company, we'll go into the SEC filings. If it's a UK company, we'll go into the *Companies Act* filings. We'll go into all of that stuff in order to validate that the intrinsic value someone has is appropriate. So we validate what they've got for buying out.

The remuneration committee chair of a FTSE 100 financial institution spoke of its difficulties with hiring people into its high rewards investment banking area:

It's a big racket isn't it? I mean, we hire people away from other companies with monstrous amounts of money which we then buy out. They've got all sorts of retention devices and we buy them out.[29] It may cost you a few million to get hold of them.

The higher levels of remuneration paid to outside hire may also reflect the market value of general management skills, rather than firm specific knowledge of internal hire.[30] These general managerial skills may be identified as superior through some kind of 'certification contest', whereby the media or even a group of peers identifies the CEO as being superior to others.[31]

A further difficult decision arises when deciding whether to offer a retention payment to an executive with an outside employment offer. Remuneration committees are frequently unwilling, rather than unable, to match an offer that will significantly disturb the pay relativities within the company. According to one remuneration committee chair, overpaying 'a bit' is acceptable because it can mitigate the risk of losing a good person, and what constitutes 'a bit' rather than 'too much' is ultimately a commercial judgment based on people impacts on the business. Remuneration committees therefore appear to have a strong sense of internal relativities[32] as well as market relativities in mind when making these types of ad hoc decisions. The key to these decisions is a pre-established policy position:

You don't make good decisions when you react in a knee-jerk kind of way and it's very hard to sustain somebody who is way out of line in the organisation. (FTSE 100 company secretary)

Corporate culture can temper the need to match outside salary offers:

If you go to investment banking: they are all complete tarts. Whoever pays the highest well, that's where they'll go. And I relate to that. In corporates like [FTSE 100 company], there's more loyalty. Some executives put money above all else. Other executives put intrinsic enjoyment of the requirements of the job, and the chemistry of them working in the company, the sort of social interaction, higher. It doesn't mean, incidentally, that one is better than the other in my opinion. (FTSE 100 remuneration committee chair)

UK practices on termination payments are a good case study in just how effective the advisory vote can be in changing remuneration practices.[33] Termination payments are governed by the terms of the employment agreement and share plans. Within these terms, committees will likely exercise some discretion in making these payments, for example by waiving performance conditions. In year 1 of the study of remuneration reports I conducted,[34] 37 companies in the sample of 73 did not have contracts that complied with the practice guidance: 12 months' notice for termination 'without cause', with a concession of up to 24 months for newly appointed executives.[35] By the last year of the study, only 13 companies of the 73 FTSE 100 companies in the sample had not made changes to fall completely into line with shareholder guidance.

The relevant guidance on the contractual terms is clear, and compliance can only be achieved in one way, and is 'rule like' rather than 'principles based'. It is easy for institutional investors and their proxy advisors to monitor compliance. This suggests that remuneration practice changes might be best achieved by a rule-like approach, but this will not be suitable for all aspects of remuneration practice. Furthermore, that shareholder guidance sets a different standard from legislation[36] has not inhibited this change in practice. However, success in achieving changes to termination payment practices can be undermined or counter-balanced by changes in practice on hiring new executives, such as guaranteed bonus payments, or 'softened' performance targets.

5.1.7 Proactive Engagement Around the Annual Review

Shareholders respond to the remuneration practices devised by remuneration committees and disclosed in remuneration reports via the strategies of engagement and voting, the last two activities in the regulated remuneration cycle. Shareholder engagement and voting are the only enforcement mechanisms for those remuneration practice rules found in shareholder guidance. Shareholders must communicate via a regulatory conversation how the practice rules they devise should apply to that company.

At least one company in the interview sample undertook proactive engagement of its key shareholders every year outside AGM season by offering one-on-one sessions for key investors, although sometimes these sessions were with ABI- or NAPF-led groups of investors. This company's secretary explained such meetings were to 'talk about the principles of the policy and also to get a flavour on how they thought the remuneration committee was doing'. From another FTSE 100 company secretary's perspective, moving the debate around remuneration upstream from the AGM allows the process to be 'constructive'. It also allows the company to set the agenda and the 'tone' of this regulatory conversation by moving it away from the specifics of any one payment or executive, onto policy and high level issues.

Aside from this company-led engagement, fund managers typically conduct one-on-one consultations annually with company management and the board, and the fund's corporate governance managers may join this meeting if the company is a governance outlier:

> We will absolutely ensure that we lead all representatives of the House, with both sides represented, because they are interested in the fundamentals of the business, and how well the company is being run, managed and remunerated, and from our perspective, it helps to have their sector experience as well as our expertise.

Remuneration committees prefer to speak with fund managers than with the fund's corporate governance managers, even if, as one remuneration committee chair observed, the fund managers' eyes 'glaze over' when the conversation turns to remuneration or other corporate governance issues.

5.2   THE MAJOR REVIEW OF REMUNERATION

At various times a company will need to undertake a more extensive review of its remuneration strategy and practices. The catalyst for the review may be a poor result on the advisory vote at the last AGM; a change in regulation surrounding a particular practice;[37] or factors more internal to the company. Remuneration committee representatives across the two jurisdictions identified the following as the catalyst for their own company's major review of remuneration:

- a change in strategy,
- a new chief executive officer,
- an acquisition or divestment,
- an incentive scheme that's not paying out,[38] and
- an incentive scheme that is misaligned.

When a company undertakes a major review of its remuneration strategy, the annual cycle of meetings is supplemented by additional meetings.

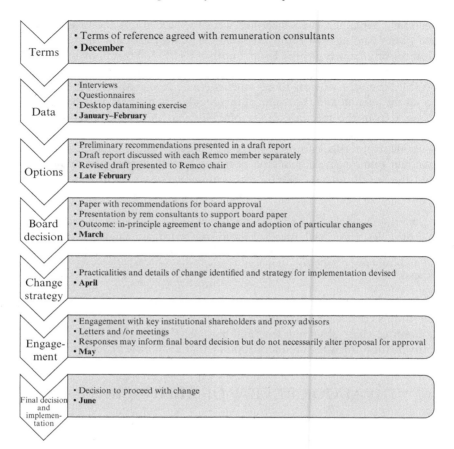

Figure 5.2   The major review of remuneration

Figure 5.2 sets out the major review process based on a generic review of the firm's overall executive remuneration strategy. The catalyst for the review will shape the nature of inquiry, the level of involvement of remuneration consultants, other external advisors and management. The major review of remuneration is also more likely to prompt companies to proactively engage with institutional shareholders as part of the decision making. The particular catalyst for the major review will influence the tone of the ensuing engagement. Engagement will typically occur after the remuneration committee and board have reached an in-principle decision to make a particular change. This exercise has two phases: a letter to the major shareholders and institutional representatives and proxy advisors, [39] with a second phase of meetings with shareholders who want to discuss the proposed changes further. Completing both stages can take at least one month, if not longer, 'if it is a particularly aggressive set of proposals' and involve the remuneration committee chair, the company secretary, HR personnel and the remuneration consultant.

Sending a letter to the corporate governance managers at fund managers describing the proposed changes is 'pretty much standard practice now', according to one company secretary. A UK remuneration consultant stated that these letters are typically

> Quite detailed . . . five, six, seven sides . . . And that letter would set out what we've had in the past, what we're proposing to do and why. It would be very detailed that letter, really because shareholders in the UK get interested in the minutiae of how all these share plans operate.

The response to the letter varies: sometimes the corporate governance people will telephone in response, or else they will request a meeting with the remuneration committee chair. Sometimes they speak directly with the committee's remuneration consultants

> even though they encourage remuneration committee chairmen to take a more active involvement. Frankly, they would rather speak to us more often than not, because we speak the same language as them. They would rather vent their spleen at us than the Remco chair. And they get it all out and it's a very cathartic experience. (Remuneration consultant)

Institutional investors and companies view this exercise differently. For companies, these discussions are not negotiations, although companies want to appear responsive. Shareholders regard the exercise as a negotiation or a dialogue. One company secretary gave an example of what would be deemed a successful negotiation by shareholders:

> We did talk to one institution and we were able to find out what really troubled them and *got them to make a much narrower point [which] we then accommodated* . . . and we stuck with our broader position with [their narrow point] carved out. (FTSE 100 company secretary)

Companies can exploit this process by

> putting a few 'Aunt Sallies' in the letter which we know aren't going to be acceptable, which we're happy to give . . . then the corporate governance bod at the shareholder can go and see his fund manager and say 'Look, they wanted this, but I've got them to stop. I didn't allow them to do that.' So everyone's a winner. *It's a bit of a game actually.* And some of the more enlightened institutional investors really know it's a bit of a game. (Remuneration consultant)

Coping with multiple consultations is difficult for institutional investors, given limited governance resources within the fund manager. This is particularly so where the major review is in response to a bad outcome on the advisory vote and involves four to six meetings. Investors are aware they may be 'gulled' by companies, in part by becoming too involved in the details and 'letting the big picture pass them by'. Institutional investors understand that companies have different reasons for consulting shareholders:

> Companies think that, because they consult, they are going to get a tick in the 'yes' box. And that is not necessarily the case. Companies get really riled when they've consulted with you and you still disagree. I mean, that's our prerogative to do that. (Corporate governance manager, UK pension fund)

Companies noted that indeed this was one of the reasons for undertaking consultations: 'Certainly the consultation and discussions do add value, in that you then know you're going to get some support and that's always well worthwhile' (FTSE 100 company secretary). It appears to work:

> But they also know that a lot of shareholders, as soon as they get a win in any part, any change, they are going to fall away and vote in favour. So it's a tactic that actually works and that's probably why they do it. (Corporate governance manager)

5.3   CONCLUSION ON UK PRACTICES

The annual review and major review of remuneration illustrate two very different sets of interaction between remuneration consultants, remuneration committees and institutional shareholders. Whether engagement changes in its format, participants and tone in the pre-AGM period is something I examine in chapter 8 below. For now, we need to understand that engagement can actually occur in a different sequence and more frequently than the regulated remuneration cycle envisages.

NOTES

1.   Main et al 2008.
2.   Bender 2004, p. 493.
3.   *The Combined Code* (2008), B.1, B.1.1 and Schedule A; Association of British Insurers 2007, p. 4; National Association of Pension Funds 2007, p. 47.
4.   Bender and Moir 2006.

5. Bizjak 2011; Faulkender 2010.
6. Bizjak, Lemmon and Naveen 2008, p, 166.
7. Garvey and Milbourn 2006, p. 199; Bertrand and Mullainathan 2001, p. 901.
8. Perkins and Hendry 2005, p. 1457.
9. Association of British Insurers 2007, p. 6.
10. National Association of Pension Funds 2007, p. 24.
11. Northern Rock plc, *Directors' Reports and Accounts 2002*, p. 18.
12. Cf. US data on shareholder proposals and the rate of growth: Thomas and Martin 1999.
13. Association of British Insurers 2007, p. 7; National Association of Pension Funds 2007, p. 24.
14. Sheehan 2011, p. 133.
15. Sheehan 2011, pp. 132–3.
16. Study Group on Directors' Remuneration 1995, paras [6.19]–[6.20].
17. Thus empirical studies reporting a positive relationship between cash compensation and accounting earnings (for example, Liu and Stark 2009) are unremarkable in that STIs are designed with these measures in mind.
18. Gregg, Jewell and Tonks 2005, p. 29.
19. O'Connell 2011.
20. Perkins and Hendry 2005, p. 1461 note that boards approach the task of setting performance targets with a range of contingencies on an 'ad hominem' basis.
21. Balsam 2011.
22. Association of British Insurers 2007, p. 13.
23. Association of British Insurers 2007, p. 12.
24. Thompson 2005 notes that the studies on LTIP and its effect on pay for performance sensitivity in the UK do not show a strong link, even when relative performance evaluation is used.
25. Over the period 2003–05, the FTSE 100 companies in my sample of 73 with a bespoke TSR comparator group (as opposed to an index such as the FTSE 100) disclosed a wide variety of practices, with anywhere between five and 42 companies in a comparator group, with an average of 18 companies.
26. Bender 2004, p. 532.
27. Ogden and Watson 2008, p. 733 report that designing the LTIP is a dynamic process, but may include revisiting previously unachievable targets.
28. Grant, Markarian and Parbonetti 2009.
29. Fee and Hadlock 2003 report the results of a US study showing executives in companies with five-year superior firm performance have enhanced opportunities in the external labour market, although the more senior the executive, the more likely he or she will be held accountable for that firm performance.
30. Murphy and Zábojník 2007 theorise that the competition in the labour market for the best CEO talent leads companies to pay more for general managerial skills than firm specific knowledge.
31. See Wade et al 2006 for the results of a US study.
32. This suggests distributive justice is determined on an intra-firm basis, as well as an inter-firm, market basis: Swanson and Orlitzky 2006, pp. 13, 23; Hermanson et al 2011.
33. This experience seems to have been forgotten: see Department for Business Innovation and Skills 2011a, pp. 21–2, proposing a binding vote on remuneration.
34. Sheehan 2007.
35. Association of British Insurers and the National Association of Pension Funds 2002, para. [2.5]; Association of British Insurers and the National Association of Pension Funds 2008, para. [3.5].
36. In the UK, offering a service contract with a guaranteed term of two years or longer without prior shareholder approval will result in that term being declared void, with a term implied to the effect of allowing a company to terminate the service contract

at any time by giving reasonable notice. *Companies Act 2006* (UK), c 46, s 189, with prior shareholder approval required under s 188. Previously the limit was five years: *Companies Act 1985* (UK), c 6, s 319.

37. For example, changes made to the taxation of pensions in the UK under the *Finance Act 2006* (UK), c 25 triggered a number of major reviews of remuneration; the change in shareholder guidance on re-tests in LTI schemes also prompted major reviews in the UK.

38. Bender 2007.

39. One UK corporate governance manager said he received around 20–30 such letters annually.

6. Australian remuneration practice – best practice?

Three key differences exist in the annual review cycle for Australian companies compared with that for the UK as set out in Figure 5.1 in the previous chapter. First, if management briefs the consultants (which was common practice),[1] a number of the decisions shown as 'remuneration committee' decisions in Figure 5.1 are actually made by management.[2] In these circumstances, there could be an iterative process, as described by this Australian remuneration committee chair:

> Normally what I do is that I sit down with the HR GM here who is very good and very experienced. We'll debate about what we are asking the remuneration consultants to do this year. Any bits of additional information we want. HR GM will then prepare the brief; I'll have a look at it and say, 'Yes: that's what we agreed' and the consultant will come in for a briefing. And occasionally, if it's a bit out of the ordinary, I'll be involved in the briefing . . . when the report comes in, HR GM will go through it, then HR GM and I will go through it. Then we'll get the rem consultants in and HR GM and I together will debate it with them. So then I guess I've a lot of rem experience: as a former chief executive, I've had this debate for 20 plus years, so I've got experience of my own, plus I sit on a number of other boards. So I'll go and have a debate sometimes with the rem people. Finally, it lands, and that will then make its way finally to the rem committee.

Alternatively, the remuneration committee might only become involved towards the end of the annual review process. One remuneration consultant described that process to me:

> In some cases we are hired as advisors to management and compile a report which is then submitted to the remuneration committee. We may be asked to attend the meeting of that committee to present the findings. Or it may be processed behind the scenes without us physically being there. That, if you like, is probably the sort of traditional, low-involvement model, which is gradually being replaced by one where we have more direct contact with the remuneration committee, to the point where the remuneration committee is effectively the hiring agency that engages our services.

The opportunities to 'cherry pick' the comparator group that such an approach concedes to management can undermine the integrity of the benchmarking exercise that forms the basis of the annual review. Yet there are also advantages in remuneration consultants speaking directly with management:

> We'll test the peer group on the chief executive. This is valuable as the CEO gives us information on which companies our client competes with for capital, labour, customers and suppliers.

> I would sometimes work with the CEO; to discuss the remuneration for his or her direct reports, but not his or her own . . . I do have an interaction but in a way that keeps it as arm's length as reasonably possible in relation to any individual's own pay . . . You can do it without that. But you do often get some useful perspectives when you understand where those executives have come from. What's their career track record, what are their core skills. In other words: what are their best employment alternatives,[3] which may or may not be the conventional ones.

A second difference to the annual review process relates to the laws surrounding related party transactions in chapter 2E of the *Corporations Act 2001* (Cth) and the reasonable remuneration exception in section 211. To ensure that shareholders do not need to approve the remuneration as a related party transaction, some remuneration committees will seek a reasonableness certification from their remuneration consultants. This can become a problem if the remuneration committee has not exclusively briefed the consultants:

> I ended up at the remuneration committee and the first question I was asked was why was it that, at the last moment, I decided not to write a letter of reasonableness to the work I was involved in. I said, *'I'm sorry. I wasn't actually involved in the work'* and there was just a gasp all around. They had actually thought that I had been involved in drafting the report.

The third and final key difference between the Australian and UK approaches relates to the decisions surrounding LTI grants. Under the ASX *Listing Rule* 10.14, an issue of securities to a director (but not a purchase on-market) requires prior shareholder approval. Thus Australian remuneration committees typically seek such approval on a two-year cycle, rather than making an annual decision on the LTI award potential. Changes to business and economic conditions in the period between shareholder approval and the date of issue of the securities can work both for and against the directors, depending on the relevant vehicle (options, performance rights or restricted shares, shares purchased with a non- or limited recourse loan from the company). It therefore becomes even more important for Australian remuneration committees to understand the likely payoffs under different performance scenarios than their UK counterparts. As one remuneration consultant noted, he plays a role in 'saving the committee from themselves'.

6.1   REMUNERATION STRATEGY

If remuneration policy contributed to corporate governance failures such as HIH,[4] there is a need to understand how remuneration policy can drive behaviour. A number of assumptions underlie the relevant guidance on the objective of remuneration policies:[5]

- Remuneration is a tool to attract and maintain talented and motivated executives.
- Remuneration can encourage enhanced company performance measured as long term growth and success on a comparative basis with the market.
- Good remuneration is balanced between short and long term performance objectives and is appropriate to the company's goals and circumstances.
- Remuneration can create executive wealth, provided it does so in a manner consistent with shareholder aspirations.

The assumption that remuneration can create executive wealth is not found in the UK guidance. While not trumpeted in statements of remuneration policy found in remuneration reports, it is clear that Australian executives have benefited from a strong growth period:

> What we've done, because the share market has gone like that for the last 16 years, we just keep giving 10 per cent a year and then a bit more occasionally and we've quadrupled his bonus and we've got a light touch on the LTI so that's proving a bit problematic and all of a sudden you've got someone earning $2 million or $3 million that was very happy on $500,000 not that long ago. (Australian remuneration consultant)

6.2   BENCHMARKING

Given the evidence of Australian management briefing remuneration consultants and earlier evidence of 'cherry picking' of comparator groups, settling the comparator group becomes more critical in the Australian context. The relevant guidance in Australia on comparator groups nominates industry, size and business focus as the relevant factors to determine the group:[6]

> Peer groups are not static, although boards want them to be . . . We ask the client to both confirm and sign off on the peer group. It is important to discuss this with the board and to arrive at a consensus on the composition of the peer group 'to get everyone on the same page' at this point. (Australian remuneration consultant)

One difficulty in Australia is the small size of that market; as one Australian remuneration consultant commented: 'We don't have 30 automakers, 30 retailers, 30 pharmaceutical companies.' As another remuneration consultant noted, accessing information about private companies and international companies that are relevant competitors for executive talent is therefore important.

> People often say, 'Well, you're not really competing with the world.'[7] For the particular company that I am in, we are. We've lost people to the world. I've poached people from the world. We are very much into the world business. They can go anywhere these people. And they do. (Remuneration committee chair)

However, not all remuneration committee chairs believe it is necessary to continuously refer back to the market via benchmarking studies:

> The only time you look at the market is to say that the potential takeout is comparable to what they might get somewhere else . . . in the end, when you're looking at that level, bearing in mind that it cascades down to everybody else, you've got to look at your own company. A construction company is different to a manufacturing company to a mining company. They've all got different incentives, problems, issues. So I think just looking at what everybody else is doing is wrong. And that's what happens.

Market data have their uses:

> I think it's useful to have some frame of reference to ensure where we want to be. Market data is only one tiny piece of information that goes into decisions about pay. And I think sometimes that people may try to oversimplify it by thinking 'I'm just going to chase the market and keep following a market reference point and keep ratcheting up pay'. (Remuneration consultant)

> You can't have everyone paying above the median . . . and it does lead to some extent to that ratcheting up effect of everyone trying to beat the others when, at the end of the day, it's not true that everyone has the best talent. (Remuneration consultant)

Australian practice is to specify an amount as fixed annual remuneration, with the executive able to designate how much of the fixed annual remuneration will be taken as base salary, non-cash benefits and superannuation. The fixed component of the package should be relative to the scale of the business measured not only in terms of market capitalisation, sales and assets, but also in terms of employee numbers.[8] ACSI further wishes to see a link between the increases in executive pay with the rate of increases applicable generally in the company and seeks justification for substantial increases in base pay.[9] IFSA seeks reasonableness and comparability with the industry as a whole as the relevant benchmark for the total remuneration package.[10]

The guidelines therefore encourage market benchmarking and also suggest that particular size measures (market capitalisation, sales, assets, employee numbers) and relativity measures (increases generally within the company, reasonableness with the industry) are pertinent. Yet benchmarking against market capitalisation, particularly in a bull market, can present an opportunity for large increases:

> If you do a market cap peer group one year and you do another one next year, you might have different companies in there and those companies might be paying more, so suddenly your remuneration arrangements are out of line. But it's not that you're out of line, it's that your peer group has changed. (Remuneration consultant)

> We select a group of companies that are of similar size and another group of companies that are roughly in the same industry . . . We take the market cap for size, revenue for size, net profits for size, employees for size, that's probably most of them. When we've done our analysis we find that the better correlation comes from market cap[11] because sometimes you get a very large company in terms of revenue but very little profit and all other factors, whereas market cap tends to distil all of those things out and comes up with a market perception of the underlying value of the entity that's being managed by top management. So we spend a lot of time selecting those two groups and we try to get a balanced group because when you do these groups they can be skewed and so . . . if we go for company size, we're trying to give an equal number of larger and an equal number of smaller . . . But we don't see it as a precise science, we see it as a bit of an art that gets you into the right ballpark and you can make some judgments with it. (Australian remuneration consultant)

This is critical when positioning the total fixed remuneration at the median of the comparator group:

> Historically, I think a lot of remuneration consultants have presented data with more of a leaning to the upper quartiles, saying 'If you want to have the best talent, you should be paying up above the median.' But the reality is, when you

stand back and look at the whole economy, you can't have everyone paying above the median . . . Statistically it just does not work. I think we do need to stand back from that and say, 'What is the compelling reason for setting target pay above the market, as opposed to actual pay when the talent actually does deliver?' . . . Shareholders don't mind executives being paid in the top quartile if they've delivered top quartile performance against whatever standards are reasonable. But to actually target the pay in the top quartile for actually just being there is just anathema to best practice. (Australian remuneration consultant)

You might get a brief. 'We're sort of anticipating a 5 per cent increase and 20 per cent uplift to our bonus opportunity because we don't think we're competitive', so the remuneration consultant can go and have a look at the broad church: 'Oh, you don't seem too badly off. However, if I eliminate health care companies, retailers and resource companies, which I don't think are relevant to your widget manufacturing, it gives me a very different picture. If I eliminate companies that are smaller than yours and include companies that are twice as large in your industry, it's quite true: your bonuses are low, proportionate to the base, your salaries are not competitive, et cetera, et cetera, and this is a sample of 50 quite relevant companies your board will be comfortable in.' So that's my model which is developing a customised [comparator group] but customised with an objective, so remuneration itself will answer the question. Or we'll undertake research which will provide an answer for the question. (Remuneration consultant)

There is another reason for finding the answer to the question:

The money is simply a scorecard that says 'Am I achieving and am I a winner?' And they really don't care whether it's a million dollars or two million or five million or ten million. But they do care relative to everybody else they know about . . . They're trying to be stars. (Remuneration consultant)

6.3   FIXED REMUNERATION

Evidence of the percentage annual increases in fixed remuneration over the period of the study for the S&P/ASX 100 and S&P/ASX 300 is presented in Table 6.1. These figures indicate that companies with larger market capitalisations tend to increase remuneration to a greater extent than companies at the median, although the rates of increase for the years 2006–08 for these two groups are constant (around 22 per cent for upper quartile ASX 300 and 11 per cent for median of the ASX 300).

Finally, in terms of fixed remuneration, it is important to consider superannuation as the practices in Australia differ from the UK in respect of pensions. There is no specific guidance on superannuation payments in either the market exchange operator *Listing Rules* and guidance, nor is there any attention given to this issue separately in the ACSI or IFSA

Table 6.1   *Percentage increases in fixed remuneration, ASX 100, 2003–07 and ASX 300, 2005–08*

Year	Upper quartile (%)	Median (%)	Lower quartile (%)
2003	n/a	26	n/a
2004	n/a	19	n/a
2005	–4	8 (2)	**14**
2006	**21.7**	9.9 (15)	0.07
2007	**23.6**	11 (–3)	3.0
2008	23	11	5

Note: The median column shows figures for the ASX 100, with the ASX 300 in brackets. The percentages shown were calculated on the dollar values reported by ACSI. The figures for the upper quartile and lower quartile are for the ASX 300 only.

Sources: Data for the ASX 100 come from Australian Council of Superannuation Investors Inc 2008, p. 9. The percentages shown were calculated by the author based on the dollar values reported by ACSI. Data for the ASX 300 come from Guerdon Associates: http://www.guerdonassociates.com (accessed 21 July 2009). There is no readily available dataset on ASX 200 companies.

guidelines. Companies are required to contribute 9 per cent of annual salary into a superannuation account for an employee under s 19(1) of the *Superannuation Guarantee (Administration) Act 1992* (Cth). However, for CEOs and other senior executives in ASX 200 companies, the actual rate of payment required under this legislation is limited to the maximum contribution base defined in s 15(1). The rest of the superannuation payment is therefore reached by agreement between the company and the employee. This lack of guidance for superannuation at the senior executive level reflects a lack of awareness of the potential size of accumulated superannuation. Typically, this is only discovered on the executive's termination or retirement from office, as was the case with David Murray, the former CEO of the Commonwealth Bank of Australia Ltd: a payment of $11.8 million in superannuation accumulated over almost 40 years of service, with 13 years as the managing director.[12]

6.4   VARIABLE REMUNERATION

Market exchange operator guidance requires performance-based remuneration to be linked to clearly specified performance targets with some preference indicated for both relative and absolute performance measures.[13] Shareholder guidance says annual bonuses should be *a reasonable and explainable multiple of base salary*, with payments in cash linked to clear performance requirements and targets,[14] and any share-based components of the annual bonus subject to the performance conditions for long term incentives.

The Australian evidence on short term incentives reveals a preference for a balanced scorecard approach[15] of key performance indicators (KPIs) across a number of financial and non-financial dimensions, or a more simple mix of financial and non-financial measures. Three remuneration consultants commented on this issue:

> I think for measuring short term performance, some sort of balanced scorecard is appropriate where financials relating particularly to return in the short run are relevant but balanced against measures around employees such as employee engagement; customers, such as customer satisfaction or retention; and maybe other groups, for example chemical companies, what are they doing to the environment, the impact on the environment and sustainability.

> Our position is that what we need is a balance of performance metrics. Any focus on one single metric will result in unintended behaviours or outcomes, so we believe it's important to capture a range of metrics that captures different dimensions of company performance.

> There has to be some measures or principles around for measures. It is probably more useful to think about: they are relevant, they are tied to the company's drivers of value, they are things the executives can influence and they don't have unintended consequences, so they don't pay out when the tide is high.

As with the UK, STI designs are the company's own handiwork:

> We tend to do relatively little work in terms of STI design . . . I think it's because STI is not a complicated design. Most people use target-based plans. Most people know they've got to select a bunch of KPIs, you've got to set some standards, rate the performance around them and attach some dollars to it. You don't have to be Einstein to do that. (Remuneration consultant)

> I'm very focused on ensuring that the short term incentives are in line with shareholders' interests, so I'm looking at the budget that's adopted by the board, the quality of that budget. I'm looking for the earnings-per-share criteria, measuring the performance of the enterprise . . . these are the sort of issues that you need to address, in my opinion, in terms of how you remunerate them, how you pay them, to keep them engaged, keep them focused. It [the STI targets] ran off the MD's, so there was an agreement between the chairman and the MD, approved by the board, which said 'These are the targets for the year. This is what we expect you to achieve.' (Remuneration committee chair)

> Who prepares the budget? Yes, the board approves it, but do they have all the information? So the whole thing is capable of manipulation. (Remuneration committee chair)[16]

There are two fundamental principles. One is that you hold people accountable for things that they have some control over . . . Second one is that you want to have their focus on the things you believe matter in terms of what the company is trying to achieve in order to deliver good outcomes to shareholders . . . The STI has to be very much focused on what are the key priorities for the business. (Remuneration committee chair)

Changes in market conditions might result in 'shifting the goal posts'; or the company's salary positioning might force it to set soft targets, so as to more or less guarantee a level of total remuneration:

We tend to have an overriding couple of criteria for most incentives. One is based on the profit we achieved last year and then there's a growth target, based on what we forecast for this year. Well the growth just isn't happening this year, so we've just moved the goal posts around a little, and we won't make last year's either, so there's been a heavy impact on the incentive component. Generally speaking the packages are 50 per cent base, 50 per cent incentive. So, as I say, we've monitored that and just look at tweaking it slightly to keep people relatively happy. (Remuneration committee chair)

It is not difficult for those KPIs to be achieved; sometimes they are removed from the list of KPIs if they are not achieved or difficult to achieve. The goal is to get the people participating in the STI as near to 100 per cent of their bonus as possible . . . People now expect a pot of gold for just doing the job. (Remuneration committee chair)

Given the heavy involvement of management in setting the parameters for the STI, what is the role of the remuneration committee? The following three quotes suggest quite different roles:

We trust the management to run the business. It's a highly technical business, they're very good at it and very well trained. And they set effectively what we bless as the short term incentive and then the budget as a whole, when we bless it. (Remuneration committee chair)

One of the things that bedevils this, and makes this quite a challenge, is that there is no agreement from clever finance types as to what 'good' looks like in a company. And 'good' looks different in different companies . . . This is not about rem, but about understanding the fundamental drivers of the company. (Remuneration committee chair)

They might have also had a discussion with the CEO about his own performance and his own payment and sometimes there's a disconnect between A and B. He or she would have thought everyone's done quite well and would be proposing to pay a marginal premium over the target incentive. The Board may have the view that that is not the case. The Board may wish to exercise discretion where they believe that, while the result was over/exceeded budget, the company's relative positioning in the market declined. (Remuneration consultant)

Does variable pay incentivise performance? These two remuneration committee chairs noted:

> At the end of the day, it's all about motivating behaviour to deliver outcomes that will be beneficial to the shareholders.

> There is no doubt in my mind that even among the rich sort of groups, the CEOs and so on, are motivated by the possibility of getting more money. So some of these LTI and even the STI can work very well. It's a rare active executive who doesn't care what he's paid.

Not all remuneration committee chairs agreed with these views:

> If I had to say what motivation comes from a salary package versus all the other factors . . . I'd say 50 per cent perhaps . . . it's really a career path.

> There's a whole lot of reasons why people are interested in working for an organisation . . . it is seen as an interesting place to work; it is seen as a source of reasonably well remunerated work.

> I have only been out of the chief executive role for three years . . . but most of my career and some of my non-executive colleagues have lived through a career where incentives/bonuses were not a key feature. The incentive was to keep your job and if you got a pay increase at the annual review you were happy . . . We grew steadily. We built our careers and our businesses and our positions in the company steadily. We didn't expect the world at 28. We didn't expect it at 48. You got it at 58. Those companies and that attitude have disappeared.

It might also depend on the economic cycle:

> I think executives like LTIs and STIs when the market is more buoyant. I think when you're in a downturn like we are at the moment, they perceive them as being much harder to achieve, again depending on what the KPIs are of course . . . I think that's when the level of the base becomes important. (Remuneration committee chair)

Remuneration consultants do not readily accept these 'incentivisation' arguments:

> They signal to people what to concentrate on, but I don't think they make any of us work any harder. Not unless it's a significant amount of reward . . . If you are a committed executive, you are going to go to work and do the right thing. And what you want incentives to do is to flag to you, out of all the things you

have to do, what are some of the priority areas. And you want them to not stand in the way of the things you need to get done . . . I think that if anyone thinks they are going to find a measure that will provide optimal performance alignment, that will change behaviours, it's a holy grail. I just don't think there is such a thing.

6.5 LTI PRACTICE

Similar to the situation in the UK described above in chapter 5, Australian institutional shareholders provide detailed guidance for long term incentives. ACSI's guidelines reflect in large part the ABI guidance noted above. IFSA's guidance note on executive equity plans reflects a number of the same positions evident in both the ACSI and ABI guidance, with a slightly different emphasis in relation to performance conditions upon criteria that will demonstrate a material improvement of the company's relative performance rather than indicators linked to general market benchmarks.[17]

Evidence from the remuneration reports reveals a few 'variations on a theme' for LTIs deployed in practice: EPS growth only, relative TSR to one or more comparators only (either an index or a bespoke comparator group), EPS growth and relative TSR,[18] relative TSR and return on equity (ROE) or return on capital employed (ROCE), or both relative and absolute TSR.[19] Bespoke comparator groups were relatively rare in the sample companies for the period studied. Of the 76 companies in the sample with TSR as a performance measure, only nine companies disclosed that a bespoke comparator group was used. The size of these groups ranged from 11 to 52 companies, with a median of 14 companies and an average of 22 companies, which reflects two companies that used comparator groups of 52 and 50 companies.

Long term incentives can be used to camouflage the true extent of the remuneration payment by setting a low absolute target that is guaranteed to pay out:

> A company might have say at a 10 per cent average TSR, but strike a hurdle at eight, but they don't publish it. It's guaranteed, unless something goes really bad. It's very easy to do. (Remuneration committee chair)

As Stapledon notes, a different way in which performance can be camouflaged is via the use of zero exercise price options that always have value for an executive as there is only a nominal price to exercise a tranche of such share-based payments.[20]

Remuneration consultants suggested there was a commonality of approach to remuneration emerging in Australia, driven by disclosure. It might instead be driven by shareholder guidance:

LTIs tend to be a longer process in that there are so many aspects to a long term incentive where various stakeholders have put their views out to the market and most boards are very conscious of not wanting to be inconsistent with the guidelines unless they have a good reason. Doesn't mean they're going to follow them blindly, but in the absence of a good reason, they'll go with the guidelines. (Remuneration consultant)

When you look at the type of long term incentive schemes' vesting patterns, performance vesting conditions, the structure of the payoff curves at the 50th and 75th percentile, the use of comparative TSR. There's a lot of commonality. And a number of examples where companies wanted to do something different, but were beaten up by the investor groups. They just submitted and went the way of others in the market. There's been a lot of 'follow the leader' behaviour that has ended up with vanilla solutions. (Remuneration consultant)

It may even be driven by the advice from remuneration consultants themselves:

I'm critical of the institutional advisors in terms of their [guidance being] actually the norm. I think we've probably also been guilty at an earlier stage of producing homogenisation, 'this is what the market's doing, so therefore it should be like that.' (Remuneration consultant)

Remuneration committee chairs justified the selection of TSR in various ways, as these three quotes illustrate:

We've had that for quite some time, the measure is total shareholder return has to be CPI [consumer price index] plus 10 per cent. We introduced this as a method of helping to retain our senior people and also aligning some of their remuneration with the interests of shareholders as well.

A long term incentive on the other hand needs to have much more of a shareholder focus.

Best practice is where you reward your key executives in a manner that aligns their interests and shareholders' interests . . . I like to tie the performance into the actual underlying performance of the entity both in terms of its numbers and its performance in terms of its share price on the LTI.

While TSR cannot be directly influenced by executives, caution needs to be exercised in interpreting its trajectory:

You'll find that our TSR is absolutely outstanding. And you'll say, 'Wow! What a clever bunch!' You'll look at the chart and ask 'Well, why did it leap up here?' Well, it leapt up here because someone tried to take us over. And so you say, 'Is that fair?' (Remuneration committee chair)

Changes in economic circumstances might mean that

> A fair number of executives have long term incentives . . . way out of the money. There's no intention of making any retrospective changes to that . . . that's what they're there for, to make sure that shareholders and management have alignment around remuneration, or at least around performance. (Remuneration committee chair)

While wealth generation is an accepted outcome of executive remuneration structures, at least according to the relevant shareholder guidance, how that wealth is generated is critical. With the strong bull market in Australia up until 2008, many senior executives were tempted to take out margin loans to acquire more shares in their company. When the market turned downwards in 2008, some executives were faced with a margin call or had to off-load their shareholding position.[21] For other executives, the change in financial position meant changes to consumer spending on lifestyle. This put the remuneration committee or the company chairman in a delicate position:

> To what extent can a chairman say to an executive, 'Are you in trouble?' They don't probe about his personal life, they don't probe about how much money he's borrowed on the new home he's built in Killara, they don't probe about anything. (Remuneration consultant)

6.6 AD HOC REMUNERATION DECISIONS

In the case of an appointment, the remuneration committee can be called upon to settle the salary package to be offered and will seek the counsel of a remuneration consultant for this purpose:

> [T]he chairman of the committee, or the managing director, or both, might seek a sign off from a remuneration consultant in relation to a payment of attracting someone which is anomalous in terms of their pay practices. And they just simply say 'Fred or Mary: we really want to get them on board. They've got a perfect background for what we want. We've got these sorts of issues: if we pay $X which, as you know is $300,000 more than we paid Jim, what implications will that have? And is that a reasonable reflection of the market and, if so, where in the market? Is it right at the top? Is it about average today? Or have we fallen behind? (Remuneration consultant)

As with their UK counterparts, Australian companies will frequently have to pay an amount equivalent to the value of surrendered equity incentives.[22]

Remuneration committees may also need to decide whether to match the offer a current executive has received from a competitor or another firm. All the remuneration committee chairs were asked if they had lost an executive due to their inability or unwillingness to trump a salary offer. In some instances, the decision not to match the outside offer is straightforward:

> We really liked him. Good operator. He was offered a job – I think on paper it looks higher than what it is – but it's a smaller company. He's a bigger pea in a smaller pod. And with us he'd be a bigger pea but in a bigger pod. And they offered him, I think it was *35% more* than what we paid him. And we deliberated – interestingly not as a committee. The CEO rang the [company] chairman and we [CEO, company chairman and remuneration committee chairman] talked about it. And we decided no, he's fantastic, but *it would send everybody upwards.*[23]

In other cases, the executive's 'heart and soul' has already left the organisation, so matching the offer might save them from leaving, 'but they're never going to be settled and happy, and if they're not settled and happy, it permeates the organisation' (remuneration committee chair). Remuneration committees therefore appear to have a strong sense of internal relativities, as well as market relativities, in mind when making these types of ad hoc decisions, although according to a remuneration consultant, they may be making judgments wearing 'rose-coloured glasses'. A tight labour market can put pressure on committees to meet market salaries, if not to remunerate in the upper quartile. The remuneration consultants interviewed all noted this issue:

> The committee sometimes [is] held to ransom by the CEO or other senior executives, saying 'if we don't put [the package] up there, we can't attract and retain such people' . . . I think some companies will have to make a decision about whether the values they are trying to portray need to be offset against a Dutch auction of paying whatever it takes to get someone from wherever, almost in a ransom-type situation.

A tight labour market can also put pressure on committees to offer retention payments, because 'you've got down time while you retrain somebody or find somebody and it all costs lots of money' (remuneration committee chair).

The other major ad hoc decision is to settle a termination payment. Legislation restricts the nature of termination payments which can be given by companies without shareholder approval[24] which, combined with continuous disclosure obligations,[25] ex-ante and ex-post[26] reporting obligations, would seem to provide, so far as regulation can in an area which governments and others believe must allow room for market forces to operate, for sufficient means by which to curb excessive payments. Shareholder guidance clarifies what shareholders will look for when assessing termination payments.[27] One remuneration committee chair remarked that one of the reasons for a ratchet in CEO salaries in Australia is 'lawyers drafting contracts'. The complexities of senior executive employment contracts may not be readily appreciated by remuneration committee members:

> They might find that of the top 20 people, half a dozen have got significant redundancy benefits plus a termination benefit, half a dozen have got pretty plain vanilla termination benefits, half a dozen have got extraordinarily generous termination benefits and there's a problem. They say 'We thought they'd all be the same' and they're not. An event will often bring forward a matter which has been sleeping and that will normally be in the contractual area. (Remuneration consultant)

6.7   PROACTIVE ENGAGEMENT AROUND THE ANNUAL REVIEW

Remuneration committees and remuneration consultants spoke of undertaking engagement as a matter of course with key institutional investors outside the peak AGM season. One remuneration committee chair noted that he likes to

> meet with the key shareholders every year and I either go and see them, or ring them and invite them in for a chat. And we discuss, not operational issues, because that's the purview of the CEO, but we discuss board governance . . . we talk to them about our policies and strategies. We talk to them about the make-up of the remuneration package . . . [This chat does] not so much add value, other than to test some ideas . . . to see what their thinking is, to see whether I'm in line with them.

Talking to the proxy advisory firms and the company's major institutional investors can help to validate the information given to the remuneration committee by the remuneration consultants. Not all remuneration committee chairs were willing to speak with the proxy advisory or governance research firms during this activity, although they were willing to meet the proxy advisors in the pre-AGM round of engagement.

Most institutional investors do not undertake routine consultations on remuneration outside the AGM season, although there might be follow-up meetings with governance outliers from the previous AGM season. The fund managers noted they had routine meetings with management throughout the year, but typically only met with the remuneration committee on an ad hoc basis.[28] ACSI might bring together a number of super funds to proactively engage with the largest listed companies on remuneration. One super fund noted that it undertook limited engagement 'with about four or five' relying primarily upon ACSI's engagement with the ASX 200. This appears to be typical and suggests superannuation funds might only engage directly with remuneration committees at unlisted companies, relying upon their investment managers, Regnan or ACSI to undertake any necessary engagement with listed companies. The difference in approach, whereby ACSI will go public with its concerns, whereas Regnan adopts a behind-the-scenes approach, creates a flexibility that one super fund alone could not achieve. For at least one remuneration committee chair, this engagement is valuable 'only in the sense that it helps to reduce a negative vote. In terms of contributing to the design, not a great deal, other than understanding what their preferences are.'

6.8 THE MAJOR REVIEW OF REMUNERATION

The process outlined in Figure 5.2 above is also followed in Australia. A major review of remuneration typically takes six months, but at least two interviewees commented that it can take up to 12 months. A longer period of review increases the likelihood that more than one round of engagement will be conducted. Remuneration consultants noted it was important to engage with the proxy advisory firms prior to making any major changes:

> If there is a major change that the company is going to go through and they want to consult them and *ensure that they have gone through due process*, they may well speak to those bodies prior to making the change. And say 'Well, look, this is where we are thinking about going: how does that sit with you; with your guidelines?' Because often the guidelines don't tell you the *interpretation* of the guidelines and you want to get a sense [of that]. There is never any certainty that what they tell you prior to you making the change is what they end up voting.

For one remuneration committee chair, engaging with proxy advisors was 'terribly important . . . probably more important than institutional investors'. This might be motivated by advice from the remuneration consultant that the proposed change will attract pushback. To avoid this, one company that decided to abandon its LTI and pay only an STI with a deferred component

> went around and they all said 'Fine, tick, tick, tick, agree with it, what you want to do' . . . they took the initiative and were prepared to go to the shareholders. (Remuneration consultant)

One company kept the whole major review away from institutional share-holders but this was

> at a time when the non-binding vote on remuneration hadn't been in place for very long and therefore practices with regard to shareholder communicating were still in their infancy. (Remuneration committee chair)

One fund manager confirmed this change in practice:

> That didn't happen initially and then, probably about 2005, 2006 they kind of discovered we existed. Now we routinely get calls or emails from companies . . . they've made changes to their long term incentive plan and just want to see what we would think about it. So that does happen more and more.

For this fund manager, engagement around anything contentious is expected: 'If we weren't approached and it was a bit of an issue, then we would have something to say about that.' Remuneration committee chairs seem attuned to the need to talk to the institutions if introducing something contentious, even if only to give them advanced notice of a change already committed to as, 'We don't come to these decisions easily. So once we've come to it, we've got to think we've made the right one' (remuneration committee chair).

Engaging with proxy advisors in lieu of direct engagement with fund managers may not be an option for all companies. Two fund managers noted they did not use proxy advisory services because

> it's a bit of a copout . . . we take the view that clients have given us money to invest on their behalf . . . *We have a duty of care to our clients to actually do the appropriate research.* Now if we start outsourcing that to third party providers, that's not providing an appropriate duty of care.

6.9 CONCLUSION

Executive remuneration links the firm's business strategy with its execution[29] by attaching a reward to successful execution.[30] In a quest for legitimacy, executive remuneration conveys the illusion, if not the substance, of sound management.[31] Performance-based pay implicitly assumes that the CEO exerts a 'disproportionate influence' over corporate performance, as well as having the leverage to direct the company's strategic destiny.[32]

Politically, the CEO has to manage the expectations of the employees, the board of directors and the company's investors. CEO terminations illustrate that poor performance is frequently measured as political failure,[33] as well as financial performance failures.[34] That performance-based remuneration motivates the CEO to perform well on both dimensions assumes a causal relationship between incentive and performance. Whether remuneration arrangements cause superior performance or merely reflect its outcomes is unclear.[35] As we have seen, remuneration consultants and remuneration committees are not universally convinced of the validity of this argument. Even within human resource management theories of performance there is a debate as to whether it is the expectancy of the reward that motivates performance[36] or whether it is the acceptance of the performance goal rather than the expectation of the reward that motivates performance.[37] As O'Neill cautions, 'there remains a significant gap between the theory and practice of pay determination'.[38]

It is also possible to simplify the remuneration committee's task to appreciate how the regulated remuneration cycle operates in practice. Let us say that, each year, the remuneration committee makes two major decisions: what to award the CEO for the financial year just concluded, given firm performance (total actual remuneration, TAR), and what potential award to offer the CEO for the next financial year, given the firm's strategy and financial goals and targets (total potential remuneration, TPR). These decisions happen in conjunction with board sign-off of the previous year's financial results and endorsement of the budget for the new financial year. This is illustrated in Figure 6.1, the company's budgeting, reporting and remuneration cycle.

Figure 6.1 mirrors the regulated remuneration cycle in Figure 2.1, with the addition of an extra opportunity for engagement prior to disclosure, but after the board has made the TPR and TAR decisions for the year. This is proactive engagement and provides an opportunity for the board to sound out shareholders on any likely 'red flags'. This is still a regulatory conversation but its content and tone are set by the board, not shareholders. That more of this kind of conversation is occurring, as the evidence in this chapter suggests, does not necessarily mean better practices are resulting.

Shareholders who issue guidance regularly update the guidance in line with this cycle. In the case of the ABI, new guidance is usually issued just prior to the new calendar year in December, so that companies with a 31 December end of financial year can take this advice on board for the coming year. ACSI typically updates its statements every two years but issued the 2005 and 2007 statements just prior to the key AGM season (September–November). This meant that many Australian boards could not take the guidance into consideration leading to delays in implementing changes to fall in line with it. ACSI's 2009 and 2011 statements were issued

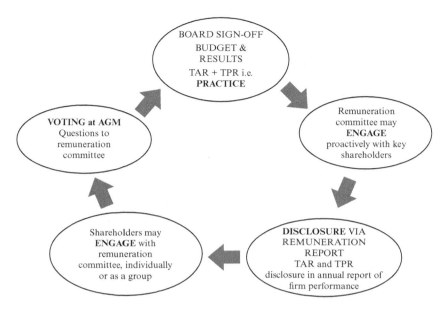

Figure 6.1   The company's budgeting, reporting and remuneration cycle

in March, thus allowing companies with a 30 June financial year end time to consider the guidance, seek advice on any changes and implement them more quickly. The constant restatement of what is good practice can have some implications for companies trying to structure remuneration policies over a three- to five-year cycle.

While remuneration committees can choose whether to adjust their practices to respond to evolving views of good practice, they must comply with legislative requirements. There can be a source of tension when legislation sets out a more generous standard of practice than shareholder guidance. Furthermore, new disclosure rules can also impact on remuneration practices but, more critically, new practices have to fit within the existing disclosure rules . . . or can they be hidden from shareholder scrutiny?

NOTES

1. Productivity Commission of Australia 2009, pp. 182–5.
2. This might explain some results obtained in earlier pay for performance studies based on Australian data. Izan, Sidhu and Taylor 1998 find no evidence of a statistically significant pay–performance relationship; Fleming and Stellios 2002 find the level of

excess remuneration is negatively related to the proportion of non-executive directors on the board. Cf. Evans and Evans 2005.

3. This information allows the remuneration consultant to determine the 'reservation wage': Diamond and Verrechia 1982, p. 276; Moore 1985, p. 40; Oyer 2004, pp. 1645–6.
4. See chapter 1, p. 3.
5. Australian Institute of Company Directors 2009, p. 16; ASX Corporate Governance Council 2003, pp. 51, 54; Australian Institute of Company Directors 2007, p. 35; Australian Council of Superannuation Investors Inc 2003, pp. 10–11; Australian Council of Superannuation Investors Inc 2005, p. 14; Australian Council of Superannuation Investors Inc 2007, p. 12.
6. Australian Institute of Company Directors 2004, p. 11; Australian Institute of Company Directors 2009, pp. 11–12; Australian Council of Superannuation Investors Inc 2007, p. 12; Australian Council of Superannuation Investors Inc 2005, p. 14; Australian Council of Superannuation Investors Inc 2003, p. 11.
7. Risk Metrics and the Australian Council of Superannuation Investors Inc 2009 casts doubt on the war for talent.
8. ASX Corporate Governance Council 2003, p. 55; ASX Corporate Governance Council 2007, p. 36.
9. Australian Council of Superannuation Investors Inc 2007, p. 12 – guidelines 14.4(b),(c).
10. Investment and Financial Services Association Limited 2007a, p. 5 (principle 3.3).
11. Garbaix and Landier 2008.
12. Sheehan and Fenwick 2008, p. 219.
13. ASX Corporate Governance Council 2007, p. 36. The guidance in box 8.1 does not distinguish between short term and long term incentives, but between performance-based and equity-based remuneration.
14. Australian Council of Superannuation Investors Inc 2007, p. 14 (guidelines 14.5(b) and (c)).
15. Kaplan and Norton 1996.
16. O'Reilly and Main 2010 note that CEOs might engage in social influence processes to increase their level of remuneration, with the opportunities to do so increasing with the number of independent directors.
17. Investment and Financial Services Association Limited 2007, pp. 7–8, principles 5.1–5.7.
18. Only 31 companies, or around 28 per cent of companies in the sample adopted this combination at some stage over the three years of the study.
19. Examples of companies with this approach include AWB Limited and Australian Worldwide Exploration Limited.
20. Stapledon 2004, p. 61; Ali and Stapledon 2000.
21. Korporaal and Meade 2008 (Eddie Groves, then CEO of ABC Learning Centres Ltd); Hartley 2008 (Greg Goodman, CEO of Macquarie Goodman Ltd).
22. Lee 2005.
23. Hamori 2006, p. 1147 reports that working for a large-sized company is likely to make an executive more visible to executive search firms and, given her other finding that perceived operational excellence is a predictor of executive career advancement, this type of career move appears consistent with this evidence.
24. *Corporations Act 2001* (Cth), s 200B(1) and the exceptions in ss 200F, 200G, 200H.
25. ASX *Listing Rules*, r 3.1; *Corporations Act 2001* (Cth), s 675(2); ASX 2003; Stapledon 2005; Sheehan and Fenwick 2008.
26. Disclosure of the key terms of service agreements with the directors is required under the *Corporations Regulations 2001* (Cth), reg. 2M.03.03, item 13.
27. The strongest statement is in Australian Council of Superannuation Investors Inc 2007, pp. 12–13.
28. North 2008, p. 513.
29. Lines 1978, pp. 9–10; Carver 2006, pp. 154, 159.
30. Pennings 2000, p. 377; McLaughlin 1991, pp. 7–13.

31. Pennings 2000, p. 380.
32. Pennings 2000, p. 374.
33. Manning and Sherwood 2008, pp. 2–3; Sonnenfeld and Ward 2007, p. 117.
34. Lucier, Schuyt and Handa 2004, p. 5.
35. Pennings 2000, p. 378.
36. Vroom 1964, p. 195.
37. Latham and Locke 1979, pp. 77–8.
38. O'Neill 2007, p. 698.

7. Disclosure

Look, to be quite honest, a lot of what happens is the CEO says, 'I want $10 million'. If you went to the market and said '$10 million', everyone would scream. So you say 'Only $2 million salary, but if they do these wonderful things, then it will be $10 million' and you structure all these wonderful things so that it is ten [million]. (S&P/ASX 200 remuneration committee chair)

The Hampel Committee in 1998 noted companies were disclosing remuneration policies 'with anodyne references to the need to "recruit, retain and motivate" or to pay "market rate"'.[1] Research one year later confirmed disclosure problems existed. A study by PricewaterhouseCoopers (PWC) for the DTI showed that while many companies in the sample analysed by PWC were disclosing in broad terms how performance was measured,[2] far fewer firms disclosed the performance measures in absolute numerical terms (for example, achieve annual net profit after tax of £x, or achieve annual profit growth of 10 per cent). Only 2 per cent of the sample disclosed this information for STIs such as the annual bonus, while 21 per cent of the sample disclosed this information for LTIs such as the share option plan.

More critically, discussion of the link between rewards and performance (the pay for performance link) was low for both general descriptions (37 per cent for STIs and 55 per cent for LTIs) and absolute numerical disclosures (17 per cent for STIs and 38 per cent for LTIs). Most companies failed to provide information to allow shareholders to make relative performance comparisons. Not only did 97 per cent of companies fail to discuss how company performance over the long term related to companies in the same sector, but 96 per cent failed to relate company performance over the long term to a well-known stock market index. Even a more general discussion on how the performance measures for incentive schemes related to long term company objectives was absent, with 95 per cent of the sample failing to disclose this information.[3]

We have already seen in chapter 1 the debate on disclosure at the time of CLERP 9 reforms that introduced the say on pay into Australian law.[4] That earlier discussion hints at the difficulties in writing disclosure laws to achieve a balance between information and comprehensive disclosure. While sunlight may be the best disinfectant, blazing sunlight leaves the viewer squinting to identify the features, seeing only the silhouette.[5] The same might be said of overly detailed remuneration disclosures:

> Reports are routinely 20 pages in length and some are over 50 pages. Both their length and complexity reflect the breadth and complexity of remuneration arrangements. They also reflect what companies consider they must do to comply with the not insignificant statutory requirements. A number of participants described the approach commonly taken by companies as legalistic 'boiler-plating' – that is, they attempt to shield themselves by using standard terms to describe arrangements. Such terminology is not particularly illuminating for investors.[6]

The bloating of remuneration reports, also observed by respondents to a 2010 consultation on narrative reporting in the UK,[7] reflects a broader trend towards longer and more complex annual reports.[8] In 2009, the FRC identified the overlapping rules on remuneration disclosure from various sources in the UK[9] before concluding: 'it isn't surprising that most preparers resort to a checklist to ensure they are compliant, rather than focusing on how best to communicate'.[10]

The usual approach to regulating executive remuneration is for government to use its law-making powers to mandate detailed remuneration disclosures. Should executive greed or excessive remuneration payments remain an issue, government will enact laws to mandate more disclosures to improve accountability and to expose the pay for performance link.[11] Is the answer to move away from prescription towards a principles-based approach?[12] Would such an approach mean that companies are better placed to 'tell their remuneration story'?[13] Or would they simply continue to supply standardised information because shareholders, remuneration consultants, accounting standards boards, management groups, accounting firms or even auditors[14] will devise the necessary standards if governments fail to do so?[15]

7.1 TARGETED TRANSPARENCY POLICIES AND RULE FORM

The remuneration report satisfies the five dimensions that Fung, Graham and Weil suggest are common to effective targeted transparency policies:[16]

- the specific policy purposes ensure the regulation is seen to not interfere with the proper operation of the markets;
- there are clear discloser targets (listed companies and particular directors and executives);

- the information is broadly defined (for example, the definitions of 'remuneration'[17] do not limit this to cash remuneration);
- there is a defined disclosure vehicle (specific types of information are required to be disclosed in a remuneration report within the annual report); and
- a mechanism to enforce disclosure exists by penalising the failure to disclose.[18]

However, sustaining such a targeted transparency policy is difficult: policy developed in response to a particular crisis motivates intended disclosers to engage in political actions to ensure the final policy and the laws imposed are weak. Disclosure laws 'degrade' over time because costs are concentrated (borne by disclosers largely) and benefits are dispersed.[19] One way in which disclosure laws degrade over time is 'boilerplate' disclosure: companies determine a particular 'magic phrase' or formula of words that will be accepted by shareholders and their proxy advisors. If anything, say on pay likely exacerbates this degradation because the 'say' in the form of the shareholder vote is a ready litmus test of the acceptance of particular words.

Targeted transparency policies are only updated when a further crisis looms to trigger a response;[20] with evidence again of political action to counter the pro-improvement disclosers.[21] Awareness of this behaviour means that governments initiating new disclosure laws have to effectively manage a campaign of public and private lobbying for 'no change'. It is important to remember that disclosure alone cannot change practice because the sanctions in the legislation target non-disclosure, not the practices disclosed. If disclosers perceive little or no benefit from making the mandatory disclosures, they may well seek to circumvent the disclosure laws. The result can be 'creative compliance',[22] where the disclosures fulfil the 'black letter' of the law but successfully avoid the spirit of the disclosure regime.[23] An effective sanction for wrong or poor practices must exist in some other part of the regulatory space for executive remuneration to achieve policy objectives directed towards practices.[24]

It is possible to see these patterns of behaviour in laws to mandate remuneration disclosures.[25] Mandatory disclosure is an important tool as it forces reluctant agents to disclose bad, as well as good, news about corporate performance, giving clues as to their own performance.[26] The news could be outcome oriented ('2005 was a poor year for the company' or 'no bonus payments were made to the senior executive team') or an assurance that a process has occurred ('the remuneration committee met three times this year' or 'the remuneration committee obtained independent advice on the incentive plans'). The substance of the disclosure rules will depend upon whether a process or an outcome forms the substantive aspect of the rule. For the remuneration-setting process via a remuneration committee, disclosure requires the company to demonstrate how the firm's remuneration practices compare with the 'best' practice: that is, confirm that the company complies or explain non-compliance. For directors' share dealing, an event, disclosure mandates the time frame within which disclosure of the event must occur: the rule is precise (three days) to ensure compliance. Disclosure of remuneration paid for a particular year (an outcome) is required under rules that are precise, clear, complex and mandatory, with legal sanctions for non-disclosure. If the goal of mandatory disclosure is to deter undesired practices, the cost of compliance with highly detailed disclosure rules might motivate executives to divert their remuneration into less readily observable forms.[27]

7.2 COMPANY PRACTICE ON DISCLOSURE[28]

The evidence of boilerplate disclosures noted in the introduction to this chapter is consistent with a compliance mentality, rather than the bespoke story-telling approach. It also reflects views expressed earlier in chapter 3 about the extent to which deviation from the best practice guidance of shareholders is permissible. Similarly, the empirical evidence of the excessive length of remuneration reports can be explained as companies taking a compliance approach driven instead by the extensive disclosures rules. It may also be the relationship between 'best practice' guidance, engagement and voting that is influencing such disclosure practices. The ABI guidelines together with the legal reporting requirements in the *Companies Act* are regarded by the UK remuneration consultants I interviewed as a starting point by providing structure for disclosures, if not necessarily the underlying remuneration practices, as 'Companies are very focused upon "How are we going to report this?"'

'Creative compliance' with the guidance might exist if, as one remuneration consultant commented, 'A lot of disclosure is optics' rather than an accurate reporting of actual practices. Another remuneration consultant downplayed this, suggesting it was a 'sugar coating of justifications for levels, rather than a deliberate hiding of information'. If shareholders value and respond to valid justifications for the quantum of remuneration paid, then this 'spoonful of sugar' may help them to digest high amounts of remuneration. A level of sugar will ultimately be misleading if it distorts the disclosed pay–performance relationship.

A broad carve-out in the regulations permits non-disclosure of 'sensitive' information and is exploited by companies in two ways: non-disclosure of measures and non-disclosure of past performance against the measures. From my own review of 219 FTSE 100 reports (73 companies for each of the years from 2003 to 2005) and 327 ASX 200 reports (109 companies for each of the years from 2005/06 to 2007/08),[29] annual bonus performance conditions are not clearly disclosed in remuneration reports,[30] although they are described; with FTSE 100 companies routinely disclosing the upper caps or limits on the annual bonus payments (either as a multiple or percentage of base salary). There is little disclosure of actual achievement of performance conditions, either in the narrative disclosures or in the financial disclosures. While shareholders support remuneration committees exercising discretion in determining such payments, they also want transparency, although as one FTSE 100 company secretary noted:

> Investors have to trust the committee. I think that there are some people who say that you have to be completely transparent about all the targets and schemes and you end up giving away what is potentially commercial information.

Yet it is precisely the relationship between the targets within schemes and the payments received by chief executives and other senior managers that lies at the heart of pay for performance.

7.3   THE ROLE OF PROXY ADVISORS IN INFLUENCING REMUNERATION DISCLOSURE PRACTICES

All the UK institutional investors interviewed use proxy advisors extensively and they all retained multiple proxy advisors. The reasons for using multiple advisors might simply be to ensure coverage of investee companies, as well as accessing a broader range of views on the remuneration report:

> The two bodies [IVIS and RREV] have complementary views, but sometimes there are differences. Both can be very useful. I can look at one that will highlight an issue which the other hasn't picked up.

The proxy advisors have differing sets of remuneration 'rules' and therefore apply different screens,[31] which can include the subscriber's own screen as a custom service. The screen of a particular proxy advisor might reflect the preferences of the particular shareholder:

I was on the committee that helped draft the rem policy of the NAPF Shareholder Affairs Committee. So it looks a lot like what our policy looks like.

We use IVIS because we believe its focus is most closely aligned with our own guidelines and it is connected with the market view as well.

It can also reflect different approaches in arriving at the final voting recommendation:

You have the ABI which is members based and they will ring up their members and say 'There is this particular issue on remuneration, how do you feel?' And their members will say 'We're happy with it' or 'We're not happy with it' and in that case they'll register a red top.

[t]he RiskMetrics (RREV) one is better just in terms of . . . it's got more detail, but they've engaged with the company: 'Here's what the company said'.

The proxy advisors' reports are crucial because the corporate governance managers only read remuneration reports identified by the advisors as problematic: 'In most cases, we know they've had the conversations already. So *we can focus on the things that matter*, rather than going through the whole thing over again.' In other words, the corporate governance managers rely upon proxy advisors to do 'first cut' on remuneration reports and to flag the issues. One corporate governance manager read the proxy advisor reports in a particular sequence:

We tend to use the ABI one most, *because they engage with companies* and they just focus on the areas where they think it's an issue, so it's a two-pager. It's a good place to start looking if you want to know what the issues are . . . And then we would probably use PIRC where *they actually give voting recommendations* . . . they are much more thorough . . . each of their reports would probably be about 20–30 pages, something like that . . . We use RREV again just for a third opinion. The good thing about the RREV stuff is they *actually have a graph on pay, so they'll tell you whether the company is actually at median*, above or below.

The evidence from the Australian interviews likewise confirms that proxy advisors are very important: it is *their* analysis of the remuneration reports and *their* recommendations on the advisory vote that identify the remuneration outliers. Retaining two proxy advisors allows for 'some form of comparison', although not all fund managers or super funds retained two advisors. A fund manager using only one advisor cited resourcing reasons for not undertaking this analysis in-house:

[They] have more resources to go into [analysing the] resolutions, *to compare CEO pay on STI and LTI and fixed pay to other top companies or similar size.* That's research that they can do which we really can't put together.

Comparative market data is valuable new information not contained in the remuneration report (which may go so far as to list out the companies in the comparator group, but does not disclose any statistical data such as median and average pay of that group). It provides a context for the remuneration reported by the company. The other valuable aspects of the proxy advisors' reports identified by interviewees are: the summary of the issues, the 'for and against' arguments and the fact that 'They do all the reading'. Institutional investors do not want to appear ill-informed about the company's practices as this can impact negatively on their existing relationship with the company. This need to maintain the relationship creates an incentive to become informed to maintain credibility, yet seemingly not so great an incentive as to encourage fund managers to invest in scaling up the in-house capacity or simply to read the remuneration reports for themselves. Finally, as a third party the proxy advisor's analysis can be used by investors against remuneration committees: 'We sometimes provide it to the company and simply say "Look, it's not just us saying this, it's an independent third party."'

In one sense, the proxy advisors are informational intermediaries or 'infomediaries'[32] because they do not provide new information but repackage information from a variety of sources into one report.[33] However, the process of devising and applying a screen invariably involves choices and professional judgments. In this sense, the role is not as neutral as 'infomediary' suggests. Some new information is provided by market comparisons for the quantum of remuneration or for company performance relative to peers in a broad index. In this way, proxy advisors communicate a view of the relevant market rates which may contradict the market remuneration consultants present to the company via the benchmarking undertaken in the annual review.

7.4 DISCLOSURE AND THE GROWTH IN EXECUTIVE REMUNERATION

Nearly all of the remuneration consultants and company representatives interviewed cited increased transparency as a source of pressure on executive salaries. The following quotes are representative of these views:

I think the fact that individual salaries linked to named people are published is probably the greatest source. It works between companies; it works within companies. There is publicity given to numbers and that generates a level of aspiration that might not have been there otherwise . . . At senior levels, it's not done overtly. (FTSE 100 company secretary)

I think markets are more transparent and all the disclosure stuff has made them more transparent. (FTSE 100 human resources director)

Number one: disclosure. Because you get disclosure, you get executives who look at all sorts of other companies, who gets paid what. (FTSE 100 remuneration committee chair)

I think disclosure has caused a lot of that. (UK remuneration consultant)

Transparency has put pressure on companies to standardise structures and their disclosure (of their remuneration practices), but it hasn't stopped the growth in quantum. (UK remuneration consultant)

One of the reasons why there is higher remuneration of executives is the remuneration report . . . I've seen it. I've had it put in my face. Someone comes along and says, 'You're paying me this. I've just looked at the annual report from that [company] and my peer is earning more than me.' (S&P/ASX 200 remuneration committee chair)

[I]t's not about the pay most times with CEOs. It's not about the absolute dollars, it's about my position relative to others. If I think I'm the leader in this sector and I'm doing the best job, I want public recognition of that. And I don't want to see that someone in another organisation who is not performing as well, is not [in] as complex [a business], whatever, is getting paid more than me. So there is a little bit of 'face' in it. And I think disclosure has really not helped it. (S&P/ASX 200 remuneration committee chair)

It's an interesting dynamic when you're looking for a CEO. Someone comes in; on paper looks good. It's very hard to sit down to say, 'I'll hire you, but I'm only going to pay you half of what the predecessor got', or something like this. They come in and they know what the person before them was getting, so they've got a base. (S&P/ASX 200 remuneration committee chair)

Number one is disclosure. Number two: the influence of global pay rates and the third is [remuneration] consultancy. Disclosure because it is seen as setting the benchmark . . . The CEOs arm themselves with it, so you've got to combat that. (Australian remuneration consultant)

Some institutional investors agreed with these views:

Disclosure, predominantly, that's been the fundamental driver of the ratcheting of pay. (UK corporate governance manager, funds management company)

There may be something to the remuneration report disclosure and increased transparency that has fed into the pay ratcheting. I'm pretty certain that's true. It's just because people are able to look at benchmarks and things now almost as a default where they may not have done that before. (UK corporate governance manager, funds management company)

I think the pressures on executives' salaries are other executives' salaries. This goes back to one of the unintended consequences of remuneration reporting and that now everyone knows not only how much everyone else gets paid but the structure within which they get pay . . . how their wealth is generated. (UK corporate governance manager)

I actually have some sympathy for the view that putting this stuff in the rem reports actually is part of the problem. Because I think there is an element of 'That person's getting paid this: so should I.'[34] Then I come back to the fact that in too many cases, the board of directors is not sufficiently strong in its view and in standing against the CEO. (Investment officer, Australian industry superannuation fund)

Others had differing views of the sources of pressure on executive salaries, from 'The greed of the executives themselves' (UK corporate governance manager, fund management company) to cynicism about how the pay ratchets come about:

I may be cynical but a couple of years ago when the share price went down and share options were under water, bonuses went up. Bonuses are still going up and whether that's down to a lot of incentives schemes not paying out in full . . . .. (UK corporate governance manager, funds management company)

I was at a seminar last year in New York. They were talking about the global market for talent. This Italian guy stood up and said, 'You talk about the global market for chief executives? 95 per cent of UK chief executives are UK citizens; 98 per cent of German chief executives are German; 97 per cent of French, 100 per cent of Italians. So where is this global competition for CEOs?' (UK corporate governance manager, funds management company)

I think it is a bit of a competitive labour market really. Obviously we have just gone through such a unique period of sustained growth . . . the labour market has been very tight, so people are well within reason to be negotiating various remuneration packages in their favour . . . you need to tread very carefully when you are talking about public disclosure of a particular remuneration package. (Institutional investor representative, Australia)

I think soft boards are one source . . . not standing up to management . . . Also talent is necessarily a source of pressure: it's more of a convenient excuse after the fact. (Investment officer, Australian industry superannuation fund)

The ratchet in remuneration is arguably better explained by benchmarking, driven from remuneration disclosures, but created by remuneration consultants in response to requests from their clients for information on 'the market'. According to one UK remuneration consultant I interviewed, many companies disclosing that they pay at the median range may not be. Statistically it is not possible for all companies in the FTSE 100 to be paying at the median, unless they are all paying exactly the same amount. So what is driving this false disclosure? It might be in response to shareholder guidance on this issue which accepts payment at the median or below, but requires a justification for payment above the median.[35] As one UK remuneration consultant noted, 'it's going to be a brave remuneration committee chairperson who can say "Well, actually, I think we should be paying below the median"'. This has implications for the growth in the size of remuneration payments:

> Without doubt, there has been this ratcheting up effect . . . the vast majority of companies will have a remuneration policy set out in the accounts which says 'We pay base salaries at the median, but provide an upper quartile opportunity through long term and short term incentives.' This is seen to be *something that is an acceptable policy to follow* by shareholders.

7.5 IMPORTANCE OF RULE-FORM

The rules on disclosure provide a striking example of the importance of rule choice as theorised by Julia Black.[36] Typically these rules are mandatory in character, with the status of a legal rule that attaches a sanction for non-disclosure (but not sanctioning the practices disclosed). In terms of the substance of the rule, such rules set out the information to be disclosed and where in the annual report it is to be disclosed (in the remuneration report, the financial statements/accounts or in the notes to the statements/accounts). In terms of rule structure, such rules tend towards precision: they are complex, they apply generally to listed companies and they seek to be clear. Complex disclosure rules may not produce usable information on remuneration practices. Yet it is not clear that a principles-based approach would produce better results.

There may be a further explanation for the complexity of remuneration reports:

> Well we certainly don't think it is because the guidelines are too descriptive because they are not, and it's not because legislation is too prescriptive, but it's probably a combination . . . probably companies are making it unnecessarily complicated.[37] Dare I say – too many lawyers getting involved.

If lawyers routinely draft remuneration reports for their clients, the success or otherwise of a principles-based approach to remuneration disclosure will depend upon how skilled lawyers are in working with principles designed for flexible application, rather than legal rules which are typically narrower in form.

Executive remuneration, whether from a human resources perspective or an economic theory perspective, is premised on the notion that linking remuneration outcomes to performance outcomes will result in better performance (or the right kind of performance, as illustrated by the post-GFC initiatives that seek to include risk elements within the determination of performance). Much of the detailed disclosure laws in the UK[38] and Australia[39] seek to expose this link. In this way, they could be said to rely upon a primary justification of being instrumental, that is, 'the subject-matter sought to be regulated will deliver the regulatory objective directly'.[40]

Yet the very substance of the rules can undermine the overall aim of these laws. Take the rules for short term incentives. A carve-out for sensitive information can be exploited by companies to justify non-disclosure. Given the annual report features historic performance data, the reasons for non-disclosure on at least an historic basis seem unsound. The persistent failure to disclose the link between remuneration outcomes and company performance makes it difficult for shareholders to decide whether the pay is rewarding good or poor performance.

Interview evidence indicates that it is proxy advisors who routinely read remuneration disclosures, while institutional investors routinely read proxy advisor summary reports on these disclosures. Boilerplate disclosures facilitate, not impede, this task by allowing proxy advisors to 'box tick' that certain requirements have been met. Thus responsibility for disclosure failures cannot be blamed solely on company directors and remuneration committees. Companies with low transparency but with strong performance track records will often be excused by shareholders.[41]

Furthermore, that the corporate governance managers resort to reading proxy advisors' reports to understand companies' remuneration reports suggests the mandatory disclosure rules are not providing what the information shareholders want: what the market thinks of the policies and how the quantum compares with the market. Proxy advisory services are essential to this task because '[the proxy advisors] have pre-digested the stuff' and provide an initial filter, although not necessarily additional expertise outside that of the corporate governance managers within fund managers and superannuation/pension funds themselves. It is also relevant to how institutional investors reach a final voting decision on the remuneration report.

NOTES

1. Committee on Corporate Governance 1998, para. [4.15].
2. This broad-brush disclosure approach was evident in 74 per cent of the sample for STIs and 57 per cent for (LTIs).
3. PricewaterhouseCoopers and the Department of Trade and Industry (1999), para. [ii].
4. See chapter 1.
5. Dew-Becker 2009, pp. 445–6.
6. Productivity Commission of Australia 2009, p. 247.
7. Department for Business Innovation and Skills 2010b, p. 32.
8. Financial Reporting Council 2009, p. 2.
9. See above, chapter 2, tables 2–3 for confirmation of the overlapping pattern of disclosure rules in the UK.
10. Financial Reporting Council 2009, p. 28.
11. A clear example of this is the 2011 reforms introduced by the *Corporations (Improving Accountability for Executive Remuneration) Act 2001* (Cth) requiring disclosures on remuneration consultants.
12. Corporations and Markets Advisory Committee 2011, pp. 70–2.
13. Corporations and Markets Advisory Committee 2011, p. 70, quoting from a submission to the inquiry by Macquarie Group Limited.
14. Palmer 2008.
15. Easterbrook and Fischel 1984, p. 687.
16. Fung, Graham and Weil 2007, pp. 39–45.
17. (UK) SI 2008/410, schedule 8, para. 17(1) defines the term 'emoluments'; *Corporations Act 2001* (Cth), s 9 defines remuneration as having the meaning given to that term by the accounting standards.
18. *Companies Act 2006* (UK), c 46, s 420 provides a specific sanction for failure to include a remuneration report; whereas *Corporations Act 2001* (Cth), s 344(1), s 344(2), are the general civil and criminal offences respectively in relation to a failure to comply with the provisions in part 2M.3 of the Act.
19. Fung, Graham and Weil 2007, p. 110.
20. Department for Business Innovation and Skills 2011a, pp. 6–7, 16–19; Department for Business Innovation and Skills 2011b, pp. 27–35.
21. Fung, Graham and Weil 2007, p. 112.
22. Parker 2002, p. 10.
23. McBarnet and Whelan 1991, pp. 850–2.
24. Department of Trade and Industry 2000a, p. 61.
25. Hill 2006, pp. 67–8.
26. Hertig, Kraakman and Rock 2004, p. 204.
27. Manne 2007, pp. 493–7.
28. See also Sheehan 2007 and Sheehan 2012 for an analysis of the first three years of disclosure in the UK and Australia under a say on pay regime.
29. See methodology appendix, A.3.
30. See Fattorusso et al 2007 for results on a study of remuneration reports for 2003.
31. Choi, Fisch and Kahan 2008, p. 44 note the heterogeneity among US proxy advisors in respect of their propensity to recommend voting against management and the factors relevant to their analysis.
32. Latham 2003, p. 92.
33. Choi, Fisch and Kahan 2008, pp. 51–2.
34. Dalton and Dalton 2008, p. 89 argue that mandatory disclosure creates a primer for executive compensation in other companies, in the process 'establish[ing] a metaphorical leader board whereby everyone can see exactly where they stand'.
35. Association of British Insurers 2004a, p. 5.
36. Black 1995.
37. Clarkson, Van Bueren and Walker 2006.

38.   *The Large and Medium-Sized Companies and Groups (Accounts and Reports) Regulations 2008* (UK) SI 2008410, schedule 8, reg. 3(2).
39.   *Corporations Act 2001* (Cth), s 300A; *Corporations Regulations 2001* (Cth), reg. 2M.3.03.
40.   Chiu 2006b, p. 260.
41.   Hebb 2006.

8. Shareholder voting

When introduced in the UK in 2002, say on pay was seen as a way to improve accountability. Voting was a public message that behind-the-scenes engagement had failed to resolve differences of opinion on the most appropriate remuneration practices for the company. Such a difference of opinion existed in 2003 in relation to 'rewards for failure': shareholders used the first year of the vote to bring about change to termination provisions within contracts.[1]

The Australian experience over the first three years of say on pay (2005–07) was very different. Figure 8.1 compares the trajectories of the 'outrage' expressed via advisory vote over the first three years of say on pay for the FTSE 100 sample (2003–05) and the S&P/ASX 200 sample (2005–07). We can see that the median level of outrage against FTSE 100 remuneration reports calmed down within three years, whereas the S&P/ASX 200 trajectory is flatter. However, this is only part of the picture. Figure 8.2 shows that the highest vote against the remuneration report increased over these first three years in Australia, whereas it decreased in the UK over the period from 2003 to 2005.

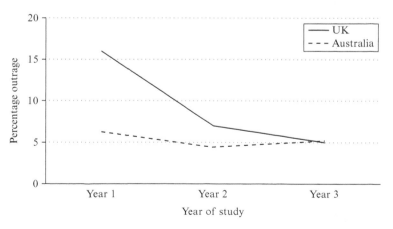

Note: For an explanation of how these values were determined, see Sheehan 2007 and 2012.

Figure 8.1 *Outrage votes: UK and Australia*

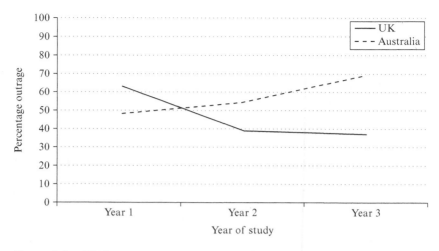

Figure 8.2   Highest outrage votes: UK and Australia

In the UK, the addition of the advisory vote has provided institutional investors in UK companies with the ability to send a message to remuneration committees; one they were prepared to use in the first three years to bring errant company practices into line with their own guidance, but used sparingly over the ensuing three years.[2] Unlike the UK, the Australian economy weathered the global financial crisis in good shape, courtesy of a mining boom and strong prudential supervision of its financial institutions by the Australian Prudential Regulatory Authority. By 2009 the situation in Australia had changed, with the Productivity Commission identifying 27 S&P/ASX 300 companies receiving substantial 'no' votes on the remuneration report in the 2009 year, ranging from 25 per cent to a staggering 81 per cent.[3] In late 2011, with the two-strikes rule in operation, over 30 companies had more than 25 per cent of votes cast against the remuneration report resolution.[4] During 2011 it became obvious that Australia's share market was not going to be insulated from difficulties in other economies.

8.1   IDENTIFYING CONTENTIOUS REMUNERATION REPORTS

We saw in the previous chapter that it is largely only the proxy advisors who read the entire remuneration report. Institutional investors first become aware of any problems with remuneration when they read the proxy advisors' reports on a particular company. This is despite the fact that UK fund managers appear to allocate resources to this task, with the average headcount per firm growing from 5.7 in 2004 to 7.7 in 2009.[5] Institutional investors in the UK will frequently contact each other if they have concerns about a company's remuneration practices, although they are conscious of the concert party provisions in the *Takeover Code*:[6]

> When you see an outlier, when you hear about a problem, we are in constant communications especially at this time of year [June]. So the email will go around 'Did you see so and so? What did you think? Let's talk about it?' So we'll compare notes. For the extreme stuff, we'll go through the ABI Council.

One FTSE 100 HR director said that some companies – such as her own – know that investor backlash is likely; although for many the first sense the remuneration committee has of a looming protest vote might be the remuneration consultants passing on news about the proxy advisors' negative recommendations (FTSE 100 remuneration committee chair). For others it is a letter from an investor explaining they will be voting against the remuneration report[7] and outlining the reasons why. These letters will typically be sent to the company secretary. Some company secretaries receive a phone call:

> One or two of the UK institutions will phone up, they will ask me some questions and then say 'Fine, thank you very much' or they will say, 'Well, on the answers given, clarification, we will probably be abstaining or voting against.'

For investors, this call is a chance for the company to provide an explanation. In the following instance, the contentious issue is a retention payment:

> We say, 'Well, okay, we understand that you need to retain a good person. But you've got a regular pay package there. It's a pretty big one. Why is this not doing the job?' And so, we'd focus on the explanation. That's always one of the key things for us . . . More often than not, we do tend to . . . we may potentially . . . shift our view favourably, because they've told us something we didn't know before.

The call from a fund management company may lead to a meeting, either individually with the concerned investor or with a group of investors which the ABI might lead. The following is an example of shareholders communicating their concerns over some relatively easy performance targets in the LTI plan:

> We met the remuneration committee chairman who came in to see us, plus another director, and they said 'Please come back to us with the figures' which we did and they were quite surprised at the levels we came back with; the first being the vesting price and second was the top performance targets which certainly were challenging enough, [but the quantum was very high]. They accepted our bottom target [suggestion] and made the [actual] target more challenging. The top end: they said 'We were so far out of kilter with everyone else' – but they did increase the performance target substantially. And so we were happy with that.

From the shareholders' perspective, the group meeting is valuable.[8] As one corporate governance manager within a UK fund manager explained:

> I think if you see eight or nine [shareholders] in one room, all more or less saying the same thing, that should be quite helpful to them. And it helps us as well because very often it's not black and white. And when you get a number of us in the room, and we all think slightly differently, and we are all pointing out, focusing on different areas, that helps us to be sure we've covered every corner and not missed something out.

Some companies are more proactive in understanding institutional investor voting intentions, as the following FTSE 100 remuneration committee chair explains:

> We normally do a ring around and consult the larger ones. Our practice is to consult the larger institutions to see if they've got any concerns they want to discuss before they put their vote in.

This may be more likely when there is a one-off payment that is likely to attract attention. One company about to make a retention arrangement for its CEO

> engaged in early dialogue with the investors. They made us aware that they were going to abstain. Some of them initially were going to vote against. Having had a dialogue and an exchange with them, they moved their vote against to voting abstentions. They understood the rationale for what we were doing. They didn't agree with it, but they understood it.

The Australian experience is slightly different from that described above for the UK. The two proxy advisors active in the Australian market over the period 2005–09 had different approaches to engagement during the AGM season. According to one S&P/ASX 200 remuneration committee chair, CGI Glass Lewis does not contact the company, whereas RiskMetrics will engage with the company prior to releasing its report to shareholders to clarify information and seek any explanations from management. This engagement precedes the final advice sent to shareholders, so is not a substitute for engagement surrounding the voting intentions of shareholders on receiving the report. Knowing the importance of gaining proxy advisor endorsement of their company's remuneration report, one remuneration committee chair who will not see proxy advisors as part of the major review of remuneration:

> Will certainly meet with them and take them through the report and invite them to come back to us as often as they need to help them understand; in order to help them have an informed judgment in terms of the analysis and the advice that they give to the institutional investors.

That does not mean that proxy advisors are welcomed or respected by remuneration committee chairs:

> The institutional investors, nearly without exception, get advice from the corporate governance gurus: RiskMetrics, CGI Glass Lewis. And they have a fairly mechanistic 'What's good? What's bad?'

> The corporate governance advisors recommended voting 'no' on the remuneration report. However, the board is closer than the corporate governance advisors and analysts to what's happening in the company, so we are staying with our decision. As a result, we are getting high levels of 'no' votes.

Sometimes the trigger for engagement by the company is a call from the fund's corporate governance manager saying they are planning to vote against the remuneration report:

> We'll send an email to the investor relations person or the CFO typically, just run them past our reasons for not voting [in favour of management]. So they're just aware that not all the votes are going their way before they have the AGM.

> We would absolutely pick up the phone and call a meeting and say, 'We disagree with this and we either want you to change it or do the following things.'

> Some companies panic and within 10 minutes you have the chairman on the phone and they'll send you more information.

According to an S&P/ASX 200 remuneration committee chair, the panic arises because 'for shareholders to vote against you on the remuneration report is a harsh statement.' Engagement at this time can involve several meetings prior to the AGM to explain the remuneration report to shareholders in an attempt to get their support. To avoid this, some shareholders do not advise the company of their voting intentions until after the

AGM, but still receive calls: '[t]hey always try and ask us how we're going to vote and we always tell them quite nicely that how we vote is between ourselves and ourselves' (UK corporate governance manager).

8.2   FINAL VOTING DECISIONS – UK

Two remuneration-related voting rights are given to shareholders of UK listed companies: an advisory vote on the remuneration report[9] and a binding vote to approve the introduction of a share plan.[10] Depending on the terms of the particular share plan, shareholders may also vote to amend the plan. No real indication is available from a resolution to approve the share plan in the UK as to the size of individual grants to any one director. One feature in the UK is the use of abstain votes and the different pattern of the use of this vote in the advisory vote when compared with the share scheme approvals.[11] This is a deliberate tactic:

> We use abstain where we can as a yellow card, to use the football [soccer] analogy. It's the first warning. We want to talk about this. And if we don't get action, then it's a red card next.

One corporate governance manager noted the different reaction of companies to an abstaining vote, rather than a vote against:

> we get a higher response rate from companies where we intend to abstain than [when we intend to] vote against. It just seems to be a tactical thing about whether they feel that we're taking into account certain things that they're doing well . . . they think that we're more reasonable and want to talk to us.

Companies are also aware that the institutional investors in abstaining

> are taking a principled position, trying to send you a message, or they are reflecting the fact that [while] they understand what you're doing, it doesn't comply with their guidelines . . . they don't particularly want to vote for it, but they don't want to vote against it either. So there is a whole series of nuances behind an abstention.

Abstaining from voting on the advisory vote seems an unnecessary nuance: there are no legal consequences from the resolution not being passed as no person's remuneration depends on the resolution passing. Understanding what drives voting decisions – remuneration quantum or its structural features[12] – might explain why this nuance exists.

When the recommendation from the proxy advisor is to vote against the remuneration report, the corporate governance managers are likely to read the actual remuneration report. In doing so, quantum may be an issue they seek to further understand:

> Most companies employ remuneration consultants. So then we know whether it's within a certain benchmark. But we definitely do look at the quantum, if the quantum is extraordinary.

For other corporate governance managers, quantum is not examined:

> This is a thorny issue, isn't it? We are a large American investment bank, it's hard to bang on about quantum . . . the line we take is that we are not afraid of large numbers.

One reason for not examining it is:

> It is quite a difficult one for us to say 'That's too much money'. And for every benchmark available, there is no benchmark that you could say simply 'This is just too much'. I think that, through experience, you get to know when an annual bonus of six or seven times salary on an annual basis is probably just a bit too generous.

For those that do examine it, what makes the quantum excessive is not based on a cap or pre-determined figure according to one corporate governance manager. Another corporate governance manager explains that it relates to

> The individual director, in terms of the contribution he's made to the overall value for shareholders as an individual, compared with the many hundreds of people that work for him . . . in some sectors, such as the banking sector, where this is more of an issue, it is something we take more cognisance of.

It may also be the quantum of an ad hoc payment that attracts shareholder attention, either a termination payment or a retention payment:

> The sort of things that really trigger a vote against automatically are ex gratia payments not in reference to performance criteria, retrospective awards, transaction bonuses for pulling off a merger – that's what they're paid to come into work for.

Some institutions are more interested in the pay–performance relationship than quantum, as economic theory predicts.[13] A vote against is likely where 'We don't think the targets are sufficiently challenging, either at the lower or top end, or if we think structurally it doesn't work.'

Structural issues are assessed against the guidance devised by the institutional investors. The selection of performance measures is a subject of intense debate, with institutional investors acknowledging that they have different perspectives:

> Certain fund management Houses prefer EPS, some prefer TSR – it's trying to get a happy medium. We are open to companies having a bespoke one, but it actually has to deliver . . . it has to show underlying improvement and be a good measure of performance. And EPS sometimes . . . can come up through acquisitions, so it's not organic [growth]. That's why it needs to be on a case by case basis.

In terms of achieving alignment, the House's own sector analysts can provide EPS forecasts for a number of years and corporate governance managers use this to determine whether actual performance reported reflects good performance. The analysis also draws upon the experience of the relevant corporate governance manager:

> I know in my head when I see a TSR plan, I might let a TSR plan that pays 30 per cent at the median go through . . . If you start to see 40 and 50 per cent, that starts to get alarm bells ringing. But a lot of it is 'seat of the pants'. There is no typical methodology.

The other trigger of a vote against can be the company's record in delivering on its previous promises in respect of remuneration:

> We will obviously check anything against prior consultation that we've had with the company. Companies do consult us prior to putting through new incentive schemes, so I will look at that to see whether they are complying with that.

With structural issues driving many, if not most, voting decisions,[14] how fund managers analyse structure is crucial. The discussion on engagement around the AGM above noted the use of proxy advisor guidance to identify the problematic remuneration reports. This activity is critical. That fund managers extensively use proxy advisors does not necessarily mean their voting recommendations are followed. Where the client mandate directs the fund manager to follow the recommendation of a particular proxy advisor, the mandate may allow for discretion to vote against or it may require the fund manager to seek the client's prior approval to vote against. Where the fund manager has discretion to decide the vote, all corporate governance managers interviewed stressed they made up their own minds and did not simply adopt the proxy advisors' voting recommendations. This might explain the results noted by Robert Daines et al in the

US context: proxy advisor recommendations to vote against management showed only a weak correlation with proxy voting outcomes.[15]

The corporate governance managers' claim of always reaching their own decision is less likely to be valid when proxy advisors endorse the remuneration report.[16] The proxy advisor's report is likely to provide sufficient information to satisfy the corporate governance manager that the House can safely support the advisory vote. Corporate governance managers do not routinely read the reports:

> We don't have the capacity to be reading through the annual reports of every single vote. But, that said, we will dip into these things when we see large ones [payments] and where we have concerns. But our starting point for the UK on a practical level tends to be the NAPF and RREV voting advisories.

Fund managers therefore appear to selectively read remuneration reports and to satisfice whenever they do read a remuneration report to confirm a few pertinent aspects of remuneration. Companies are likely to know of this habit and disclose remuneration to highlight these aspects of their remuneration practices so as to make shareholder monitoring easier via 'optics'.

While the voting recommendation is made by the corporate governance manager, all interviewees confirmed that individual fund managers within the House have the final say on how the vote will be cast. In practice, only a recommendation to vote against or vote abstained would be reviewed by a fund manager, as a vote for the resolution is not a vote against management:

> I'm not allowed to vote against any resolution without the fund manager's prior approval. Because that means if I vote in isolation, the executives could ring up the fund manager and say 'Why are you voting against?' . . . And sometimes on the issue of remuneration, what I think is black and white, there is a good reason why someone has been paid x, y and z but it is not public knowledge. Particular circumstances are not in the public domain, but the fund manager is aware of them and this is another reason why fund managers need to sign off.

Typically the decision being made by the fund manager 'won't be the difference between a for and an against, it's more nuanced as to whether we go abstain or whether we hit them with a full against'. That corporate governance managers do not have the final say on the voting decision indicates that this role provides a service to the fund managers. An alternative model observed in one of the fund managers is a committee system for deciding contentious proxy votes, involving senior analysts, fund managers and representatives of leading clients, together with the corporate governance manager. In this model, the final voting decision represents a consensus of these alternative viewpoints, influenced by the House's own commercial relationships.[17]

8.3   FINAL VOTING DECISIONS – AUSTRALIA

Only one of the six fund managers interviewed might consider voting abstained; the other interviewees were adamant that they only ever voted for or against a resolution. The same was obvious from the super fund representatives interviewed, with only one suggesting the super fund would consider voting abstained or vote withheld. There are no 'nuances' to interpret as with abstaining votes in the UK and where the issue hangs in the balance, it may well tip in favour of management.

This different pattern of voting behaviour is partly explained by the drivers of the voting decision. Australian institutional investors say they are attentive to quantum issues, relying on proxy advisor analysis for this information. Quantum may be an issue that drives the final voting decision:

> Our view is the quantum of remuneration should reflect, again not the competitive universe necessarily, but what degree of influence management can actually have on the bottom line result.

One superannuation fund representative noted that decisions on quantum were difficult to make:

> If I channel Buddha it's okay. You know, it's dangerous playing those sorts of games. You're not close enough to the decision making and responsibility and what not . . . I think the annual remuneration or the fixed and variable remuneration is probably a decision best left for the board.

The source of the comparative information on quantum comes from proxy advisor reports, or it could depend upon the fund manager's assessment of the quantum relative to 'the size of the company, its profits and the history and performance of the executives' (Australian fund manager). It could also be the quantum of an ad hoc payment (for example, a termination payment) that is the issue: 'You shouldn't walk out with a wheelbarrow full of money if you've buggered up the company and too many people do.'

For a few investors, structure was *the* issue: whether it fitted within the structure for the particular industry or, alternatively, whether the structure is 'skewed towards long term outcomes'. While quantum and the structure of the remuneration are issues, there is also the 'bigger picture' of the structure of the board, the structure of the remuneration committee. If the remuneration committee is completely independent, then we would be more inclined just to let them get on with the job and not nit pick every single thing they're doing.

Two remuneration consultants noted that shareholders were starting to influence the quantum of remuneration, especially in relation to termination payments, although with proxy advisory firms reporting benchmark remuneration data, 'it is starting to get to the issue of whether it is a *reasonable quantum* or not'. The proxy advisor's assessment of the reasonableness of quantum identifies the remuneration reports that have quantum issues. Whether shareholders support the remuneration report depends on who makes the ultimate voting decision. As one S&P/ASX 200 remuneration committee chair noted, the 'mum and dad investors' are outraged with big payouts, whereas 'the fundies don't mind the high dollars'. She saw 'the instos' as being quite flexible and willing to engage in discussion regarding the company's policies and practices and how these compare with the guidelines. The dilemma for the institutional investors is the corporate governance advice they have obtained.

Proxy advisor recommendations are important to the fund managers' final voting decision, with a recommendation to vote for the particular resolution accepted by both fund managers and super funds without further analysis:

> If both research providers are recommending to vote for [on all resolutions], then we pretty much waive looking at that meeting; because if they haven't come up with an issue, then it's very unlikely we will come up with an issue.

However, if the recommendation from the proxy advisor is to vote against any of the resolutions,

> we would delve into that more and give it more thought and that could be anything from public coverage to individual company information that we might have . . . We'll actively consider our vote as distinct from passively going along with what the proxy voting service might advise.

The final decision within the fund manager varies between Houses. The decision might be made by the individual portfolio manager or fund manager, a team of fund managers, or a separate committee of fund managers and corporate governance representatives. Superannuation fund trustees may retain voting discretions, although one super fund representative noted this was problematic because fund managers are closer to companies and their management than the trustees. One way around this problem is to seek the views of the fund manager before reaching a voting decision:

> Firstly, we want them to be engaged in the process, so that they actually think about it more and then incorporate it into their own thinking about stocks . . . they also seem to have better knowledge about the company. The proxy advisors tend to do a fairly black and white process . . . rather than looking at whether there's something about a particular company which makes the structure of the remuneration, as distinct from the report itself, appropriate to that company.

For those superannuation fund trustees who delegate the decision making to the external fund managers, the mandate can require they vote in accordance with the recommendation from the proxy advisory firm unless the fund manager decides that a different decision is justified.

Remuneration committees are critical of the use of proxy advisor services:

> the trustees . . . are not commercial people. They've got legal liability and they've set up these protocols to protect themselves. One of which is 'get advice, cast your vote' . . . if you ignore it, it exposes you.

Remuneration committees frequently accuse foreign investors of 'slavishly' following the proxy advisors' voting recommendations.[18] Yet remuneration committees also fail to appreciate that this frequently works in their favour. A recommendation to vote 'for' the remuneration report will usually be followed without question by subscribers to the proxy advisory services. Furthermore, while a negative recommendation from the proxy advisor may attract a voting sanction, this may not be fatal to the resolution ultimately passing with the requisite majority.

8.4   PUBLICATION OF VOTING RECORDS

The fund management houses and companies interviewed all provided their clients with a record of their voting, typically on a quarterly basis, including an explanation of why the fund manager voted against management. The report can be very detailed, showing the voting record for each company by resolution, or else it can be a summary report with high level statistics and more detailed commentary on the significant votes against management (one UK corporate governance manager within a funds management House said a 'summary report' can be 34 pages long). A third alternative is a customised report for the client based on their portfolio. One reason for detailed disclosure to clients is to satisfy compliance requirements:

> Some clients prefer the 110 pages, meeting by meeting, resolution by resolution. Tends to be the Americans . . . tends to be the clients who don't care about it. They want to know that it's happened [so] they can tick the box and move on.

Public disclosure of the voting record for UK fund managers in the sample was infrequent[19] and, when it occurred, typically only presented aggregate data on votes for, against and abstained across all investee companies, and did not disclose those resolutions or companies where the fund voted against management. One justification for this type of public disclosure was to avoid being labelled as a governance activist, according to one corporate governance manager I spoke to. The institutional investor representatives were unanimous in supporting disclosure of the voting record to the client, but less certain of the need for public disclosure:

> The big worry about the requirement to publish the voting record by law is that it would end up diminishing the quality of the engagement that people have with companies because it would become too much in the public domain.

While fund managers could get away with not voting when company performance was strong, the situation has changed and 'there is a lot of feeling that we have to be seen to be doing *something*'. Voting on remuneration-related resolutions is an important stage in the regulated remuneration cycle. Institutional investors' own guidance shapes their voting habits and government-sponsored initiatives such as the *Stewardship Code* in the UK have not altered this self-regulatory approach. There is clearly a gap between the transparency expected of listed companies and that expected from institutional shareholders. The argument against mandatory disclosure of the institutional investor's voting record made by one interviewee – 'it wouldn't be fair, if you don't make my Aunt Doris disclose how she voted' – does not take into consideration the interests of beneficiaries in how investee companies are governed. It also means that an important aspect of the regulated remuneration cycle is unable to be monitored externally by government or other stakeholders. Efforts to give shareholders increased say on remuneration-related issues[20] might be ill-judged regulatory initiatives if there is no external accountability for whether or how shareholders have voted.

Demands for more accountability from institutional investors raise several questions. Should 'accountability' be broadly or narrowly defined? What is the vehicle for communication? How do the answers to both of these questions shape the message given as 'the account'?[21] Assuming this accountability is reduced to written form as mandatory public disclosure, the risk is mis-specifying the appropriate rule dimension by drafting a precise rule which is then followed by disclosers to the letter. In other words, is accountability in this context best achieved by the 46 page, company by company, resolution by resolution account of voting, or via 'exception' reporting?

8.5   CONCLUSION

While agency theory views performance-based executive remuneration as a way of ensuring the desired performance by executives and hence the desired company performance, the evidence in this chapter suggests the monitor of performance and the monitor of remuneration are not one and the same person.[22] This separation is what Hu and Black describe in another context as decoupling of the economic rights attached to shares from shareholder rights such as voting.[23] In this context, it suggests that decisions about appropriate remuneration are not related to the investment decision.[24] Even though there are fewer corporate governance professionals within Australian fund managers and super funds in both countries, the dialogue between fund managers as investment decision makers and the company is unlikely to be with the remuneration committee.

The evidence presented in this chapter highlights how engagement around shareholder 'rules' on remuneration, particularly practice rules on structure, functions as a regulatory conversation. The quality of engagement is pivotal to ensuring good remuneration practices because it is how boards are held accountable in what Roberts describes as an intelligent accountability:

> not a mere showing or making visible of the self against a pre-determined set of categories, but rather involves active enquiry – listening, asking questions and talking – through which the relevance or accuracy of indicators can be understood in context . . . *It is typically a face-to-face encounter*, rich with information, in which communication is less easily stage-managed and rhetoric can be constantly compared to actual practice. (Italics added)[25]

Of the two shareholder-oriented activities within the regulated remuneration cycle, engagement and voting, engagement is less visible as both companies and investors prefer meeting behind the scenes. The advisory vote on the remuneration report is valued as a signal to the company about its executive remuneration practices, but requires both shareholders and remuneration committees to return to engagement to identify the specific issues and then to work within the remuneration guidance largely developed by shareholders for a solution.

Institutional investor rule making on remuneration practice provides all-important balance to the development of practice by remuneration consultants in response to remuneration committee and management demands. If shareholders do not like the practices observed in companies, they may have themselves to blame.

NOTES

1. See above chapter 5.
2. Gilshan and PIRC Limited 2009, p. 13.
3. Productivity Commission of Australia 2009, p. 283.
4. Boyd 2012.
5. Investment Management Association 2009, p. 11.
6. The concert party provisions in rule 9.1 of the *Takeover Code* (2002) deem a group of individual investors to be acting in concert in certain circumstances, which may trigger an obligation to make a bid to acquire the company if the combined voting rights exceed 30 per cent of the voting rights in the company and one of the party acquires a further interest in the company, which Davies notes is not restricted to shares (Davies 2008, pp. 1012–13). This is more likely to be an issue where several shareholders requisition or threaten to requisition a general meeting to vote on 'a board-control'-seeking resolution: notes to rule 9.1. The Takeovers Panel clarified its interpretation of these provisions in September 2009: Panel on Takeovers and Mergers 2009, paras [1.2], [1.4].
7. IMA survey data indicate close to 100 per cent of fund managers surveyed either always or mostly advise management in advance of their voting intentions: Investment Management Association 2009, p. 21.
8. It can overcome the 'free-rider' problem of acting alone: Nisar 2005, pp. 64–5.
9. *Companies Act 2006* (UK), c 46, s 439(1), formerly *Companies Act 1985* (UK), c 6, s 241A(1).
10. Approval via ordinary resolution is required under the FSA Handbook, LR 9.4.1(2)R.
11. Evidence of the level of 'conscientious abstentions' from IMA surveys shows a trend of 15 per cent of all fund managers votes for the year to 30 June 2003, decreasing to 13 per cent for the year to 30 June 2005, with a more dramatic decline to 7 per cent for the year to 30 June 2006: Investment Management Association 2009, p. 22.
12. For details of US experience on shareholder proposals and the influence of quantum and dilutive nature of stock option plans, see Morgan, Poulsen and Wolf 2006; Thomas and Cotter 2007.
13. Hölmstrom 1999 and 1979; Jensen and Meckling 1976; Shavell 1979.
14. Gilshan and PIRC Limited 2009, p. 13.
15. Daines, Gow and Larcker 2010, p. 460. Cf. Alexander et al 2010 pp. 4444–5 (proxy advisor recommendations are a good predictor of the outcomes of director election contests in the US).
16. Selvaggi and Upton 2008, pp. 15–16 shows that for each year in the period 2004–07, the number of 'red tops' (the highest level of concern) for remuneration reports was about 33 (2004), 37 (2005), 25 (2006) and 26 (2007) (these calculations are based on the information in table 1 and figure 1). Thus less than 8 per cent of all tops awarded in each of these years were red tops assigned for remuneration issues. The ABI is more likely to issue an amber top (average rate of 32.8 per cent of observations, compared with 9.4 cent for red tops). It was not possible on the information disclosed to calculate the rate of amber tops assigned to remuneration reports.

17. Myners Review of Institutional Investment for HM Treasury 2001, p. 91.
18. Australian Institute of Company Directors 2011, pp. 64–5; Semple and Friedlander 2010; Duran 2010; Urban 2010; Cornell 2008.
19. This is also confirmed by Trades Union Congress (TUC) surveys of fund managers' voting behaviour. In its 2006 survey, it noted that only four of the 34 organisations responding to the survey publicly reported their full voting record, while three disclosed aggregate results. The TUC noted that 'despite the Government's decision to take a power that would mandate disclosure [a reference to regulations power in the *Companies Act 2006* (UK), c 46, s 1277], which gives a clear signal that public disclosure is desirable, many fund managers will not embrace transparency voluntarily': Trades Union Congress 2006, p. 43.
20. See chapter 10 below.
21. Messner 2009, p. 934.
22. An observation noted by John Hendry et al in their interview study of UK institutional investors: Hendry et al 2006, p. 1112.
23. Hu and Black 2006, pp. 814–16; Yermack 2010.
24. Ingley and van der Walt 2004, p. 539. Being active on remuneration may not be value maximising for shareholders: Romano 2001, p. 203.
25. Roberts 2009, p. 966. An alternative description is that of 'socialising accountability': Nisar 2005, p. 63.

9. Limits of institutional shareholders as 'regulators' of executive remuneration

Institutional shareholders clearly play the pivotal regulatory role in say on pay, undertaking three different roles within the regulated remuneration cycle. Yet the mixed evidence from the UK and Australia of how pay practices changed following the introduction of say on pay suggests that they are not necessarily successful regulators. This chapter examines two important limits on institutional investors' regulatory capacities: their preferred model of investment and their ability to act as norm entrepreneurs for executive remuneration practices within investee companies.

9.1 ONE PREFERRED MODEL OF INSTITUTIONAL INVESTMENT

The assumption that institutional investors want to act as regulators of executive remuneration through rule making, monitoring disclosures, engagement and voting may only be true for certain types of institutional investors and not universally true, despite the rhetoric of 'responsible investment' or the notions of 'stewardship'. The Walker Review of corporate governance in UK financial institutions views stewardship as offering social legitimacy to significant holders of stock in listed companies, with obligations and attentiveness to the performance of companies over both the short and long term required horizons.[1] Stewardship creates expectations on institutional share owners akin to those in a large family shareholder in a family company.[2] As a concept it extends the moral expectations of the owner beyond those anticipated under the concept of 'fiduciary capitalism'.[3]

One presentation of the differences in investors' approach to engagement is the two paradigms identified by Nisar: the arm's-length approach and the engagement approach. The former paradigm is reactive to performance and uses voice to engage in a company-oriented manner, as opposed to the issues-oriented approach of the engagement paradigm.[4] Governments make policies premised on this latter paradigm, even though they acknowledge alternative investment approaches exist. Take for example the UK *Stewardship Code*: while its aim is 'to help improve long term returns to shareholders', institutional investors are free to choose whether to engage, based on their investment approach.[5] A decision to be a passive investor may reflect commercial realities.[6] A selling strategy may not lead to better absolute returns than some form of governance, stewardship or engagement activity, even though '[t]he absolute return that can accrue to investors from engagement initiatives is not measurable, not least because there are so many drivers of performance.'[7] The choice of strategy can also reflect the incentives for fund managers to increase assets under management and invest in an index to diversify investments, rather than undertaking strategies to improve the performance of portfolio companies.[8]

Pension and superannuation funds are likely to use a mix of passive and active strategies:[9]

> The managers have got benchmarks in the listed space to achieve. That's how we purchase the product. If they have benchmarks for the small caps, which are where we have our active managers, what we look at is the absolute return that we receive. We expect them to go 'under the bonnet' as it were; [that] they go through that process of examining all the information. We also have some equities managers who are essentially index managers chasing a little bit of alpha, so for them invested company performance is less of an issue. (Investment officer, Australian industry superannuation fund)

As for active engagement,

> It will vary by company and the size of our holding. Where we are a large investor in a large company, then that engagement is on a fairly ongoing basis, so it won't just be around the annual report or the quarterly updates. (Corporate governance manager, Australian funds management company)

> We view it as our fiduciary duty and we vote everything we can. (Corporate governance manager, Australian funds management company)

> It's certainly something that we assess and we are looking at it increasingly now when we select fund managers. I wouldn't say that it's the absolute fundamental make-or-break in selecting a fund manager . . . (Corporate governance manager, UK pension fund)

For superannuation funds, taking a particular stance via engagement has to be balanced against the outsourcing of the investment decision:

> In employing the managers you are outsourcing your investment of those funds and it can be complicated if you start telling the manager how to invest or what

decisions to make in relation to corporations in which they invest. (Corporate governance manager, Australian industry superannuation fund)

This assumption of one model of investment is also reflected in transnational-level initiatives such as the United Nations' *Principles of Responsible Investment*.[10] While government policies are premised on a belief that 'engaged and active owners lead to better companies', the equation for institutional investors is 'engaged and active owners lead to better companies and higher shareholder returns'. As we have seen in relation to the levels of voting support for remuneration reports over the years, good corporate performance reflected in strong share price growth and high or consistent dividend payments might weaken the resolve of the otherwise 'engaged' institutional investor. More critically, the link between shareholder activism and investee company corporate governance is not easily observed. While research has shown private engagement has led to outperformance,[11] its private nature means it is impossible to measure on a large scale. Econometric-based studies that seek to measure the relationship between corporate governance and firm performance yield mixed results,[12] and give rise to technical problems due to relationships between the variables or factors of corporate governance being measured, not to mention establishing cause and effect.[13] If there is no clear link between better corporate governance and firm performance, engagement and voting on executive remuneration resolutions may be ultimately futile activities.

9.2   INSTITUTIONAL INVESTORS AS 'NORM ENTREPRENEURS'

It is questionable whether institutional investors can successfully fulfil the role of norm entrepreneur for executive remuneration; aside from the difficulties noted in chapters 3 to 6 as to whether investor guidance leads or merely responds to innovation by companies. Three questions warrant close analysis: do institutional investors want to play the role of executive remuneration norm entrepreneur; what norms really matter to institutional investors; and what territory is best covered by institutional investors?

We have already seen how institutional investors play a key role in any market-based regulatory system for executive remuneration in three ways: by promulgating guidance on what are best or good remuneration practices, by engaging with companies on that guidance and by voting on remuneration-related resolutions where permitted by law. If this market-based system is not working, then institutional investors are partly to blame. The first way in which institutional investors are to blame relates to their role as norm entrepreneurs, that is, people interested in changing social norms.[14] In devising and promulgating principles and rules on executive remuneration, institutional investors have encouraged performance-based pay without setting any meaningful limits on what quantum of remuneration is acceptable, given firm performance, and what amount is excessive, given strong firm performance. Furthermore, some of the so-called principles are actually treated by investors and companies alike as rules. This means that principles designed for flexible application become ossified into narrow interpretations that can result in poor remuneration practices. The 'vanilla-isation' of remuneration practice in the UK is one such example. Earnings per share growth over and above a measure of inflation, together with total shareholder return relative to an index, are not necessarily the only ways to measure performance over a three-year time horizon. Yet within the first three years of the advisory vote in the UK, these two measures had become the standard measures in FTSE 100 long term incentive schemes.[15]

The second way institutional shareholders are responsible relates to inconsistent monitoring and enforcement via engagement and voting. The opportunity for shareholder engagement in a market-based system depends in part on the extent of legal rights given to pass resolutions on remuneration: such rights exist in the UK and Australia. Voting against remuneration report resolutions does not communicate the relevant norm, but signals disagreement. We have seen how engagement can occur pre-AGM in respect of the remuneration report (initiated by institutional investors or representative organisations) or outside the AGM season on remuneration policies (initiated by remuneration committees). The tone of these latter conversations is set by company management who initiated the conversation. The regulatory conversation that follows a significant vote against is where the norms – the principles in the various guidelines – are translated into agreed rules for that company going forward. If this occurs during a major review of remuneration, there might be six months of delay before the final new policy is disclosed as extensive engagement on the proposed changes occurs.

With governments now stepping in to change executive remuneration norms relying on 'vivid rhetoric'[16] such as 'extreme capitalism' and 'extreme greed', institutional shareholders have to reconsider their role as executive remuneration norm entrepreneurs. Do institutional shareholders still want to play this role? Or should they abdicate the role of executive remuneration norm entrepreneur to governments and prudential regulators?

9.2.1 Norms of Executive Remuneration

'Norms' have been defined as 'informal social regularities that individuals feel obligated to follow because of an internalised sense of duty, or because of fear of external non-legal sanctions or both'.[17] Sunstein defines norms as 'social attitudes of approval and disapproval, specifying what ought to be done and what ought not to be done'.[18] In respect of corporate law, Ferran notes that the success of social norms lacking a legal backing 'depends on most individuals in the business, investment and financial communities approving of compliance and disapproving of non-conformity'.[19] Eisenberg argues that the norms observable in corporate law can be categorised into three kinds: behavioural patterns, behavioural practices and obligational norms.[20] Behavioural patterns appear from Eisenberg's analysis to be almost instinctive responses or habits, 'that neither entail a sense of obligation nor are self-consciously adhered to or engaged in', with behavioural practices 'distinguishable from behaviour patterns by self-conscious adherence, yet lacking any sense of obligation'.[21] Obligational norms are distinguishable by the sense of obligation that is both self-consciously imposed yet responds to external criticism of non-compliance. The internal sense of obligation relies upon 'complex phenomena of internalisation of normative behaviour'.[22] A shaming sanction can be an effective style of external criticism,[23] although internalisation of the norm may be more effective in ensuring compliance.[24] Do institutional shareholder rules have the status of obligational norms?

Executive remuneration is seen to be a social practice occurring within a market environment with legislative interventions designed to ensure market efficiency.[25] Norms are thus likely to play a pivotal role in shaping remuneration practices. Gopalan suggests three competing norms exist for executive remuneration: greed is good, pay equity is desired, and contributions to performance should be reflected in pay outcomes.[26] Greed drives quantum in remuneration when boards agree to executive demands for more and more remuneration. 'Ethical egoism'[27] combines with managerial power to create an opportunity for rent extraction.[28]

Pay equity in executive remuneration likewise drives quantum, not only in terms of 'who should get what' – what constitutes a just reward for the specific executive based on the 'justice evaluation' of the particular situation – but also how justice evaluations shape future conduct.[29] This pay equity can be reflected in terms of differentiating pay within the firm,[30] as well as between firms, or within the community of stakeholders that surrounds a firm.[31] Distributive justice arguments take different forms, which Harris summarises as justice as fairness; justice reflecting the capabilities approach (Amartya Sen and Martha Nussbaum);[32] and justice in acquisition and transfer of property (Robert Nozick). Of these three approaches, Harris uses Rawls' notions of the 'difference principle' and the 'open position'[33] to focus on the processes by which the firm first selects the executive and then justifies the distribution of compensation to that executive and to the firm's other stakeholders. The challenges of setting pay levels at hire to achieve pay equity can be achieved *in form* by matching levels and structures within the firm or other firms, but undermined *in substance* by guaranteeing bonus payments or through the use of golden parachute provisions.[34] It is reflected in notions that 'The Talented' can justifiably receive higher wages if all agree to it and the amount paid reflects the market.[35] The role of the market in setting executive remuneration levels is acknowledged[36] and seemingly accepted without question.[37] Thus pay equity is likely to be referenced to the external market, with some consideration of internal sensitivities to other members of the top management team, while disregarding the pay gap between senior executives and entry-level employees.

While some would like executive remuneration to be based on objective criteria such as 'a metric, value or standard rather than some arbitrary decision made by ill-informed board members',[38] selecting these criteria is not a neutral exercise.[39] Any number of benchmarks could be chosen: average worker salary, company size, market comparison by industry and size, and value generation.[40] This leads to the third norm identified above: pay for performance. Carried to its extreme, this norm implies that no limits should exist on pay if performance is unlimited. This norm, if internalised, would justify extreme risk taking on the basis of enhancing performance, with the executive entitled to be rewarded for outperforming some previously set benchmark. Remuneration practices around short term incentives are based on annual budgets, with performance described as 'threshold', 'on target' and 'stretch'. The 'performance' part of this norm is contestable: is it individual performance or company performance or both that should be paid for, over and above the 'coming to work' salary? If it is company performance, should that be expressed solely in terms of financial performance indicators? If it is individual performance, is it truly possible to say what difference any one individual made in an organisation of thousands, albeit that individual is the CEO? Why does 'threshold' performance below the budget targets deserve recognition via payment of a performance bonus? To attain the level of 'stretch' performance, do the means justify the ends? Where it is a mix of these criteria, say one-third individual performance, two-thirds financial performance, is this the right mix? If paying for performance seeks to address the agency problem, it might not be working;[41] and this may be due to companies choosing the wrong performance measures and setting the wrong targets.

Bebchuk and Fried suggest a fourth norm: the tendency to conform to remuneration arrangements in other firms.[42] This norm relates both to structures that match other firms but also to benchmarking quantum. It is related to the norms of pay equity and pay for performance. This norm is not only internalised by executives but by remuneration committees. It is reflected in the adoption of a standard set of remuneration practices across firms, irrespective of firm size and industry. We have seen in chapters 4 to 6 just how pervasive the practice of benchmarking is, while remaining sceptical of claims that disclosure is driving quantum increases (chapter 7).

9.2.2 Are Institutional Investors Executive Remuneration Norm Entrepreneurs?

The previously noted definition of norm entrepreneurs from Sunstein ('people interested in changing social norms') warrants further examination. As Gopalan notes, 'norm entrepreneurs do not create new norms for altruistic reasons: acting as a norms entrepreneur can result in economic benefits'.[43] Clearly if institutional investors are to play such a role, economic benefits have to exist; a point often raised in the literature on responsible investing[44] and shareholder activism.[45] What economic benefits exist for institutional investors in setting norms for executive remuneration? Clearly norms relating to share-based payments are highly relevant, if such plans are dilutive or do not adequately link remuneration outcomes to performance as experienced by shareholders (such as shareholder return). The same rationale exists in respect of norms for other remuneration practices: the norms should be those that lead to economic benefits that flow to the shareholder. Yet if remuneration consultants and some remuneration committee chairs are ambivalent about the incentivising potential of executive remuneration – an ambivalence some institutional investors share – then pay for performance norms may not lead to better corporate performance.

It is possible to exploit dissatisfaction with existing norms to create new norms and this is more likely when a tipping point is reached to push norms in new directions.[46] The global financial crisis of 2008 was a tipping point, with new norms being written for remuneration practices in the banking and financial services industries, with mixed success.[47] The primary source for these new rules can be linked to the Financial Stability Board's *Principles of Sound Compensation Practices* and their local adoption.[48] Whether this push in a new direction represents merely incremental change or a fundamental change depends in part on how the entrepreneurs exploit the dissatisfaction. Perhaps to a larger measure it also depends upon whether behaviour aligned with the norm is no longer acceptable, even in private moments. Exploiting such private dissatisfaction is what Sunstein argues can be used to bring about fundamental change by

> Signalling their own commitment to change, creating coalitions, making defiance of the norms seem or be less costly and making compliance with the new norms seem or be more beneficial.[49]

While it is too soon to determine if measures designed to reduce excessive risk taking will ultimately be effective, it is not at all apparent that without some extra pressure assisted by media coverage that the annual bonus culture in such institutions is being reshaped.[50] If anything, the last three years should have called into question the need for annual bonus payments at all for chief executives and other senior executives. There is also a moral issue for chief executives who accept high pay in the face of redundancies or strained economic circumstances.[51] The evidence in chapters 5 and 6 however shows that the quantum of remuneration is important to senior executives, reflecting their relative value vis-à-vis other senior executives.

If institutional investors want to be norm entrepreneurs for executive remuneration, how can each of these activities be undertaken by them individually? Braithwaite and Drahos see norms as a generic category that includes rules, principles, standards and guidelines.[52] This broad view therefore includes the types of statements about remuneration practice made by institutional investors. The norms of remuneration are found in guidance issued by institutional investor organisations (such as the ABI, NAPF and ACSI) and individual institutional investors. How institutional investors decide on the appropriate norms is also relevant to the norms thus created. As discussed above in chapter 3, it is clear that institutional investor representative organisations largely adopt a consensus approach to norms setting. For an institutional investor organisation, typically a specialist committee will be tasked with developing a draft set of guidelines for circulation and comment from the members before a final set of guidelines is reached.

Given institutional investors are setting remuneration norms via their guidelines, how are changes in practice to comply with the guidelines not reflecting shareholder-friendly practices? What is not clear is whether the norms espoused in these guidelines reflect widespread existing practices (that is, norms that are already followed by most companies) or represent aspirations of what practice should be (norms followed by only the better performing companies). Perhaps the consensus view of the appropriate norms set by shareholders might reflect cognitive biases among institutional investors: how institutional investors are remunerated might be reflected in the norms they set, such as accepting that executives should be paid for achieving short term performance,[53] or that executive performance is best measured by relative total shareholder return. Institutional investors might be preferring practices they can readily understand rather than practices that are necessarily better.

9.2.3 Norms Espoused by Institutional Investors

To identify the relevant norms for institutional investors, I focused upon the guidelines issued by the ABI, NAPF, ACSI and IFSA/FSC, that is, the two main institutional investor representative organisations in the UK and Australia respectively. The first norm identified above by Gopalan – greed is good – is conflated with the second norm, pay equity – to arrive at a norm of paying sufficient to attract, retain and motivate executives without paying too much or ensuring the pay is reasonable and aligned with shareholder interests. It is important to note that the guidelines do not expressly say 'greed is good', nor do they say 'greed is bad'. The guidelines suggest that deciding what is 'too much' requires some sense of pay equity as well as a sense of paying only for performance.[54] For example, the ACSI guidelines suggest that an appropriate comparator group for benchmarking remuneration is one based on industry, size and business focus.[55] Shareholder guidelines endorse a norm of market-based remuneration. This means that in profitable times, when human capital is scarce, shareholders will tolerate pay that is in line with the market, given firm performance. If the market rate at this time is generous, perhaps excessive by community standards, shareholders will accept it. Conversely, in leaner times, such as the present, market-based remuneration should be reflecting the decreased profitability of companies. Yet chief executive salaries continue to grow at rates that cannot be explained by increases in inflation.[56] Institutional shareholders do not share the same market benchmarks for assessing quantum with 'mum and dad investors'.

The third norm of pay for performance receives more detailed attention in shareholder guidance, not merely in terms of measures of performance,[57] but also in norms such as no rewards for failure,[58] no ex-gratia termination payments, reasonable contractual provisions for terminations and no hedging of unvested performance-based remuneration. Thus a norm exists that the alignment of shareholder and executive interests is both valuable and achievable by remuneration structures with performance measures linked to shareholder return. This reflects the optimal contract from economics.[59] A further norm is that variable remuneration should be paid only for achieving *superior* performance. However, as noted earlier,

actual short term incentive plans begin to pay out for 'threshold' performance against an undisclosed (either ex ante or ex post) target. Institutional
investors might reasonably question why they have been unsuccessful in
achieving this norm in practice.

The fourth norm of conformity in pay practices is not solely based
on how remuneration consultants undertake the task of advising
remuneration committees; it reflects the actions of institutional investors in enforcing their own guidelines. A norm of market-based remuneration would encourage conformity of pay practice. Proxy advisor
scrutiny of remuneration reports further encourages conformity as companies learn via observation which pay practices will pass through that
filter. That conformity exists is not necessarily a bad thing; however,
it makes it difficult for a norm entrepreneur to introduce a new norm
unless there are a number of firms who are identified as leaders and
who readily adopt that norm. Others, seeing their example and that
institutional investors are reacting positively to that practice, will also
adopt it.[60]

9.2.4   Have Institutional Investors Failed as Norm Entrepreneurs?

The evidence suggests that, in the absence of an external pressure to
monitor such as poor investment performance or government pressure,
institutional investors turn a blind eye to remuneration practices, particularly when economic conditions are favourable. Firstly, executive
remuneration has continued to grow both in the UK and Australia since
the introduction of the vote. I accept that some growth is to be expected:
what is not readily apparent is why the rate of growth is as high as it
is, nor why the gap between average earnings and CEO earnings has
widened. For example, the Productivity Commission has noted that
CEO pay for the S&P/ASX 100 has grown in real terms by an average of
8–9 per cent per annum over the period from 1993 to 2008. It notes this
equates to remuneration of 17 times average annual earnings in 1993 to
50 times average annual earnings in 2008.[61] The evidence from the UK
is similar.[62]

Secondly, institutional shareholders are not always consistent in voting
against remuneration practices. A couple of specific examples illustrate
the problem. While shareholders voted against Macquarie Banking
Group's 2007 remuneration report in numbers, they overwhelmingly
supported the 2006 remuneration report, although the performance
in 2007 was superior to that achieved by the bank in 2006 and any
structural issues identified in 2007 also existed in 2006. Qantas Airways
Limited's 2005 remuneration report contained evidence of potentially

high termination rewards to its then chief executive Geoff Dixon, yet was overwhelmingly supported. When Dixon left Qantas in 2009, the report attracted censure for payment of $11 million for the financial year ended 30 June 2009, when he worked for only one-quarter of that financial year. To examine the UK, the record for the advisory vote for the Royal Bank of Scotland from 2003 to 2009 shows that the lowest level of support received for the remuneration report was 84 per cent in 2003, followed by 85 per cent in 2005. In all other years from 2003 to 2009, the remuneration report has received over 90 per cent of votes in favour of the resolution to adopt it. Yet, as we have already seen, it was always apparent from those reports that the annual pension payable to the chairman was going to be high.[63]

While the public (and thus governments) might be concerned about the absolute quantum it is not clear that institutional investors share this concern, or that they are necessarily troubled by 'undeserved high rewards'.[64] When examining the norms actually espoused by a select group of institutional investors, it is clear that absolute quantum is not the issue, but quantum relative to the market, given firm performance, is. Thus a remuneration norm of greed is good is not challenged by institutional investors under circumstances of good company performance. Pay equity as a norm is endorsed by institutional investors through their norm of setting pay at market levels. While information on the market may not be provided by companies, it is typically provided by proxy advisors in their analysis of the remuneration report. If the proxy advisors do not find the pay is outside the market rate, given firm performance, it will not warrant adverse comment or a voting recommendation against the report. Finally, pay for performance as a norm is accepted by companies and institutional investors. Thus pay that broadly reflects performance, using metrics identified by shareholders as relevant, will be accepted by them. Therefore many of the norms of executive remuneration internalised by company management are endorsed by institutional investors, and practices that conform with the norms are endorsed. This suggests either that the norms encourage the wrong behaviours (greed is fine if performance exists), the content of the norms is unclear (for example, pay for performance as an institutional investor norm appears tolerant of allowing companies to begin paying for performance that is less than superior) or that monitoring of uptake of the norms is weak. Furthermore, a preference for institutional investors for behind-the-scenes engagement means that a shame sanction, even if imposed, lacks a public dimension. In other words, executive remuneration norms do not have the status of obligational norms. This casts doubt on the ability of the advisory vote to create a shame sanction.

9.3 SOME QUESTIONS FOR INSTITUTIONAL INVESTORS

To determine whether institutional investors can continue to play a role as norm entrepreneurs for executive remuneration, institutional investors must ask themselves a series of questions. I do not offer any answers to these questions in this book; rather I suggest that answers are necessary before deciding how best to act in a newly emerging regulatory environment for executive remuneration.

First: *do institutional investors truly want to be norm entrepreneurs for executive remuneration?* From experience, such investors know that monitoring executive remuneration is no easy task. Remuneration structures are complex; remuneration reports are overly long, with myriad details and seemingly no easy way to make sense of them. This might explain why government initiatives to give institutional investors greater say on remuneration decisions are not a cure-all: investors may not believe that all remuneration practices warrant their close inspection. Proxy advisory firms, widely retained by institutional investors, undertake the detailed reading and analysis of remuneration reports and disclosures. Institutional investors use these reports to identify the potential remuneration outliers. Depending upon the mandate given to the fund manager, deciding not to follow a proxy advisory firm's voting instruction might require an ex-post explanation to the pension/superannuation fund client. Thus the room to manoeuvre is really with firms that are identified as potential outliers and the quality of the proxy advisory firms' screening processes is critical. Why not leave it entirely up to the proxy advisory firms to set remuneration norms, given they are doing so currently by default through their screening activities?

However, if the answer to the first question is yes, institutional investors want to play the role of norm entrepreneur, our second question is *what norms* really *matter to institutional investors?* Of the norms identified earlier, arguably it is pay for performance that matters most to institutional investors. Governments are concerned with extreme levels of remuneration and have political imperatives to seek to limit this remuneration. Governments also have the legislative powers to mandate disclosure and voting on particular resolutions. Shareholder norm setting in these areas is probably a suboptimal use of resources because, given a choice to comply with a shareholder norm on disclosure or a legal requirement on disclosure, the latter will prevail. Thus shareholders may want to devote less time to creating detailed disclosure principles, focusing instead on remuneration practice principles and the norms underlying these principles. Proxy advisory firms would seem to cover most of the details of remuneration, while the media can play a role in highlighting particularly high payments and the overall market.

Clearly company performance is pivotal for institutional investors, and so pay for performance-type measures might best be described and monitored by these investors. A number of these investors will have access to company management in relation to company performance issues, although the mismatch cycle between remuneration disclosures and performance discussions makes it less likely that the routine briefings or conference calls could be used to raise remuneration-type issues. Furthermore, institutional investors are better placed than governments and prudential regulators to make assessments of company performance, provided appropriate risk disclosures are available to such investors.

9.4   CONCLUSION

I concede the above analysis offers no ready solutions for institutional investors to adopt. Indeed it may be impossible for institutional investors to reject the role of norm entrepreneur in light of initiatives such as the *Principles of Responsible Investment* and government pressures within individual jurisdictions to be active owners. This creates an opportunity for institutional investors to further refine this role to focus on executive remuneration norms that truly matter to institutional investors, knowing that others will be monitoring and enforcing other aspects of remuneration. Lobbying these other actors in response to formal requests for submissions on policy changes creates the opportunity to influence the norms set by other actors, although many institutional investors and superannuation/pension funds seem to prefer undertaking such activities via representative groups and not directly. However, this latter avenue should not be overlooked as another way of ensuring investor-preferred norms are adopted by investee companies. Some of the recent Australian reforms to termination payments can be linked to institutional investor submissions on the issue.[65]

As the regulated remuneration cycle illustrates, focusing just on disclosure and on voting rights is necessary, but not sufficient, to change remuneration practices. In their own norm-setting activities, institutional investors can return to some core activities, based on their interests in firm performance. It is unlikely that other monitors have either the expertise or intense interest in doing so. Therefore, in setting norms for executive remuneration, the opportunity presented by the global financial crisis is for institutional investors to rethink norms of company performance,[66] and how remuneration can be best aligned to achieve this.

NOTES

1. Walker 2009, p. 62.
2. Organisation for Economic Cooperation and Development 2011a, p. 15.
3. Hawley and Williams 2000, p. 58.
4. Nisar 2005, p. 16.
5. UK *Stewardship Code*, p. 1. Cheffins 2010, pp. 1013–14.
6. Walker 2009, pp. 61–2.
7. Walker 2009, p. 64.
8. Organisation for Economic Cooperation and Development 2011a, pp. 9, 12.
9. Myners Review of Institutional Investment for HM Treasury 2001, p. 81 notes this is a strategic choice with passive investing being 'a legitimate strategy for an investor who values its tangible cost advantages over the possibility of achieving additional return through stock selection'.
10. United Nations Economic Programme Financial Initiative 2006.
11. Becht et al 2008.
12. Gold 2006, pp. 145–6.
13. Brown, Beekes and Verhoeven 2011, pp. 105–9.
14. Sunstein 1996, p. 909.
15. Sheehan 2007.
16. Sunstein 1996, pp. 949–50.
17. McAdams 1997, p. 340.
18. Sunstein 1996, p. 914.
19. Ferran 2001, p. 404.
20. Eisenberg 1999, p. 1254.
21. Eisenberg 1999, p. 1256.
22. Scott 2002, p. 1604.
23. Gopalan 2007b, p. 4.
24. Gopalan 2007a, p. 775.
25. Hill 1996, p. 233; Cheffins 1997, p. 211.
26. Gopalan 2007a, p. 783.
27. Rodgers and Gago 2003, p. 191.
28. Bebchuk and Fried 2004, p. 76.
29. Jasso and Meyersonn Milgrom 2008, pp. 124–5.
30. Swanson and Orlitzky 2006, pp. 20, 25.
31. Harris 2006, p. 70.
32. According to Harris, this approach would simply ask how executive remuneration enhances individual capabilities or deprivations for the firm's stakeholders: Harris 2006, p. 76.
33. Harris argues that different remuneration payments for the CEO and the entry-level worker are justified if they represent the best allocation of the firm's money and are to every stakeholder's advantage, and, more importantly, that the CEO position is open and available to all: p. 71.
34. Cf. Evans and Hefner 2009.
35. Shaw 2006, p. 97.
36. Holmström 1981.
37. Dine 2006, p. 82.
38. Petel 2003, p. 388.
39. This is recognised in initiatives such as the Walker Review with its draft Code of Conduct for remuneration consultants in the UK: Walker 2009, pp. 131–6. Although the Code primarily aims to neutralise the effects of conflicts of interest on the advice given, its emphasis on transparency in selecting comparator groups recognises that professional judgment is involved and any advice is context specific.
40. Kandel 2009, pp. 411–12.
41. Harris 2009.

42. Bebchuk and Fried 2004, p. 75.
43. Gopalan 2007b, p. 31.
44. For example, see United Nations Environment Programme Finance Initiative 2005; United Nations Environment Programme Finance Initiative 2009; Wen 2009.
45. For example, see Chiu 2008.
46. Sunstein 1996, pp. 929–930.
47. Craig and Solomon 2009; Hughes 2009.
48. Financial Stability Board (formerly Financial Stability Forum) 2009.
49. Sunstein 1996, p. 929.
50. Murphy 2012.
51. Moriarty 2009.
52. Braithwaite and Drahos 2000, p. 19.
53. For example, the more recent policies issued by various institutional investor groups endorse short term bonus payments linked to profits or other key performance indicators: Association of British Insurers 2011, p. 7; National Association of Pension Funds 2009, p. 26; Australian Council of Superannuation Investors Inc 2011a, p. 22.
54. Association of British Insurers 2011, p. 9.
55. Australian Council of Superannuation Investors Inc 2009, p. 18.
56. Australian Council of Trade Unions 2010; Stensholt and Durkin 2010; Australian Council of Superannuation Investors Inc 2011b.
57. Association of British Insurers 2011, pp. 12–13; Australian Council of Superannuation Investors Inc 2011a, pp. 22–3.
58. Association of British Insurers 2011, pp. 4–5; Australian Council of Superannuation Investors Inc 2011a, p. 21.
59. Jensen and Meckling 1976; Shavell 1979.
60. See above chapter 2, Figure 2.4.
61. Productivity Commission of Australia 2009, p. 30.
62. High Pay Commission 2011.
63. Sheehan 2011, pp. 132–3.
64. Mitchell, O'Donnell and Ramsay 2005, p. 444.
65. A clear example of such success is the reduction in the termination payments threshold in Australia to the 12 months' base salary advocated publicly by ACSI since 2005.
66. Enderle and Tavis 1998; cf. Jensen 2001.

10. The advantages and limits of say on pay as a regulatory technique

When say on pay was first introduced in the UK, at least one interviewee thought 'That's a stupid idea. What's the point of that?' A similar view was expressed in submissions to the Joint Committee on Corporations and Financial Services in 2004 that considered the bill to introduce say on pay into Australian law:[1]

> If the objective of the proposed changes is to provide shareholders with an opportunity to express their views on remuneration, then a provision requiring the chair to invite debate on this topic is far more appropriate than a 'chocolate teapot' provision, such as s 250R(2), which simply permits the board to pay lip-service to the members while incurring substantial and unnecessary costs for the company.[2]

The UK corporate governance manager first quoted above soon came to see the value of the advisory vote:

> The fund managers are a pretty conservative bunch. They spend a long time building up these relationships, they are long term shareholder investors in these companies and they know the companies well. *It's a big deal to vote against a binding issue.* To have a non-binding vote is quite a good safety valve.

Other UK fund managers also stressed the impersonal nature of voting against the advisory vote:

> Having the advisory vote is good in that it has 'de-personalised' the vote against the executive director or the executive chairman if you have concerns over his/ their remuneration. Because you don't really want to penalise the director concerned by voting against his or her re-election, as that is quite specific.

The FTSE 100 remuneration committee representatives I interviewed had a different view of the advisory vote and the corporate governance managers within funds managers and pension funds:

> Corporate governance people well . . . they are a sort of necessary evil. (FTSE 100 remuneration committee chair)

You know the people who are doing the compliance and remuneration issues and governance issues in the institutions tend to be failed fund managers who didn't quite make it. (FTSE 100 remuneration committee chair)

The more vociferous tend not to be the larger [shareholders]. We tend to be closer to the ones that are larger and so there is perhaps a bit more continuous influencing going on rather than a one-off shot 'This is what we are doing' – and them over-reacting. (FTSE 100 company secretary)

At least one S&P/ASX 200 remuneration committee chair I interviewed thought that say on pay

has been a big step forward. I was sceptical at first. I thought all we were going to get was a heap of protests that the board is just going to ignore because it's non-binding. That hasn't been the case. People have voted with reasonably good intent. And boards in the main are listening.

For UK investors, this need to de-personalise the vote on remuneration issues might reflect the 'fat cat' debate in the UK during the 1990s and early 2000s where remuneration became highly personalised (as it has again more recently with Fred Godwin and Stephen Hester from the Royal Bank of Scotland). However, if the de-personalised nature of this vote means shareholders are more likely to use it to signal disagreement, initiatives introducing a binding vote, such as those examined below, may not improve accountability or remuneration practices as intended if institutional shareholders are reluctant to 'just vote no'.

The second value of the say on pay from the perspective of institutional shareholders is that it has led to an increase in engagement and dialogue, as well as improving remuneration disclosures. As one UK corporate governance manager commented:

It's been valuable in terms of, certainly in the UK, increasing dialogue between investors and the company. I think that the disclosure we have now is a lot more transparent than what we had before the regulations came into play . . . It is a great platform to engage with companies.

The desire to engage is not limitless:

We sit with the fund managers for a reason. If they are happy campers and they've made, our clients have made, a lot of money, the share price is going the right way, then we are less concerned. If executive managers are trousering large awards for poor performance, that elevates them up the queue and that's when the engagement kicks off. (Corporate governance manager, UK funds management house)

Remuneration consultants in the UK confirmed that the vote had forced shareholders to become more involved in remuneration, with one commenting that such involvement was

> not always willingly frankly. Traditionally, before the vote, the only thing shareholders ever got really excited about were long term incentive plans and service contracts. That's where the only bun fights ever were. Salaries weren't particularly relevant. Annual bonuses weren't particularly important either. But the vote has caused shareholders to look at all elements of the package.

The third value of say on pay for institutional shareholders is that, despite its advisory status,

> It does seem to have an effect. It allows us to raise concerns but the concerns can be acted on. The company realises it has to face this vote each year. I think it focuses their minds. (UK corporate governance manager, funds management company)

The imperative to act might depend on the strength of the signal sent by shareholders:

> Ten per cent is a threshold where you would expect the remuneration committee to think about what went wrong and up to 25 per cent means they would have to do something about it, a change is required. (UK corporate governance manager)

Shareholders regarded the advisory vote as valuable in sending a message, even if it is done in a formalised way, because of the publicity this can generate:

> If shareholders have an adverse review of the remuneration reports, then it comes out into the public forum, it at least gives the companies a little bit of food for thought.

As with the appetite for engagement, there is a limit to how much publicity is desirable:

> when it becomes more high profile, confrontational and can impact on reputation . . . the share price as well might suffer. And you don't want that. So what we tend to do is to try and iron out all of these issues beforehand. (Corporate governance manager, UK fund management house)

For one Australian fund manager interviewed, the fact the vote is advisory only '[means] that you feel you can vote against without it affecting too much'. Shareholders believe companies do notice the signal, although one superannuation fund representative noted it only had an impact when

> it's a particularly egregious payment . . . [when] it looks like serial pillaging, it will upset enough institutional investors. [Otherwise the company] can modify their behaviour and get away with it.

From the perspective of an S&P/ASX 200 remuneration committee chair, a good outcome on the advisory vote 'validates what the committee is doing'. One remuneration committee chair who had experienced a high level of votes against the remuneration report noted 'the press obviously hammered me', while another in similar circumstances noted the advisory vote was

> Problematical . . . [the remuneration report] comes out 18 months later [than the timing of decisions] and people forget what it was like at the time . . . when you realise how [shareholders] function, it's not really a powerful message.

Yet there is value in 'focusing the minds of the remuneration committee . . . which is, I suppose, a good thing' (Australian ASX 200 remuneration committee chair).

It is by no means clear that when companies respond and change their practices that these changes lead to better practices. The levels of executive remuneration have continued to increase in both jurisdictions,[3] while the gap between executives' salaries and ordinary employees' salaries has also increased. However, over time the ability of the advisory vote to trigger engagement and changes to practices wanes:

> What's interesting the UK market is that two–three years ago if you got 5 per cent vote against your remuneration report, that'd be quite strange. If you got 10 per cent you'd be worried. And some corporates are taking the view now that if it passes, it passes. It's only a non-binding vote anyhow. Seventy-five per cent is good enough. (UK institutional investor representative)

> I'm not sure that I can say that as a result of a sustained discussion with an institutional investor that we changed a metric in a policy or something like that . . . I think that if we ended up in the situation that Glaxo had four or five years ago, where they all just said 'We just don't like this at all and we're going to vote against' then you may well find that you'd take a different view. (FTSE 100 company secretary)

> There are individuals in the group who have a different idea, but the group controls the extreme individuals who bang on about their pet subject. And let's face it: if one individual votes against it, so be it. It's not going to be the end of the world. (FTSE 100 remuneration committee chair)

> A couple of years ago we went through a huge trend of consultation whereby remuneration committees wrote to investors on almost a weekly basis asking them for views and advice on their plans that they were thinking about being introduced. That seems to have waned slightly. (UK corporate governance manager, pension fund)

These different views hint at difficulties reconciling actual practices with the policy goals behind say on pay: it would curb excess because it creates a mechanism for shareholders to hold the company (via the board of directors and remuneration committee) to account for their actual practices. The empirical evidence presented above in chapters 4 to 6 indicates the remuneration committee's task is both complex and political. In arriving at an independent view, and not simply approving a management-sponsored proposal, the remuneration committee must proactively make an informed decision relying on multiple sources of information. The various laws, rules and guidance within the regulatory space for the activities of practice and disclosure add a further layer of complexity, although most of the real decisions turn on positioning of overall remuneration, annual increases, setting short term incentive targets and determining whether those targets have been satisfied.

The task is also political because of internal dynamics of companies and boards of directors, as well as the various external pressures on the committee from shareholders, governments and the media. This interplay of complexity and politics impacts on the ability of remuneration committees to deliver the remuneration norms for practice outcomes espoused in government policy goals. In other words, achieving the desired restraint on quantum is difficult if market salary data and pressure from executives weigh in favour of higher and higher remuneration.

10.1   IMPROVED ACCOUNTABILITY

The policy goals for accountability in the UK and Australia draw attention to the remuneration committee process. While remuneration committees in Australia and the UK struggle to maintain strict independence from management, resolving these issues via regulation (including the company's constitutional arrangements) is not straightforward. Difficulties arise in practice due to reliance upon management for company information and data, if not outright reliance on management to provide a report for the committee's discussion and a recommendation for the committee's approval. In focusing upon independence of the remuneration committee, government and shareholder initiatives might be missing the larger picture. The regulatory framework does not have sufficiently clear guidance on what good remuneration outcomes look like, but instead relies heavily upon guidance on process that companies can hide behind.

As discussed previously in chapter 2, the rules for remuneration practice focus on two issues: the remuneration committee decision-making processes and the structure of remuneration packages. Remuneration committees need an unbiased remuneration policy and a way of monitoring the outcomes of decisions made under this policy. Yet the guidance on what the remuneration policy should seek to achieve consists of high-level principles that readily accommodate both good and bad practices. A principle that the company's remuneration practices retain key executives supports the use of retention payments, even though the remuneration committee representatives interviewed appear sceptical about the benefits of doing so. It also supports benchmarking and, potentially, paying well above the market rate.

It is also important to acknowledge the reality of the relationships between non-executive directors and company management. Personal factors *will* influence directors' judgments.[4] This is particularly evident when the committee makes an ad hoc decision to hire, retain or terminate an executive by applying the general remuneration policy in a specific instance to a particular executive. Independence can be viewed as creating a division based on suspicion of executive directors by non-executive directors, or as a state of mind that non-executive directors bring to deliberations and decisions that benefits both the board as a whole and the executive directors.[5] The above analysis suggests that any regulation of remuneration committees needs to take a pragmatic view of the committee's information needs and the available sources to satisfy those needs. Good judgment is as essential a characteristic of good directors as independence. Unsurprisingly, 'good judgment' has yet to be captured in regulation. It is not sufficient to be accountable: the directors on the remuneration committee also need to be competent.

10.2 BETTER REMUNERATION PRACTICES

Two particular issues are highlighted by the evidence: the role of remuneration consultants in providing market advice and the influence of guidance on actual remuneration practice.

10.2.1 Remuneration Consultants

All remuneration consultants interviewed acknowledged that they owed a duty of care to their clients. They did not speak of care in terms of the accuracy of the market advice, but rather whether the advice was independent and 'rigorous'. Unlike auditors, remuneration consultants do not require any special training; there is no system of professional standards, methods or rules to work within to produce 'rigour'. Remuneration consultants communicate the market to remuneration committees by providing market data for a comparator group. Given the evidence suggests that this is a key input to decisions on quantum (either as part of the annual review or as an ad hoc decision), achieving fair and responsible remuneration requires more attention to how remuneration consultants perform this task.

While disclosing the material advisors to the remuneration committee creates a reputational risk for these advisors, the reality is that the business market in Australia is small. As one remuneration consultant noted, 'bad news travels twice as fast as good news', although it only travels within the non-executive directors' network, rather than being publicly available to shareholders. Likewise, one UK remuneration consultant interviewed suggested there were only about 50 individuals who act as remuneration consultants to large companies in the UK. This is a small enough group for directors to become familiar with. In other words, publicity via disclosure is targeting the wrong issue.

The evidence suggests a set of standards for remuneration consultants is needed if remuneration committees are to demonstrate they have remunerated fairly, responsibly and reasonably. These might be along the lines of accounting or auditing standards that describe how to conduct a benchmarking exercise, annual review and major review, as well as how to prepare and present remuneration data. While regulatory attention is focusing upon the conflicts of interest that can exist for remuneration consultants,[6] a more pertinent need is to settle on a set of standards for such things as comparator group selection, selection of incentive measures and benchmarking. While remuneration consultants in the UK have come together in an affiliation to develop a code,[7] no professional association currently exists for remuneration consultants in Australia. In other words, there is no obvious body to devise and promulgate these standards. In terms of legislative solutions, merely disclosing the name of the remuneration consultants, the nature of their services and their independence will not overcome biased comparator group selection and the remuneration decisions that flow from this.

10.2.2 Influence of Guidance on Pay for Performance

There are clear distinctions between the influence of shareholder guidance on STIs, LTIs and ad hoc payments. In terms of practice for STIs, remuneration committees make choices so as to align the senior executives to achieve the corporate goals set by management and endorsed by the board. In terms of what company remuneration policies should achieve, the STI presents the opportunity to create true best practice for the firm and to achieve the kind of alignment as predicted by the optimal contract and the motivation literature.[8] The broadly worded guidance for STIs, combined with 'commercial in confidence' carve-outs in the mandatory disclosure rules for the actual performance targets, make it difficult to assess whether the STI is aligned with performance, however it is specified within the STI scheme. In other words, a law appears to inhibit rather than promote pay for performance, because companies know that shareholders are not able to accurately monitor performance achieved on the STI criteria.

While STIs can be tailored to the company's circumstances and strategy, the same cannot be said of LTIs, where the particularised nature of the guidance has a clear influence on company practice. The 'vanilla-isation' of approach to LTIs in the UK, irrespective of the company's industry and position in the business cycle, is an example of where narrowly worded guidance may work against the achievement of best practice. While there is a standard suite of approaches in Australia, there is more choice allowed – at least during the period studied – for differences in practice. This suggests a difference in approach between UK institutional investors and Australian institutional investors in enforcing their own guidance. While this guidance and its adoption would suggest measuring pay for performance is easy for LTIs, the use of fair-value accounting to derive a value for the benefit granted, combined with a definition of 'remuneration' that specifically excludes the gain on share-based payments on exercise,[9] means the remuneration actually received by the executive is never truly disclosed.[10] Hence it is impossible to determine whether remuneration is aligned with performance from the company's own disclosures. Additional information is needed to determine this. For institutional shareholders, this information is provided by proxy advisor analysis. Ordinary shareholders are left to determine this as best they can. If the aim of the remuneration report is for the remuneration committee to provide information to shareholders, viewed either as a targeted transparency initiative or a goal of providing information on remuneration practices, it may not be providing the information shareholders actually require.

10.3   THE ROLE OF INSTITUTIONAL INVESTORS

The evidence highlights a number of conflicts within and between three activities undertaken by institutional investors in the regulated remuneration cycle. Institutional investor rule making plays an important role in the regulated remuneration cycle by providing most of the rules for remuneration practice. We have seen how company remuneration practices reflect this guidance. Remuneration committees and their consultants are more likely to follow the guidance if there is a synergy between this guidance and the engagement and voting practices of institutional shareholders. The evidence on voting presented above in chapter 8 indicates that voting decisions largely reflect shareholders' assessment of structure (thus suggesting this synergy exists) although excessive ad hoc payments will also attract a voting sanction. Proxy advisors' reports are critical inputs into both of these decisions because institutional investors lack the resources, or, perhaps more correctly, fail to allocate sufficient resources to this activity. This means the proxy advisors' recommendations can be highly influential, but more typically support a vote for the report than a vote against it.

Both the UK and Australian governments encouraged greater shareholder engagement on executive remuneration as a way of improving board accountability, with the advisory vote as a signal of shareholder sentiment. Institutional investor voices are modulated from the private whisper of engagement to the loud public shout[11] of the advisory vote. As the governments expected, the advisory vote provides leverage for shareholders to encourage reluctant remuneration committees to engage. What they perhaps did not expect is that remuneration committees would respond by creating additional opportunities for engagement that undermine shareholders' ability to hold boards accountable. While still 'engagement', two of the engagement opportunities examined allow remuneration committees to exploit this regulatory conversation for their own ends by shifting engagement away from the advisory vote to earlier in the regulated remuneration cycle (prior to disclosure in the remuneration report). At this time, shareholders are relying largely on their own resources to respond to the company's initiatives, although remuneration committees also court proxy advisors during this process. More engagement does not necessarily mean board accountability has improved or that institutional shareholders are being more diligent. Both sides may well be gaming the vote via their engagement activities.

10.4   ADVANTAGES OF SAY ON PAY

There are many advantages of say on pay as a regulatory technique that make it an ideal choice for governments to respond to public ire about the levels of executive pay. The first of these advantages is that say on pay respects the authority of the board of directors by allowing shareholders only an advisory vote, rather than a binding vote, on the remuneration report. Secondly, it respects the market mechanisms for setting the price for executive labour and does not impose government control over the levels or structure of executive remuneration packages. Thirdly, an advisory say on pay for shareholders is cheap for governments to implement. It requires little government expenditure in monitoring because shareholders and the media will monitor remuneration practices and voting outcomes; the government needs only to confirm that listed companies have included a remuneration report and that an advisory vote on that report has been held as part of the AGM. It does not cost too much to impose sanctions as any sanction relates to the failure to either make the required disclosures or to conduct the vote, which is binary in nature (yes, it occurred or no it did not) and no costs are incurred to impose a sanction against the board or the company for the remuneration practices. It satisfies the political need to do something in response to moral panic at the sight of executive greed.

It also *appears* to have an effect.[12] Engagement between boards of directors and major shareholders becomes more frequent.[13] Companies attract high levels of votes against the remuneration report and, at least initially, many of these companies change their ways.[14] Shareholders soon overwhelmingly support remuneration reports:[15] an indication that they are happy with the practices disclosed. Yet with new economic crisis, such as the GFC and its aftermath, fresh evidence of the high levels of executive remuneration comes to light, bringing with it a renewed call for governments to do something.

10.5   LIMITS OF SAY ON PAY

Even without the economic crisis that began in 2008, it is clear that say on pay has some limits as a regulatory technique. Disclosure (the pay) and voting (the say) alone cannot change practices towards government-preferred practices because shareholders, not governments, make the rules about remuneration practices and enforce those rules through engagement. Thus the synergies between rule making on practice, engagement and voting are key to changing remuneration practices and institutional shareholders hold that key. Shareholder accountability for these activities has been largely lacking in Australia, with the Cooper Review of Australia's superannuation system in 2009–10 forgoing the opportunity to make such a requirement, although making recommendations on governance arrangements.[16] It is also too soon to judge how effective the UK

Stewardship Code will be in ensuring greater levels of shareholder accountability. As with director accountability, this reform has failed to describe in clear terms what the outcome of having more accountable institutional investors is.

As we saw in chapter 2, the enforcement options available for good remuneration practice with an advisory say on pay are severely limited. The relevant laws clearly state that no person's remuneration is affected by the outcome of the vote alone. As we have seen, the regulated remuneration cycle and the advisory vote within that cycle are premised on the understanding that shareholders will engage boards in regulatory conversations to move remuneration practices towards shareholder-preferred practices. A vote against the remuneration report signals this conversation has failed to achieve the desired changes. It is not the end of the regulatory conversation. The evidence in chapters 5 and 6 indicates that the remuneration committee may respond to a negative voting outcome by undertaking a major review of remuneration. A 'dialogue' (not a negotiation) about the proposed practices will be instigated by the remuneration committee, not its shareholders, and the tone of the regulatory conversation will change as a result of when it occurs in the cycle. More activity in the form of engagement does not necessarily mean better practices are adopted following these conversations: a 'one size fits all' approach to executive remuneration structures is not necessarily a good outcome,[17] if one accepts that performance targets motivate performance and pay reflects the result of that performance. It is also clear that the rate of growth in executive remuneration has not slowed.[18]

The principles paradox identified by Julia Black[19] is evident in executive remuneration where the supposed advantages of principles-based regulation are not achieved because participants cannot or do not distinguish between principles and rules. We have seen how UK remuneration practices, and to a large extent Australian remuneration practices, have fallen into one model of remuneration: fixed pay (base salary and pension/superannuation benefits) revised annually after benchmarking exercise; an annual STI based on company profit and perhaps other strategic goals where actual performance against goals is not explicitly linked to the STI paid; and LTI awarded annually, with 50 per cent based on EPS growth goals and the remaining 50 per cent based on relative TSR performance goals.

It is by no means clear why this so-called best practice is actually 'best'. Careful drafting is needed to ensure that principles do actually allow for flexible application by paying attention to the structure of the rule. That said, the various rule makers within the regulated remuneration cycle should not retreat from making narrower rules where substantive compliance can only be achieved in one way. 'If not, why not' or 'comply or explain' should be reserved for those practices where compliance via different routes is not only feasible, but desirable.

10.6   FRESH GOVERNMENT INITIATIVES?

Governments now tend to respond to such failures by directly intervening in the regulated remuneration cycle. Instead they may need to make *facilitative rules* to enable the regulated remuneration cycle to work better, rather than to make substantive rules on practice. For example, if a credible peak is needed for the enforcement pyramid for good remuneration practices, maybe the threshold to call a meeting to remove one or two directors could be lowered. If levels of institutional shareholder voting are of concern, introducing rules to allow for direct electronic voting (bypassing the convoluted system of proxy appointments and instructions) and to require an audit trail might reduce the incidence of lost votes. Governments have, however, sought to make *substantive rules* on practice (for example, on termination payments in Australia[20] and proposed rule on termination payments in the UK[21]) and, in the case of Australia at least, a raft of new offences relating to remuneration decision making that alters the tension of the policy tightrope.

That governments are increasingly resorting to new substantive rules on remuneration practice, relying on their artillery of public law sanctions to achieve what shareholders, armed with voting rights cannot do alone, may have unintended consequences. A recent example is the deliberations of the Australian Department of Treasury on whether mechanisms to claw back bonus payments in circumstances where the financial statements are materially mis-stated are necessary.[22] If the 'squeezing the balloon' argument raised in relation to changes to the termination provisions rings true for any unfavourable changes to executive remuneration practices,[23] these amendments will be paid for with fresh consideration, most likely in the form of higher fixed pay.

These government initiatives lead us to a bigger question: why is it in the government's interest – and hence the public interest – to interfere in company affairs by making laws about executive remuneration? The High Pay Commission in the UK identifies three problems with executive remuneration practices: they damage companies; they are bad for the UK economy; and they have 'negative impacts on our society as a whole' in two ways. First, they damage public trust in UK companies and that loss of trust is paid for by job losses among ordinary employees. Secondly, executive remuneration practices lead to gross inequalities of income.[24]

Improving the UK economy by regulating executive remuneration is premised on the notion of pay for performance and, more particularly, that superior performance can be motivated and thus achieved by the correct pay structures and rewards. We have seen in chapters 5 and 6 that remuneration consultants largely dismiss such arguments, although these arguments are accepted by remuneration committees and shareholders alike.

Gross inequalities are also an appropriate policy issue for governments. A conceptually difficult issue in liberal economies is how far government should intervene to address inequalities, rather than providing for a minimum level of income through social security benefits such as aged and other pensions, unemployment benefits, access to free healthcare and education, and other welfare benefits. It is not at all clear, however, that this is the motivating rationale for regulating executive remuneration. Company directors believe government policies over-emphasise executive remuneration over other corporate activities. As one Australian remuneration committee chairman told me, 'In dollar terms, this is one of the smallest decisions we make.' Yet with the amount of law reform in this area over the past 10 years, it is clear that governments feel obligated to try to influence the outcomes of this smallest decision.

10.6.1   Remuneration Committees

One way to improve accountability is to change the way in which the boards of companies make remuneration decisions. The first and obvious way to do so is to regulate the remuneration committee. The Department for Business Innovation and Skills consultation on executive remuneration in 2011 considers different ways to reconfigure the remuneration committee, including adding employee representatives to the committee.[25] The Productivity Commission of Australia's proposals to reform remuneration committees have been adopted by amendments to the ASX *Listing Rules* to require companies in the S&P/ASX 300 to have a remuneration committee of only non-executive directors;[26] and by the ASX Corporate Governance Council through amendments to its guidance on practice to require a remuneration committee of at least three members, with an independent chair and a majority of independent directors.[27] These rules can be undermined by practices within companies to allow the CEO and other executives to routinely attend remuneration committee meetings 'by invitation'.

10.6.2   Remuneration Consultants

The second strategy for governments is to focus on remuneration consultants. The remuneration report in the UK has required disclosure of material advisors to the remuneration committee since its inception. Following the Walker Review, remuneration consultants set up an industry body, the Remuneration Consultants Group, and devised a code of practice.[28] That code was reviewed in 2010–11 by Dr Martin Read and it is likely that the code will be further enhanced in early 2012.[29] More recently the Department for Business Innovation and Skills has queried whether further transparency on the use of remuneration consultants would be achieved by requiring boards to disclose the levels of fees paid, in the process drawing an analogy with the company's auditors.[30]

It is important to remember that remuneration consultants provide data and advice to inform the decision making of directors, rather than performing a certification or verification function. As noted in the *Voluntary Code of Conduct in Relation to Executive Remuneration Consulting in the United Kingdom*, issued by the Remuneration Consultants Group in 2009:[31]

> In this connection it is important to clarify the role that executive remuneration consultants fulfil. Their role is to provide advice and information which they believe to be appropriate and in the best interests of the company. Their input should take fully into account the *Combined Code* principle that pay should be sufficient, without being excessive, to attract, retain and motivate executives of the right calibre. The purpose of their input is to support robust and informed decision making by the company on remuneration matters.

Australia has only required disclosure of remuneration consultants since July 2011. However, a more important move is the creation of new offences in relation to giving remuneration advice to anyone other than a non-executive director in a company.[32] Focusing on the decision making of the board of directors and how the exercise of independent judgment may be compromised is the correct approach, rather than an approach based on creating offences in relation to the giving of remuneration consulting advice. A comparison between the role of remuneration consultants and the role of auditors clarifies the very different roles these two advisors play in company affairs.

An audit of the financial reports is required by section 301(1) of the *Corporations Act 2001* (Cth). The integrity, reliability and credibility of financial reports are important to shareholders and other company stakeholders, and to the financial markets more generally. As Ramsay notes:

> Audited financial statements are an important part of the financial information that is available to the capital markets and an important part of effective corporate governance.[33]

This justifies the registration of auditors under part 2M.4 of the *Corporations Act 2001* (Cth), and the requirements for auditor independence in sections 324CA, 324CB and 324CC. The auditor is required to form an opinion on several matters listed in s 307; conduct the audit in accordance with the auditing standards (or else commit an offence of strict liability per s 307A(3)); retain audit papers for seven years (or else commit an offence of strict liability per s 307B(2) for an individual auditor or audit company or s 307B(4) for a member of an audit firm); make a declaration of independence *to the board of directors* under s 307C(1) (individual auditor), s 307C(3) (lead auditor for an audit firm or audit company); and comply with the audit report content requirements in s 308, which includes an audit opinion on the remuneration report (in terms of whether it complies with the requirements of s 300A) (with a strict liability offence in s 308(5) for an offence based on ss 308(1), (3), (3A), (3C) or (4)).

The statute also recognises the importance of the auditor's role by giving the auditor certain powers: for example, the auditor has a power to obtain information under s 310 as a right of access to the books of the company and, providing the request is reasonable, to require any officer to give the auditor information, explanations or other assistance for the purposes of the audit or review. Officers of the company are under complementary statutory obligations found in s 312 to allow access and give information.

A final requirement is that an auditor must avoid a conflict of interest situation. 'Conflict of interest situation' is defined in s 324CD(1) and incorporates the concept of not being able to exercise objective and impartial judgment in relation to the conduct of the audit, and allows for this to be assessed objectively by a reasonable person with full knowledge of all relevant facts and circumstances in s 324CD(1)(b). There are also further independence requirements that take the form of identifying persons and entities covered[34] by the requirement to take all reasonable steps should a conflict of interest situation arise,[35] and define several relationships as relevant for this purpose.[36] It is clear auditors play a very different role to remuneration consultants.

Remuneration consultants are also in a different role from experts who write reports on proposed transactions, such as a merger or acquisition,[37] a scheme of arrangement[38] or a compulsory acquisition of capital.[39] ASIC's *Regulatory Guide 112: Independence of Experts* identifies independence of reports as important to security holders because 'they will assume that an expert report is an independent opinion and will be misled if the opinion is not'.[40] As Brooking J notes:

> they are supposed to be for the protection of individuals who are being invited to enter into some kind of transaction. Unless high standards are observed by

those who prepare these reports, there is a danger that systems established for the protection of the investing public will, in fact, operate to their detriment through reliance on these reports and the reputations of those who furnish them.[41]

The Act provides for particular disclosures to be made by these experts,[42] including disclosure in their report of relationships and fees: this is the model that has been used for the proposed amendments to the remuneration report (s 300A(1)(h)).

It is clear that remuneration consultants fulfil a different function in the companies they advise. They are not auditors; nor are they providing expert reports on a transaction proposed by management, with the report being provided to shareholders to assist in their decision making. A different type of initiative which has been endorsed by the Corporations and Markets Advisory Committee[43] is to develop a different kind of remuneration consulting standard from the original *Voluntary Code of Conduct* by focusing on the nitty-gritty of how remuneration consultants undertake benchmarking exercises and the other technical aspects of the role. In this way, a system of professional standards, methods and rules will exist for remuneration advice.

10.6.3 Regulating the board of directors

A different way to improve accountability is to enhance the ability of shareholders to appoint and remove directors as rights separate from remuneration issues. The Walker Review recommended annual re-election for boards of quoted companies,[44] a recommendation taken up by the Financial Reporting Council.[45] The Australian solutions seek to override the 'no vacancy' rule found in some company constitutions. A no-vacancy rule allows the board of directors to declare there are no vacant seats on the board, even though the maximum number of directors permitted by the company's constitution has not been reached. Previously shareholders who have tried to submit candidates for election have been told, 'Sorry, there is no vacancy on the board.' Electing their own candidates requires a successful challenge to displace an incumbent director and then a resolution to elect the new director. The amendment requires that a resolution to declare 'no vacancy' is to be passed by the shareholders in general meeting. [46] In a different approach also aimed at changing the composition of the board, the Department for Business Innovation and Skills has sought views on allowing shareholders and employees to have a voice on the board's nominations committee.[47]

The two-strikes rule warrants closer examination as a regulatory mechanism for improving accountability. The Productivity Commission of Australia's final report in December 2009 concluded that some companies had failed to respond adequately to large votes against the remuneration report, evidenced by consecutive votes against the remuneration report over the period 2007 to 2009.[48] Most still achieved sufficient support for the remuneration report resolution to pass. However, evidence of a lack of responsiveness was sufficient for the government to act by imposing distinct obligations on the company for each strike. Following a vote of 25 per cent or more against the remuneration report (year 1), the remuneration committee must explain in the following year's remuneration report (year 2) how it took shareholders' views into account in settling that year's (year 2) remuneration policy. If 25 per cent or more of shareholder votes are against the remuneration report in year 2, a resolution to remove the entire board of directors must be voted on at that same AGM. If that vote is passed by a majority of votes, then the company has 90 days to replace the board of directors (other than the executive directors) or else conduct a further general meeting to re-elect the board.

Unsurprisingly, the measure was controversial when proposed, being announced with the release of a Department of Treasury Consultation Paper on 20 December 2010 and a one-month window for submissions at a time when Australia is typically enjoying its summer holidays. It has also proved controversial in practice. In the first six months of its operation since coming into force on 1 July 2011, at least 30 Australian companies have received a 'first strike'.[49] We shall only see in the second half of 2012 whether the threat of attracting a second strike is sufficient incentive for companies to amend their practices to shareholder-preferred practices. Some company boards of directors may choose to 'shoot it out' with their shareholders, confident that while the 25 per cent are unhappy with practices and incurring a second strike, they hold sufficient votes for any spill resolution to pass. As one executive chairman who is also a majority shareholder commented publicly:

> If we receive a second strike again next year, we will be left in the farcical position of the board being subject to a spill. If that happens, I will use my votes to ensure all directors are voted back in immediately.[50]

With the two-strikes count to begin again at the next year's AGM after a spill resolution, the two-strikes requirements may undermine the operation of the regulated remuneration cycle by reducing the effectiveness of the advisory vote as a public signal of shareholder dissatisfaction.

10.6.4   Disclosure

While disclosure alone cannot change practice, it can have an indirect effect on practice, thus presenting a less invasive legal reform. What has become the 'best practice' position on hedging policies (ASX Corporate Governance Council, UK *Corporate Governance Code*) started through shareholder demands for these disclosures.[51] Many companies had to introduce such policies so that they could comply with this requirement.[52] If the practice is sufficiently important, one of the regulators in the remuneration cycle has to devise a rule directly about the practice. The advantage of others (such as institutional shareholders) making such rules is that they are more nimble rule makers than the parliament. By mandating disclosure of the company's position on the particular practice, the parliament can support the rule-making activities of others in the regulated remuneration cycle.

However, each new disclosure requirement adds to the length of already bloated remuneration reports. We have also seen how remuneration disclosures quickly tend towards boilerplate to facilitate shareholder monitoring. While the Corporations and Markets Advisory Committee did not recommend an overhaul of the current Australian disclosure laws, it did tinker with some provisions.[53] By way of contrast, the Department for Business Innovation and Skills has signalled a far-ranging review of narrative reporting, including the remuneration report to be included within a proposed Strategic Report, although some of the details will be in the Annual Directors' Statement and incorporated by cross-reference.[54]

It is not apparent that either government fully appreciates the imperatives driving companies towards 'cosmetic compliance' with the disclosure laws. First, directors largely disagree with named disclosure, even if they concede that some disclosure of executive and director remuneration is warranted. Secondly, there are many detailed and rule-like (rather than principles-like) laws for disclosure, thus driving compliance towards 'the letter of the law' rather than its spirit. Thirdly, directors know institutional investors 'satisfice' when reading remuneration reports by relying on proxy advisors to undertake the detailed analysis. Feeding that analysis via disclosure based on 'optics' makes it more likely that the 'compliant remuneration practice' boxes will be ticked. While it is beyond the scope of this book to suggest a methodology for such a study, disclosure compliance behaviours need to be better understood before effective disclosure laws can be written. This assumes that some of these factors can in fact be overcome by writing the right law: they might prove to be too dominant within the directors' compliance mind-set. Only once government has this evidence will it be in a position to understand the impacts of writing a rule requiring disclosure of the total remuneration received by the director or executive in the year reported.[55]

10.6.5 Taxation Law

Taxation law presents a further alternative regulatory approach for governments, although it has not been used extensively by either the UK or Australian governments for executive remuneration. The US government in 1991 (with effect from 1992) attempted to control the size of executive remuneration paid without reference to company performance by introducing s 162m into the Internal Revenue Code to limit the deductibility for companies of compensation with no performance conditions attached (unless shareholder approval obtained). It quickly resulted in an increase in base salaries to the threshold specified.[56] Selective taxation reforms were also used by the US government to curb excesses in financial institutions receiving government bailout funds under the Troubled Asset Relief Program (TARP) scheme.[57]

While the Australian government has not used taxation laws to address some of its policy goals for executive remuneration, it is clear that tax laws will impact on remuneration practices. The original formula for termination payments in part 2B.2 of the *Corporations Act 2001* (Cth) was linked to the tax deductibility of superannuation payments.[58] When remuneration practices shifted away from base salary plus an annual bonus plus superannuation (the standard 1970s–1980s approach) towards a total remuneration approach with short term and long term incentives, the law did not change with it. When companies could not make the new practices fit within the old laws, they would either work around them or seek shareholder approval to make a termination payment in excess of seven times average annual remuneration awarded over the previous three years.

A more controversial and recent taxation law amendment was to adjust the date on which the individual incurred a taxation debt for share-based payments,[59] followed by a punitive tax on superannuation contributions in excess of statutory caps.[60] These two reforms were not restricted to directors and executive officers, but had broader impact. Deploying taxation law in this manner creates an incentive for executives to demand, and companies to supply, tax-effective remuneration arrangements; circumventing the effectiveness of policy aims of the law to reduce payments or to raise revenue to facilitate government programmes to redistribute income. In the words of Kevin Murphy, it is bad policy and bad law.[61]

A further difficulty with using taxation laws to achieve changes in remuneration practices is that it distorts the regulated remuneration cycle by 'trumping' shareholder guidance about the structural aspects of remuneration. It also puts pressure on governments to enforce the public law sanctions introduced, which has cost implications. Government regulators may not necessarily want to prioritise enforcement of executive remuneration taxation laws over other, more critical taxation issues, although the Australian experience with the superannuation shortfall illustrates that incentive might depend upon Treasury and Australian Taxation Office projections of the likely revenue to be raised via enforcement activities. A lack of consistent enforcement will not go unnoticed by companies or executives. The challenge for governments is managing expectations when the popular view is that imposing higher rates of taxation is necessary, if not sufficient, to address the widening income gap.[62]

10.6.6 Make the Advisory Vote a Binding Vote

Is the answer to the lack of enforcement options for good remuneration practices to make the vote on the remuneration report somehow binding? For the UK and Australia it is not possible to make the resolution 'to adopt the remuneration report' binding because a failure to adopt the report appears meaningless, as the remuneration has been paid and the emphasis to date in disclosures has been on historical results, not forward-looking statements of remuneration policy. Recently the Department of Treasury argued:

> A binding vote on remuneration would absolve directors of their responsibility to shareholders on remuneration issues, and would also undermine their capacity to make key decisions affecting the performance of the company. As a result, the accountability of directors would be diminished, along with the ability of shareholders to hold directors to account on remuneration issues and the company's overall operations.[63]

The Australian regulatory solution in 2011 was to enact the 'two strikes' rule discussed earlier, which has a direct accountability mechanism built into it.

The proposed UK solution is to give shareholders a binding vote on future remuneration policy,[64] as the UK Secretary for Business, the Hon. Vince Cable, announced in early 2012.[65] Should the vote fail to be passed by the required majority, the company will continue with the current policy. Logically speaking, a company introducing a new policy following a strong vote against the remuneration report in a previous year will most likely be supported by shareholders who do not wish to see the old practices continue (even though they have for the year of the review).[66] The extent to which 'dialogue' between remuneration committees and institutional investors leads to investor-preferred practices and better remuneration practices remains to be seen. UK institutional investors may well be in for another year or two of 'almost weekly discussions' with remuneration committees.

Two different binding votes may be better able to address concerns on the level of pay. The first type of binding vote is to require shareholder approval of a grant of securities (such as options, or another form of share-based payment) and not just on an issue of new securities as currently permitted by the ASX *Listing Rule* 10.14;[67] or to approve the terms of a share plan in the UK.[68] The second type of binding vote seeks to restrict rewards for failure by targeting termination payments, making all such payments, and not just those below a certain threshold, subject to shareholder approval. Not excluding contractually provided for payments from being subject to shareholder approval might be a better, more manageable reform than requiring shareholder approval of the employment contract.[69] As with disclosure rules, it is important to ensure that a carve-out from the requirements to seek shareholder approval does not undermine the intention of the general rule. The advantage of these kinds of binding votes is that they prevent such payments occurring as shareholders may vote in sufficient numbers such that the resolution does not pass the required ordinary majority. The drafting challenge is to ensure that if a threshold is chosen to limit shareholder approval to only 'substantial' payments, it does not establish a new level of payment.

10.7   CONCLUSION: RESETTING THE TENSION ON THE POLICY TIGHTROPE

Devising solutions to the problem of executive remuneration requires an accurate assessment of the nature of that problem. To date, this assessment has been undertaken by different investigators with different agendas. The result of all this activity is a regulatory framework that relies on a mix of state and non-state actors undertaking their roles with diligence and being held accountable by other actors for their actions. This is at once its strength and its weakness. The different regulatory actors do not necessarily agree there is in fact a problem with executive remuneration, let alone agree on what the solution to that problem might be.

Governments that respond to mass public demands for action by legislating on executive remuneration risk creating unrealistic expectations of what such legislation can achieve. With the passage of time and the swing back to economic prosperity following the latest financial crisis, salaries will again rise, institutional investors will be less inclined to take principled positions on poor practices and regulators may be distracted by more pressing problems. Policy goals expressed in terms of outcomes (no fat cats, that pay is aligned with performance, improved accountability) are unable to be achieved by say on pay because the policy outcomes have not been defined in more meaningful ways. Regulating executive remuneration requires good policy goals that also describe the policy outcomes that are then translated into a variety of principles and rules. It can be difficult to demonstrate a positive impact of policy upon the social practice of executive remuneration and the economic benefits that flow from such regulation.[70] Both qualitative and quantitative analysis should be deployed to do so.[71]

Without a fundamental change in the structure of companies and the extent to which outsiders can intrude into company decision making, it is ultimately the company's primary decision-making bodies – the board of directors and the shareholders in general meeting – who are best placed to decide what is appropriate for their company. There is a need to ensure that each body exercises its powers responsibly and accounts to others (which may include others outside the company) not only for the fact of exercising powers, but also for the outcomes that follow. If anything has been lacking in the regulation of executive remuneration via say on pay, it is consistent diligence by shareholders to act as effective regulators of executive remuneration within the regulated remuneration cycle.

Rather than pursuing a futile quest for *the* answer, governments and the voters who elect them to office may have to console themselves with imperfect solutions to executive remuneration problems.

NOTES

1. Joint Committee on Corporations and Financial Services 2004, pp. 84–5.
2. UTS Centre for Corporate Governance 2003, p. 21.
3. Department for Business Innovation and Skills 2011a, p. 8; Durkin and Stensholt 2011; but see Australian Council of Superannuation Investors Inc 2011b, p. 7.
4. Bebchuk and Fried 2004, pp. 31–2; O'Reilly III and Main 2007, pp. 8–9.
5. Roberts, McNulty and Stiles 2005.
6. The emerging empirical literature from the USA is focused on independence, although it does not find evidence that cross-selling of services (a proxy for independence from management) leads to higher CEO pay: Cadman, Carver and Hillegeist 2009, p. 19; Murphy and Sandino 2010.
7. First recommended by the Walker Review, Walker 2009, pp. 125–6 and 170–6, and now found in Remuneration Consultants Group 2009.
8. Vroom 1964; Latham and Locke 1979; Herzberg, Mausner and Snyderman 1957; McClelland 1975; Finkelstein and Hambrick 1988.
9. *The Large and Medium-Sized Companies and Groups (Accounts and Reports) Regulations 2008* (UK) SI 2008/410, schedule 5, para. 9. The definition of 'remuneration' in the *Corporations Act 2001* (Cth), s 9 refers to the definition in the relevant accounting standard.

10. Sheehan 2006, p. 34.
11. Hawley 1995, p. 430.
12. Ferri and Maber 2009; Alissa 2009.
13. Gilshan and PIRC Limited 2009, p. 14; Productivity Commission of Australia 2009, p. 281; Department for Business Innovation and Skills 2011a, p. 20.
14. Sheehan 2007.
15. Department for Business Innovation and Skills 2011a, p. 20 comments that the high level of dissent observed in 2009 (one-fifth of FTSE 100 companies had more than 20 per cent of the shareholders 'withhold support' on the advisory resolution) has subsequently waned.
16. Super System Review 2010, pp. 32–4.
17. Gordon 2009.
18. Conyon and Sadler 2010, p. 304; Ferri and Maber 2009; cf. Carter and Zamora 2008.
19. Black 2008.
20. *Corporations Amendment (Improving Accountability on Termination Payments) Act 2009* (Cth).
21. Department for Business Innovation and Skills 2011a, pp. 22–3.
22. Department of Treasury, Commonwealth of Australia 2010.
23. Durkin 2010; Hepworth and Kitney 2010.
24. High Pay Commission 2011, pp. 8–11.
25. Department for Business Innovation and Skills 2011a, pp. 27–8.
26. ASX, *Listing Rules*, rule 12.8 for S&P/ASX 300 companies.
27. ASX Corporate Governance Council 2010, p. 37 (recommendation 8.2).
28. Remuneration Consultants Group 2009.
29. Remuneration Consultants Group 2011a; Remuneration Consultants Group 2011b.
30. Department for Business Innovation and Skills 2011a, p. 19.
31. Remuneration Consultants Group 2009, p. 2.
32. *Corporations (Improving Accountability on Director and Executive Remuneration) Act 2011* (Cth), schedule 1, inserting sections 206L.
33. Ramsay 2001, para.[4.01].
34. Section 324CE(5) (individual auditor), s 324CF(5) (audit firm) and s 324CG(9) (audit company).
35. A suite of offences is created in sections 324 CE(1) and (2) (individual auditor), ss 324 CF(1) and (2) (audit firm) and ss 324CG(1) and (2) (audit company).
36. Section 324CH(1).
37. Section 648A.
38. Section 411(13) and *Corporations Regulations 2001* (Cth), r 5.1.01(1).
39. Section 667B.
40. Australian Securities and Investments Commission 2007, para. RG112.5.
41. From the judgment in *Phosphate Co-operative v Shears (No 3)* (1998) 14 ACSL 323 at 339.
42. Section 648A(3) and s 667B(2).
43. Corporations and Markets Advisory Committee 2011, p. 37.
44. Walker 2009, p. 12.
45. *UK Corporate Governance Code* (2010), p. 17 (Code provision B.7.1).
46. *Corporations (Improving Accountability on Director and Executive Remuneration) Act 2011* (Cth), schedule 1, inserting s 201P.
47. Department for Business Innovation and Skills 2011a, pp. 23–4.
48. Productivity Commission of Australia 2009, pp. 294–300.
49. Boyd 2012.
50. Grigg 2011.
51. Australian Council of Superannuation Investors Inc 2006.
52. Sheehan 2012.
53. Corporations and Markets Advisory Committee 2011, pp. 8–11.
54. Department for Business Innovation and Skills 2011b, pp. 27–35.

55. Department for Business Innovation and Skills 2011b, p. 29; Corporations and Markets Advisory Committee 2011, pp. 121–4.
56. Perry and Zenner 2001; Ferris and Wallace 2009; Dew-Becker 2009, pp. 446–8.
57. The major initiative in the USA is the *Emergency Economic Stabilization Act of 2008*, 12 U.S.C. 5221, as amended by the *American Recovery and Reinvestment Act of 2009*, Pub L No 111-5, 123 Stat 516, §7001. Additional amendments to the *Internal Revenue Code*, 26 U.S.C. § 162(m)(5) (2008) reduce the deductibility of compensation paid to particular executives whose firms sell 'troubled assets' to $500,000 (from $1,000,000). Golden parachute payments have been even further restricted under § 280G(e) with the imposition of an additional tax of 20 per cent imposed on a 'covered executive' who receives an *excess* golden parachute payment, defined as a payment in excess of three times the base amount (the tax is imposed on the payment less the base amount). The obligation on TARP recipients to comply with this provision is found in the amended *Emergency Economic Stabilization Act of 2008*, 12 U.S.C. 5221, § 111(b)(1)(b). See also 31 CFR §§ 30.1–30.11.
58. Sheehan and Fenwick 2008.
59. *Tax Laws Amendment (2009 Budget Measures No 2) Act 2009* (Cth); Durkin 2011.
60. Walsh 2011a and 2011b; Patten 2011.
61. Murphy 1995.
62. This is a particularly vigorous debate in the UK. See HM Treasury 2009 and HM Treasury 2010 (for example, p. 122 on individual tax rates) for budget measures designed to address the gap by taxes. As to the gap between 'the city' and British businesses, see Cable 2012b.
63. Corporations (Improving Accountability on Director and Executive Remuneration) Bill 2011, Explanatory Memorandum, p. 43.
64. Department for Business Innovation and Skills 2011a, pp. 21–2.
65. Cable 2012a.
66. Sheehan 2012.
67. See Productivity Commission of Australia 2009 pp. 287–91.
68. FSA, UK *Listing Rules*, R 9.4.1.
69. Department for Business Innovation and Skills 2011a, pp. 22–3.
70. Organisation for Economic Cooperation and Development 2011b, p. 44.
71. Productivity Commission of Australia 2011, pp. 97–117.

Methodology appendix

To allow for a comparison of the operation of the new regulatory framework following the adoption of a disclosure and vote regime, a decision was made to focus on the first three years of operation in each jurisdiction only. A sample group of listed companies was drawn for both jurisdictions. These samples form the basis for the interview studies reported in this book. They also form the basis for the content analysis of changes to remuneration practices, reported in Sheehan 2007 and Sheehan 2012.

A.1   UK COMPANIES

The FTSE 100 was taken as the population from which to draw a sample of companies for analysis. A company was included in the study if it satisfied the following criteria:

- the company was a constituent member of the FTSE 100 as at 1 January 2003, 2004 and 2005, and still existed in 2007 (at the time of the interview study);[1]
- the company conducted an advisory vote on the remuneration report at its 2003 AGM;
- the company disclosed the proxy voting instructions received/results of the poll conducted on a resolution;
- the listed securities were voting securities.[2]

On this basis, 73 companies were included in the sample.

A.2   AUSTRALIAN SAMPLE

The S&P/ASX 200 was selected as the relevant index from which to draw a sample. A company was included within the sample if it satisfied the following criteria:

- the company was a constituent of the S&P/ASX 200 as at 1 July 2005, 2006 and 2007;

- the company still existed in 2009 at the time of the interview study;
- the company had a vote on the remuneration report at the AGM held during the period 1 July 2005 to 1 July 2006;
- the company disclosed proxy voting results for each year.

On this basis, 109 companies were included in the sample.

A.3 ANNUAL REPORT AND REMUNERATION REPORT ANALYSIS

To understand company practice, the annual reports were obtained for every company in the sample for the first three years of the advisory vote. For the UK these are the annual reports covering the AGMs held in 2003–05. For Australia, these are the annual reports covering the AGMs held between the period 1 July–30 June in each of the years 2005–07.

A.3.1 UK Sample

Four particular disclosures were reviewed to understand the firm's remuneration practices:

- the corporate governance statement for details about the remuneration committee and the attendance at meetings;
- the directors' report for information about the board and substantial shareholders;
- the directors' remuneration report;
- the notes to the accounts for further information about share-based payments.

The first year's remuneration report was reviewed and the company's practices in respect of base pay, short term incentives, long term incentives, pension and contracts summarised into tabular form for easy comparison. The second year's remuneration report was then compared with the first year's report to identify any changes or modifications. The third year's remuneration report was then compared with the second year's report and any further changes noted. Because some of the details in relation to share plans were found in notices of meeting, these too were included when relevant. The data were then summarised into three tables for easy reference: short term incentives, long term incentives and contracts.[3] This summary informs the analysis of these particular practices in chapters 4 and 5.

A.3.2   Australian Sample

The same four disclosures identified above were reviewed for each of the 109 companies in the Australian sample over the period 2005–08:[4] corporate governance disclosures, the directors' report, the remuneration report and the notes to the accounts. Due to some early duplication of reporting requirements between the legislation and accounting standards, the notes to the accounts contained detailed remuneration disclosures for the key management personnel. Notices of meeting were also reviewed where relevant to understand any changes proposed to share-based remuneration.

Company practice on base salary, short term incentives, long term incentives and contracts was noted, with STI, LTI and contracts summarised in tables. The first year's report formed the baseline from which subsequent practice was viewed. As with the UK study, the data were summarised into tables for short term incentives, long term incentives and contracts.[5] This summary informs the analysis of company remuneration practices presented in chapters 4 and 6.

A.4   INTERVIEW STUDIES

Two separate interview studies were undertaken for each jurisdiction. To understand the experiences of companies working with the regulated remuneration cycle, remuneration committees and remuneration consultants were interviewed. The analysis of these interviews forms the basis of chapters 3 to 6.

The second interview study seeks to understand the experiences of shareholders responding to company practice. For this study, institutional investors and their representative organisations were interviewed. This evidence informs the analysis in chapters 3 to 8 and 10. Ethics committee approvals for both the UK and Australian interview studies were obtained from the University of Melbourne Human Ethics Advisory Committee.

A.4.1   UK Study

The interview study of remuneration committee representatives and remuneration consultants was conducted in November–December 2007. The purpose of the interview study was to explore how companies worked within the regulatory framework and to go beyond written disclosure to the 'black box' of boardroom practices.[6] Semi-structured interviews were conducted with representatives of both groups. All interviewees consented to the interview being taped. Transcripts were prepared from the recordings.

A.4.1.1 FTSE 100 remuneration committee representatives
The original sample of FTSE 100 companies was further refined in light of a number of privatisations and takeovers. To be included in the interview study, a company had to still exist as a listed company on the LSE in 2007, although it did not need to still be a member of the FTSE 100. Based on these two criteria, 70 companies were selected. For each company, the corporate governance statement in the directors' report and the directors' remuneration reports from the annual reports and accounts for each of the AGM years 2002–07 were reviewed and the remuneration committee chair at the time of each AGM identified. The company secretary as of late 2007 was also identified. Interview requests were sent to the current remuneration committee chair via the company secretary. Of the 70 invitations sent, five remuneration committee chairs and four company secretaries who act as the secretary of the remuneration committee agreed to participate in face-to-face interviews. Low rates of participation by executives in surveys are not unknown.[7] Section A.6 below sets out the interview questions.

A.4.1.2 UK remuneration consultants advising the FTSE 100
Remuneration consultants were identified from disclosure in directors' remuneration reports.[8] This list of firms was then discussed with a former UK-based remuneration consultant to check whether the list represented the major firms in the UK. The websites and publications for these firms were reviewed to attempt to identify the relevant consultant and to obtain contact details. Where no consultant could be identified by name, the firm was dropped from the sample. Invitations to participate were sent to 11 remuneration consulting firms, with five consultants agreeing to partici-pate. The interview questions for remuneration consultants are set out in section A.7 below.

A.4.2 UK Study of Shareholder Practice

To identify a sample of UK-based institutional investors, a number of sources of information were used.

A.4.2.1 UK fund managers
An initial list of key fund managers was taken from the IMA list of the top 20 retail and institutional fund managers as at March in each of the years 2001 to 2008 inclusive.[9] This process resulted in a list of 38

companies. As the IMA's list does not distinguish between retail and institutional fund managers, whereas this study focuses on institutional investors, a list of the top investment managers and advisors to pension funds for 2007[10] was also used to identify the main institutional fund managers. Each fund manager's website was then reviewed for details of its corporate governance and shareholder engagement policies and published voting records. A final list of 32 fund managers was obtained. Letters were sent to each of these managers, with six funds accepting. All participants are corporate governance professionals with the fund manager. Two representatives were interviewed for two of the six funds that participated.

A.4.2.2   UK beneficial owners

To identify a sample of beneficial owners, the *Pensions and Investment* Top 100 pension funds published in September 2007 was used to identify the largest UK occupational pension schemes. Twenty-seven UK schemes were identified. A search of the internet sites for each scheme was then conducted to identify whether a corporate governance and engagement policy was issued, and whether a voting record was published. A number of the UK's largest occupational pension schemes belong to public companies; many of these schemes did not have separate websites or else did not release information to non-members. Therefore, a decision was taken to focus upon industry schemes (such as the Railways Pension Funds and the University Super Scheme, USS). The website for each of these schemes was reviewed to locate the corporate governance and engagement policies of the scheme. The key corporate governance person was also identified. Where no such person was identified, the senior investment officer was noted. Letters were sent to these five funds with regrettably only one positive response. The questions for institutional investors are set out in section A.8 below.

A.4.2.3   Institutional investor representative groups

Institutional investor representative groups are responsible for producing shareholder guidance on remuneration practices in investee firms. The key institutional investor groups in the UK for remuneration practice are the ABI and NAPF. Other institutional investor groups produce guidance for their own members on engagement and voting, but do not produce specific guidance for investee companies. This latter group includes the IMA and the Association of Investment Companies. Given the interest in engagement and voting, all were approached and three accepted. The questions for institutional investor representative groups are set out in section A.9 below.

A.4.3 Australian Study of Company Practice

To understand practices within firms, an interview study was conducted with remuneration committee representatives and with remuneration consultants. As with the UK study, many interviews were conducted face to face, with the remainder via telephone. All but one interviewee consented to be taped. My notes of interview were forwarded to this interviewee; the remaining interviewees were provided with a transcript of their interview.

A.4.3.1 Remuneration committee representatives

For each company in the initial sample of 109 companies, the 2008 remuneration report and the corporate governance statement within the same annual report were reviewed to identify the current chair of the remuneration committee or the equivalent committee within the company. Companies originally within the 109 sample that no longer existed[11] or were in some form of external administration[12] were not approached. Letters were sent to the remuneration committee chair via the company secretary. Of the 94 companies approached, 12 interviews were conducted, all with remuneration committee chairs. The questions put to these chairs are the same as those used in the UK study.

A.4.3.2 Remuneration consultants

As Australian companies are not required to disclose the material advisors to the committee, remuneration consultants active in the Australian market were identified using recent media articles quoting remuneration consultants. This was supplemented by internet searches of company websites. Nine firms were identified on this basis. Of this group, six firms accepted. In one instance two consultants from the same firm took part in the interview, making seven remuneration consultants in total. The questions put to the Australian-based remuneration consultants are the same as those used in the UK study.

A.4.4 Shareholder Responses – Australia

A different sample selection process was undertaken in Australia, with the sample of beneficial owners drawn first, and the fund managers involved with this sample of super funds subsequently identified.

A.4.4.1 Australian beneficial owners

To identify superannuation funds, I focused on the industry super funds.[13] The members of the ACSI as at 1 April 2009 were identified from the ACSI website. The 2008 annual report for each fund was then reviewed to confirm that the fund invested in Australian equities and to identify the relevant fund managers. Where no fund managers were identified by asset class, the super fund was dropped from the sample. A final list of 23 funds was obtained and each fund's website reviewed to identify the chief executive officer, chief investment officer and/or chief governance officer. Of the 23 invitations sent to these funds, five funds accepted, with one fund represented by two interviewees.

A.4.4.2   Fund managers

To identify institutional/wholesale fund managers, the managers of Australian equities for the 23 industry funds were identified from the annual reports and confirmed by reviewing the industry funds' websites. This resulted in a list of 80 fund managers. I then cross-checked the fund managers across industry funds to identify funds with two or more industry super fund clients. This analysis resulted in a list of 35 fund managers. Details for the fund managers were obtained from Morningstar and supplemented by reviewing the relevant fund managers' websites. Invitations were sent to these fund managers, with six funds accepting. The participants are a mix of fund managers, corporate governance managers and a compliance manager. The interview questions are the same as those used for the UK study of shareholder practice set out below.

A.4.4.3   Institutional investor representative groups

There are a number of institutional investor groups active in the Australian market but these groups have differing levels of interest in developing specific guidelines on executive remuneration. These groups were initially identified from the membership list of the ASX Corporate Governance Council. I eliminated those groups representing management (such as the Group of 100 representing the CEOs of S&P/ASX 100 companies). The website for each of the remaining groups was reviewed to confirm it issued guidelines on corporate governance. A group was dropped from the sample if it did not issue such guidelines. Five groups were approached and two accepted. The questions put to these interviewees are the same as those used for the UK study.

A.5   STRENGTHS AND LIMITATIONS OF SMALL INTERVIEW SAMPLE

The regulated remuneration cycle presented in chapter 2 is a regulatory space in which authority is shared between a number of regulators, including the government. Obtaining 'behind the scenes' information on how this regulatory space worked in practice required interviews with a variety

Table A.1   Summary statistics of interviews undertaken with company and shareholder representatives, UK (2007 and 2008) and Australia (2009)

	Survey group	UK	Australia
Company representatives	Remuneration committees	9	12
	Remuneration consultants	5	6
Shareholder representatives	Institutional investors	7	11
	Representative organisations	3	2
	TOTAL	24	31

of participants. Interviewing a small number of representatives should be sufficient to understand how the process works from an inside perspective. More interviews would add nuances of experience and interpretation but would probably not tell a dramatically different story.

The number of interviews with each group is necessarily small to allow for a manageable research process, with the method of sample selection using defined criteria to identify representatives of the target populations of interest (listed companies, remuneration committees, remuneration consultants and institutional investors). Aside from the UK pension funds, there are multiple representatives from each group (with remuneration consultants being particularly well represented) and the similarities in the interview evidence between the small numbers of participants within each group paint a sufficiently clear picture of how the process generally works.

Understanding the complexity behind the publicly disclosed outcomes of remuneration decisions (remuneration reports and proxy voting/poll results) is just one source of information used, first, to develop the regulated remuneration cycle model and, secondly, to draw generalisations about how that cycle works in practice. The interviews confirm what the public disclosures reveal, and vice versa, while also extending into the private domain of company decision making. The interviews by group are summarised in Table A.1.

A larger sample of interviewees from each group is unlikely to have revealed different information about the general operation of the framework, but could provide further case examples of where particular problems had been encountered. Given the media interest in these extreme cases, a number of facts are publicly known. Whether the participants would have been willing to go on the record with statements about these examples remains unknown. It is believed they would be unlikely to do so.

Other interview-based studies on executive remuneration specifically or institutional investors generally, typically interview participants from only one group. Ruth Bender's UK-based study takes a vertical sample of 40 representatives within 12 FTSE 350 companies.[14] Brian Main et al's study of remuneration committees involves 22 interviews with remuneration committee members who sit on 35 remuneration committees distributed across the FTSE 350 and private companies.[15] Stapledon's study of UK and Australian institutional investors interviewed fund managers, pension/superannuation fund trustees and institutional investor representative groups, conducting 27 interviews in total.[16] Similarly, Hendry et al interviewed 14 company representatives and 18 institutional investor representatives: a total of 32 interviews.[17] A 2007 study by Anderson et al of Australian institutional investors involved 13 interviews, with a mixture of fund managers, superannuation funds and shareholder representative groups.[18] The choice of a narrower focus in these studies allows for a larger number of interviews within a particular group. By way of contrast, this book draws evidence from two jurisdictions and seeks perspectives from a range of insiders to more fully understand what effect the legal reforms have had on the activities of key participants in the regulated remuneration cycle.

A.6   INTERVIEW QUESTIONS – REMUNERATION COMMITTEE REPRESENTATIVES

Development of executive remuneration practices
1   Does your company uses remuneration consultants to assist with the development of your executive remuneration strategy?
2   How did you select your executive remuneration consultants? If you use more than one firm, how do you separate the areas of concern? Why do you use more than one firm?
3   Describe the interaction with the remuneration consultants.
4   Have you undertaken a major review of your remuneration practices since 2001? If so,

    a.   When did this occur? Have you undertaken more than 1 review? What was the catalyst for the review/s?

    b.   What assistance did remuneration consultants provide?

5   What assistance do remuneration consultants provide in relation to the annual review of remuneration?

6   How do you validate the information they are giving you with respect to market practice on executive remuneration?

7   How did you choose the performance criteria to use in your

    a.   Short term incentive scheme

    b.   Long term incentive scheme

8   What criteria do the company use to measure company performance?

9   In your opinion, are remuneration consultants now an essential advisor to the remuneration committee? How comfortable would you feel 'going it alone' without such advice?

10   In your view, what is 'best practice' executive remuneration?

11   Remuneration consultants have been blamed for ratcheting up executive remuneration: what do you think are the sources of pressure on executive salaries? How real is the pressure on you as the chair of your company's remuneration committee to pay at the market rate, and more particularly, to remunerate in the upper quartile?

12   Have you 'lost' an executive to another company due to the inability to trump a salary offer? In retrospect, do you feel the decision to not meet the salary offer was the best decision?

13   In your experience, how important is remuneration (structure and quantum) to executives?

Relationship with institutional investors

14   Have your key institutional investors abstained from voting on the advisory vote on the remuneration report?

    a.   In which year?

    b.   Did they advise you of this intention? At what time?

    c.   If the contact was prior to the AGM, what effect did it have on the conduct of the AGM?

    d.   Were there other key institutional investors who adopted the same approach?

15   Have your key institutional investors ever voted against a remuneration report?

    a.   In which year?

    b.   What communication did you have with the institutional investor in relation to their decision to vote against the proposal? At what time did this occur?

16   Have your key institutional investors abstained from voting on a binding remuneration resolution?
     a.   In which year?
     b.   Did they advise you of this intention? At what time?
     c.   If the contact was prior to the AGM, what effect did it have on the conduct of the AGM?
     d.   Were there other key institutional investors who adopted the same approach?

17   Have your key institutional investors ever voted against a binding remuneration resolution?
     a.   In which year?
     b.   What communication did you have with the institutional investor in relation to their decision to vote against the proposal? At what time did this occur?

18   Have you ever initiated communications with your key institutional investors in relation to your company's executive remuneration practices?
     a.   In which year/s?
     b.   Timing of communication: release of remuneration report, prior to AGM, post-AGM, on new appointments, sounding out new remuneration proposals prior to final board decision?
     c.   Who was that communication with?

19   What was the outcome of the direct communication?
     a.   AGM related: withdrawal of binding resolution, influenced presentations at the AGM on executive remuneration
     b.   Non-AGM related: adopted proposed remuneration changes, revised remuneration arrangements

20   In your experience, are institutional investors willing to accept deviations from best practice executive remuneration that are well explained ('comply or explain')? In other words, do you think institutional investors are flexible in applying their own guidelines or have they adopted a box-ticking approach?

21   Describe an interaction with a key institutional investor that has added value to your executive remuneration processes.

22   Have you experienced intervention by key institutional investors in relation to executive remuneration that you felt was 'wide of the mark'? Describe that experience. What impact, if any, did it have on the ongoing relationship?

23   Do you think the senior executives and executive directors of your key institutional investors should be subject to the same level of disclosure of their annual remuneration?

A.7 INTERVIEW QUESTIONS – REMUNERATION CONSULTANTS

1 Describe the process of interaction with the remuneration committee. How do you balance working with a number of remuneration consultants (e.g. pension/actuarial advisors, performance measurement advisors)?
2 What role do remuneration consultants play in educating the remuneration committee on executive remuneration practices?
3 What level of awareness do Boards in general have on executive remuneration?
4 What kinds of interaction do you have with executive directors; and non-executive directors at the companies you advise?
5 In your view, what is the catalyst for changes to executive remuneration?
6 What constitutes 'best practice' executive remuneration? How do you know it is 'best'?
7 How influential are best practice guidelines issued by institutional investors in shaping the structure of executive remuneration?
8 Have the investor guidelines led to homogenous or 'vanilla' remuneration practices or is there still room for innovation? Who or what drives that innovation?
9 Do investors influence the quantum of remuneration paid? If so, is such influence appropriate?
10 Remuneration consultants have been blamed for ratcheting up executive remuneration: what do you think are the sources of pressure on executive salaries? How real is the pressure on remuneration committees to pay at the market rate, and more particularly, to remunerate in the upper quartile?
11 In your opinion, which performance metrics are the most valid for measuring executive performance?
12 Have you ever walked away from a client?
13 Do you believe you owe your clients a duty of care? If so, what does that encompass?

A.8 INTERVIEW QUESTIONS – INSTITUTIONAL INVESTORS

Corporate governance statement/proxy voting policy
1 Do you publish a corporate governance statement that specifies how you select companies to invest in and outlines your voting policies?

2 How do you use this statement? *Or* What is the purpose of this statement?
   a. What does it say about executive remuneration?
   b. What is your company's position on voting?
   c. Do you publish a voting record?

Voting on remuneration report vote

3 Do you *routinely* vote on the advisory vote on the remuneration report?
4 What influences your decision whether to vote or not?
5 Have you ever *abstained* from voting on the advisory vote on the remuneration report?
   a. In which year?
   b. Give a specific example and explain why.
6 Have you ever voted against a remuneration report?
   a. In which year?
   b. Give a specific example and explain why.
7 What communication did you have with the company in relation to your decision to vote against the proposal? At what time did this occur?
8 In your view, how valuable is the advisory vote?
9 What effect do you see the vote having on your investee companies?

Voting on binding remuneration resolutions

10 Do you routinely vote on binding remuneration resolutions?
11 Have you ever abstained from voting on a binding remuneration resolution?
   a. In which year?
   b. Give example to explain why.
12 Did you communicate your choice to abstain from voting to the company? At what time did this occur?
13 Have you ever voted against a binding remuneration resolution?
   a. In which year?
   b. Give example to explain why.
14 What communication did you have with the company in relation to your decision to vote against the proposal? At what time did this occur?
15 In your view, how valuable is the binding vote on remuneration resolutions?
16 Have you ever voted at an AGM on a binding remuneration resolution and the advisory vote on the remuneration report?
17 In which year?
18 Did you vote in favour of both resolutions?

Relevance of the disclosure in the remuneration report

19 Which parts of the remuneration report, if any, do you routinely peruse in relation to your investee companies?
    a. Statement of board policy for determining remuneration of directors, secretaries and senior managers
    b. Statement of relationship between that policy and company performance: forward looking and historic performance
    c. Remuneration table of current year and previous year [salary, STI, non-cash benefits, post employment benefits, LTIs, termination benefits, share-based payments]
    d. Disclosure of provisions of executive service contracts
    e. Tables disclosing details of share-based remuneration (long term incentives and share options)

Use of proxy advisors

20 Do you use a proxy advisor?
21 Name of proxy advisor?
22 What type of advice do they give? For example, do you subscribe to a service for all your companies or is there some other service they provide?
23 What aspects of the advice given are most helpful?
24 In deciding whether or how to vote, what weight do you give to the proxy advisor's advice?

Use of best practice guidelines

25 Do you use best practice guidelines to determine whether or how to vote?
26 Which guideline/s do you use?
27 How valuable are the guidelines?
28 Do you look at the overall quantum of remuneration?
29 If so, how do you determine whether the overall quantum is acceptable or excessive?
30 Do you have access to market data on remuneration for the positions at your investee companies? If so, what is the source of that information?
31 Remuneration consultants have been blamed for ratcheting up executive remuneration: what do you think are the sources of pressure on executive salaries? How real is the pressure on company remuneration committees to pay at the market rate, and more particularly, to remunerate in the upper quartile?

Company performance

32 How do you assess investee company performance?
33 What metrics do you routinely examine?

34   What is the source of that information – company annual reports, quarterly updates, company forecasts, road shows, broker reports, other?
35   How frequently do you review investee company performance?

Engagement with remuneration committees
36   How frequently do you communicate directly with the remuneration committee at your investee companies?
     a.   Annually.
     b.   Semi-annually or quarterly.
     c.   Ad hoc basis.
37   Who initiates the direct communication?
     a.   Your initiative (why), investee company initiative (who in company specifically and why), representative body request (who and why), coalition of institutional investors as part of a campaign (why).
     b.   Timing of communication: release of directors' remuneration report, prior to AGM, post-AGM, on new appointments, sounding out new remuneration proposals prior to final board decision.
38   When you initiated the dialogue, what was the outcome?
     a.   Withdrawal of binding resolution, change to remuneration practice, no change to remuneration practice.
     b.   Other outcome (please specify).

A.9   INTERVIEW QUESTIONS – INSTITUTIONAL INVESTOR REPRESENTATIVE GROUPS

Development of best practice executive remuneration guidelines
 1   Describe the process your organisation uses to develop its guidelines on executive remuneration.
 2   How frequently are these guidelines updated?
 3   What internal processes exist for approval of these guidelines? Is there a process to allow member input into draft guidelines?
 4   Do you seek the views of listed companies or remuneration committees as part of the process of updating your guidelines?
 5   In your view, what drives changes in executive remuneration practices?
 6   What makes the practices in your current guidelines 'best'? In other words, what is 'best practice' in executive remuneration?
 7   Remuneration consultants have been blamed for ratcheting up executive remuneration: what do you think are the sources of pressure on

executive salaries? How real is the pressure on company remuneration committees to pay at the market rate, and more particularly, to
remunerate in the upper quartile?

Guidelines on voting
  8 Describe the process your organisation uses to develop its voting
     guidelines.
  9 How frequently are these guidelines updated?
 10 What internal processes exist for approval of these guidelines? Is
     there a process to allow member input into draft guidelines?
 11 Do you seek the views of listed companies as part of the process of
     updating your guidelines?
 12 Should institutional investors be required by law to vote?
 13 Should institutional investors be required by law to publish their
     voting records?
 14 In your view, is there pressure upon institutional investors to vote at
     AGMs?
 15 Is the decision to abstain from voting on a resolution a valid
     alternative for institutional investors?

NOTES

1. A company was included in the sample if it was a member of the FTSE 100 as at 1
    January in each of the years 2003–05. This excluded companies that did not stay in the
    FTSE 100 for the whole three years but were still listed on the London Stock Exchange
    (for example, Bradford & Bingley plc). It also excluded companies that were taken
    over or merged with another FTSE 100 company (for example, Abbey National plc,
    Allied Domecq plc). Companies with a dominant shareholder (> 50 per cent) were also
    excluded as the relevant advisory vote could never fail to pass.
2. For example, United Utilities 'A' shares and the ordinary shares of United Utilities Ltd
    are listed on the London Stock Exchange and both are constituents of the FTSE 100 for
    the relevant period. The 'A' shares do not have voting rights and were thus excluded.
    Another example is Schroders N/V.
3. The tables are on file with the author.
4. For some companies, the first three years of operating with the new regime are financial
    years 2006–07–08.
5. These tables are on file with the author.
6. Roberts, McNulty and Stiles 2005, p. 19; Pettigrew 1992, p. 178.
7. Gay 2001, p. 158, citing Pettigrew 1992, p. 164.
8. Disclosure of the remuneration consultants is required under *The Large and Medium-
    Sized Companies and Groups (Accounts and Reports) Regulations 2008* (UK) SI
    2008/410, schedule 9, paras 2(1)(b),(c) (formerly *Companies Act 1985* (UK), c 6, sched-
    ule 7A, part 2(1)(b)(c)).
9. http://www.investmentuk.org/statistics/fum/default.asp (accessed 27 May 2008).
10. Obtained from http://www.pensionfundsonline.co.uk/leaguetables/investment.aspx
    (accessed 31 May 2008). Information on the top 20 advisers is reported by the website,
    relying upon the information disclosed in the 'Blue Book': AP Information Services

2007 (*Pension Funds and Their Advisers 2007*). The ranking is based on the number of funds each investment manager represents.

11. For example, Zinifex Ltd.
12. For example, ABC Learning Centres Ltd, Commander Communication Ltd.
13. Australian Prudential Regulatory Authority 2007; Department of Treasury, Commonwealth of Australia 2001.
14. Bender 2007, p. 712 (table 1). The main interviewees were HR professionals (12), with five remuneration committee chairs, five other non-executive directors and three company secretaries. Five consultants (executive search and remuneration) were also part of the 35 interviewees.
15. Main et al 2008, p. 228.
16. Stapledon 1996.
17. Hendry et al 2006, pp. 1107–9.
18. Anderson, Marshall and Ramsay 2007, p. 81.

Bibliography

Adams, Renée (2009), 'Asking directors about their dual roles', Working Paper, available at http://ssrn.com/abstract=1362339 (accessed 8 March 2012).

Aggarwal, Rajesh and Andrew Samwick (1999), 'Executive compensation, strategic competition and relative performance evaluation: Theory and evidence', *Journal of Finance* **54**: 1999–2043.

Alexander, Cindy R, Mark A Chen, Duane J Seppi and Chester S Spatt (2010), 'Interim news and the role of proxy voting advice', *Review of Financial Studies* **23**: 4419–54.

Ali, Paul and Geof Stapledon (2000), 'Having your options and eating them too: Fences, zero-cost collars and executive share options', *Company & Securities Law Journal* **18**: 277–82.

Ali, Paul U, Geof Stapledon and Martin Gold (2003), *Corporate Governance and Investment Fiduciaries*, Pyrmont: Lawbook Co.

Alissa, Walid M (2009), 'Boards' response to shareholders' dissatisfaction: The case of shareholders' say on pay in the UK', Working Paper, available at http://ssrn.com/abstract=1412880 (accessed 30 September 2011).

AMP Capital Investors (2007), *Corporate Governance Report*, Sydney: AMP Ltd.

Anderson, Kirsten, Shelley Marshall and Ian Ramsay (2007), 'Do Australian institutional investors aim to influence the human resource practices of investee companies?', Research Report, Centre for Corporate Law and Securities Regulation and Centre for Employment and Labour Relations Law, The University of Melbourne.

AP Information Services (2007), *Pension Funds and Their Advisers 2007*, London: AP Information Services and IPE International Publishers Ltd.

Armour, John (2008), 'Enforcement strategies in UK corporate governance: A roadmap and empirical assessment', European Corporate Governance Institute, Law Working Paper no. 106/2008.

Armour, John, Simon Deakin and Suzanne J Konzelmann (2003), 'Shareholder primacy and the trajectory of UK corporate governance', *British Journal of Industrial Relations* **41**: 531–55.

Armour, John, Henry Hansmann and Reiner Kraakman (2009), 'Agency problems and legal strategies', in Reiner Kraakman et al (eds), *The Anatomy of Corporate Law: A Comparative and Functional Approach*, 2nd edition, Oxford: Oxford University Press, pp. 35–53.

Association of British Insurers (2011), *ABI Principles of Remuneration*, London: ABI.

Association of British Insurers (2009), *Executive Remuneration: ABI Guidelines on Policies and Practices*, London: ABI.

Association of British Insurers (2007), *Executive Remuneration: ABI Guidelines on Policies and Practices*, London: ABI.

Association of British Insurers (2004a), *Principles and Guidelines on Remuneration*, London: ABI.

Association of British Insurers (2004b), *Annual Report 2003–04*, London: ABI.

Association of British Insurers (2002), *Guidelines on Executive Remuneration*, London: ABI.

Association of British Insurers and the National Association of Pension Funds (2008), *Joint Statement on Executive Contracts and Severance*, London: ABI.

Association of British Insurers and the National Association of Pension Funds (2002), *Best Practice on Executive Contracts and Severance: A Joint Statement*, London: ABI.

ASX Corporate Governance Council (2010), *Corporate Governance Principles and Recommendations with 2010 Amendments*, 2nd edition, Sydney: ASX Corporate Governance Council.

ASX Corporate Governance Council (2007), *Corporate Governance Principles and Recommendations*, 2nd edition, Sydney: ASX Corporate Governance Council.

ASX Corporate Governance Council (2003), *Principles of Good Corporate Governance and Best Practice Recommendations*, Sydney: ASX Corporate Governance Council.

ASX Ltd (2010), *Listing Rule Amendments – New Requirements for a Remuneration Committee and a Company Trading Policy: Exposure Draft*, Sydney: ASX Ltd.

ASX Ltd (2003), *Continuous Disclosure and Chief Executive Officer Remuneration*, Sydney: ASX Ltd.

Austin, Robert, Harold Ford and Ian Ramsay (2005), *Company Directors: Principles of Law and Corporate Governance*, Chatswood: LexisNexisButterworths.

Austin, RP and IM Ramsay (2010), *Ford's Principles of Corporations Law*, 14th edition, Chatswood: LexisNexisButterworths.

Australian Council of Superannuation Investors Inc (ACSI) (2011a),

ACSI Governance Guidelines: A Guide for Superannuation Trustees to Monitor Listed Australian Companies, Melbourne: ACSI.

Australian Council of Superannuation Investors Inc (ACSI) (2011b), *CEO Pay in the Top 100 Companies: 2010*, Melbourne: ACSI.

Australian Council of Superannuation Investors Inc (ACSI) (2009), *ACSI Governance Guidelines: A Guide for Superannuation Trustees to Monitor Listed Australian Companies*, Melbourne: ACSI.

Australian Council of Superannuation Investors Inc (ACSI) (2008), *CEO Pay in the Top 100 Companies: Research Paper prepared by RiskMetrics – ISS Governance Services*, Melbourne: ACSI.

Australian Council of Superannuation Investors Inc (ACSI) (2007), *ACSI Governance Guidelines: A Guide for Superannuation Trustees to Monitor Listed Australian Companies*, Melbourne: ACSI.

Australian Council of Superannuation Investors Inc (ACSI) (2006), *Disclosure Implications for Executive Hedging of Long Term Incentives*, Melbourne: ACSI.

Australian Council of Superannuation Investors Inc (ACSI) (2005), *ACSI Governance Guidelines: A Guide for Superannuation Trustees to Monitor Listed Australian Companies*, Melbourne: ACSI.

Australian Council of Superannuation Investors Inc (ACSI) (2003), *ACSI Governance Guidelines: A Guide for Superannuation Trustees to Monitor Listed Australian Companies*, Melbourne: ACSI.

Australian Council of Trade Unions (2010), 'The remuneration of CEOs and executive chairs of companies in the ASX/S&P 50 index 2010', *ACTU Executive Pay Watch 2010*, available at http://www.actu.org.au (accessed 8 March 2012).

Australian Government (2010), *Response to the Productivity Commission's Inquiry Report on Executive Remuneration,* Attachment to The Hon Wayne Swan MP, Senator Nick Sherry and Chris Bowen MP, 'Government responds to the Productivity Commission Report on Executive Remuneration' (joint media release no. 033, 16 April).

Australian Institute of Company Directors (AICD) (2011), *Institutional Share Voting and Engagement: Exploring the Links between Directors, Institutional Shareholders and Proxy Advisers*, Sydney: AICD.

Australian Institute of Company Directors (AICD) (2009), *Executive Remuneration: Guidelines for Listed Company Boards*, Sydney: AICD Publications.

Australian Institute of Company Directors (AICD) (2004), *Remuneration Committees: Good Practice Guide*, Sydney: AICD.

Australian Investment Managers' Association (AIMA) (1995), *Corporate Governance: A Guide for Investment Managers and a Statement of Recommended Corporate Practice*, Sydney: AIMA.

Australian Investment Managers' Association and the Australian Institute of Company Directors (AICD) (1994), *Employee Share Scheme Guidelines and Executive Share Option Guidelines*, Sydney: AIMA and AICD.

Australian Prudential Regulatory Authority (2007), 'A recent history of superannuation in Australia', *APRA Insight* **2**: 3–10.

Australian Securities and Investments Commission (ASIC) (2007), *Regulatory Guide 112: Independence of Experts*, Sydney: ASIC.

Australian Stock Exchange (1994), *Disclosure of Corporate Governance Practices by Listed Companies*, Sydney: Australian Stock Exchange.

Ayres, Ian and John Braithwaite (1992), *Responsive Regulation: Transcending the Deregulation Debate*, Oxford: Oxford University Press.

Baillie Gifford & Co. (2008), *Global Corporate Governance Principles and Guidelines*, Edinburgh: Baillie Gifford & Co.

Balsam, Steven (2011), 'The impact of firm strategy on performance measures used in executive compensation', *Journal of Business Research* **64**: 187–93.

Barclays Global Investors (2008), *Corporate Governance Policy*, London: Barclays Global Investors Ltd.

Barclays Global Investors Australia Limited (2007), *Proxy Voting Policy*, Sydney: Barclays Global Investors Australia Ltd.

Barnett, Anthony (1998), 'How company chiefs line their pockets', *The Observer* (London), 5 April, p. 7.

Barnett, Anthony (1997), 'Moment of truth for "stakeholding"', *The Observer* (London), 3 August, p. 6.

Bebchuk, Lucian and Jesse Fried (2004), *Pay Without Performance: The Unfulfilled Promise of Executive Compensation*, Cambridge, MA: Harvard University Press.

Bebchuk, Lucian and Holger Spamman (2010), 'Regulating bankers' pay', *Georgetown Law Journal* **98**: 247–87.

Becht, Marco, Julian Franks, Colin Mayer and Stefano Rossi (2008), 'Returns to shareholder activism: Evidence from a clinical study of the Hermes UK focus fund', *Review of Financial Studies* **22**: 3093–129.

Bender, Ruth (2007), 'Onwards and upwards: Why companies change their executive remuneration schemes, and why this leads to increases in pay', *Corporate Governance: An International Review* **15**: 709–23.

Bender, Ruth (2004), 'Why do companies use performance-related pay for the executive directors?', *Corporate Governance: An International Review* **12**: 521–33.

Bender, Ruth (2003), 'How executive directors' remuneration is determined in two FTSE 350 utilities', *Corporate Governance: An International Review* **11**: 206–17.

Bender, Ruth and Lance Moir (2006), 'Does "best practice" in setting executive pay in the UK encourage "good" behaviour?', *Journal of Business Ethics* **67**: 75–91.

Bennett, Bruce, Michael Bradbury and Helen Prangnell (2006), 'Rules, principles and judgments in accounting standards', *Abacus* **42**: 189–204.

Berle, Adolph and Gardiner Means (1933), *The Modern Corporation and Private Property*, New York: The Macmillan Company.

Bertrand, Marianne and Sendhil Mullainathan (2001), 'Are CEOs rewarded for luck? The ones without principals are', *Quarterly Journal of Economics* **116**: 901–32.

Bizjak, John (2011), 'Are all CEOs above average? An empirical analysis of compensation peer groups and pay design', *Journal of Financial Economics* **100**: 538–55.

Bizjak, John, Michael Lemmon and Lalitha Naveen (2008), 'Does the use of peer groups contribute to higher pay and less efficient compensation?', *Journal of Financial Economics* **90**: 152–68.

Black, Julia (2008), 'Forms and paradoxes of principles-based regulation', *Capital Markets Law Journal* **3**: 425–57.

Black, Julia (2002), 'Regulatory conversations', *Journal of Law and Society* **29**: 163–96.

Black, Julia (1995), 'Which arrow? Rule types and regulatory policy', *Public Law*, Summer: 94–117.

BlackRock Investment Management (UK) Limited (2007), *Global Corporate Governance*, London: BlackRock Investment Management (UK) Limited.

Blue, Tim (1998), 'Investors still in the dark', *The Australian* (Sydney), 30 September, p. 40.

Boyd, Tony (2012), 'New year, new approach to executive pay', *Australian Financial Review* (Sydney), 5 January, p. 48.

Braithwaite, John (2009), 'Restorative justice for banks through negative licensing', *British Journal of Criminology* **49**: 439–50.

Braithwaite, John and Peter Drahos (2000), *Global Business Regulation*, Melbourne: Cambridge University Press.

Brown, Philip, Wendy Beekes and Peter Verhoeven (2011), 'Corporate governance, accounting and finance: A review', *Accounting and Finance* **51**: 96–172.

Cable, Vince (2012a), 'Executive remuneration', Speech delivered to the Social Market Foundation, 24 January 2012, available at http://www.bis.gov.uk/news/speeches/vice-cable-executive-pay-remuneration-2012? (accessed 25 January 2012).

Cable, Vince (2012b), Speech delivered at Mansion House, 7 March.

Cadman, Brian, Mary Ellen Carver and Stephen Hillegeist (2010), 'The incentives of compensation consultants and CEO pay', *Journal of Accounting and Economics* **49**: 263–80.

Carpezio, Alessandra, John Shields and Michael O'Donnell (2011), 'Too good to be true? Board structural independence as a moderator of CEO pay-for-firm-performance', *Journal of Management Studies* **48**: 487–513.

Carter, Mary Ellen and Valentina Zamora (2008), 'Shareholder remuneration votes and CEO compensation design', Boston University Working Paper.

Carver, John (2006), *Boards That Make a Difference*, 3rd edition, San Francisco: Jossey-Bass.

Cassell, Michael (1996), 'Open season on fat cats', *The Financial Times* (London), 6 June, p. 17.

Chalmers, Kerryn, Ping-Sheng Koh and Geof Stapledon (2006), 'The determinants of CEO compensation: Rent extraction or labour demand?', *British Accounting Review* **38**: 259–75.

Chancellor, Alexander (1997), 'Pride and prejudice – bonus balls', *The Guardian* (Manchester), 7 June, p. 7.

Chapple, Larelle and Ernest Cheung (2005), 'Disclosure of proxy voting information by Australia's managed investment schemes', *Australian Accounting Review* **15**: 75–83.

Cheffins, Brian (2010), 'The *Stewardship Code's* achilles' heel', *The Modern Law Review* **73**: 985–1025.

Cheffins, Brian (1997), *Company Law: Theory, Structure and Operation*, Oxford: Oxford University Press.

Cheffins, Brian and Randall Thomas (2001), 'Should shareholders have a greater say over executive pay? Learning from the US experience', *Journal of Corporate Law Studies* **1**: 277–315.

Chiu, Iris H-Y (2008), 'The meaning of share ownership and the governance role of shareholder activism in the United Kingdom', *Richmond Journal of Global Law and Business* **8**: 117–60.

Chiu, Iris H-Y (2006a), 'Delegated regulatory administration in mandatory disclosures: Some observations from EU securities regulation', *International Law* **40**: 737–72.

Chiu, Iris Y-Y (2006b), 'The paradigms of mandatory non-financial disclosure: A conceptual analysis, part I', *Company Lawyer* **27**: 259–68.

Choi, Stephen, Jill Fisch and Marcel Kahan (2008), 'Director elections and the role of proxy advisers', University of Pennsylvania Law School, Institute for Law and Economics Research Paper no. 08-18.

Ciro, Tony and Michael Longo (2010), 'The global financial crisis: Causes and implications for future regulation, part 2', *Journal of International Banking Law and Regulation* **25**: 9–18.

Clarke, Thomas (2007), *International Corporate Governance: A Comparative Approach*, Abingdon, UK: Routledge.

Clarkson, Peter, Ami Lammerts Van Bueren and Julie Walker (2006), 'Chief executive officer remuneration disclosure quality: Corporate responses to an evolving disclosure environment', *Accounting and Finance* **46**: 771–96.

Coffee, John (1994), 'Market failure and the economic case for a mandatory disclosure system', *Virginia Law Review* **13**: 717–53.

Collins, Hugh (2004), 'Regulating contract law', in Christine Parker, Colin Scott, Nicola Lacey and John Braithwaite (eds), *Regulating Law*, Oxford: Oxford University Press, pp. 13–32.

Committee on Corporate Governance (1998), *Final Report*, London: GEE Publishing.

Committee on the Financial Aspects of Corporate Governance (1992a), *Report of the Committee on the Financial Aspects of Corporate Governance*, London: Gee and Co Ltd.

Committee on the Financial Aspects of Corporate Governance (1992b), *The Financial Aspects of Corporate Governance: Code of Best Practice*, London: Gee and Co Ltd.

Committee on Oversight and Government Reform (2008), *CEO Pay and the Mortgage Crisis*, 7 March, Serial No. 110-81, Washington, DC: US GPO.

Companies and Securities Advisory Committee (CASAC) (2000), *Shareholder Participation in the Modern Listed Company*, Sydney: CASAC.

Congressional Oversight Panel (2009), *Special Report on Regulatory Reform: Modernizing the American Financial Regulatory System: Recommendations for Improving Oversight, Protecting Consumers, and Ensuring Stability*, Washington, DC: US GPO.

Conyon, Martin (1997), 'Institutional arrangements for setting directors' compensation in UK companies', in Kevin Keasey, Steve Thompson and Mike Wright (eds), *Corporate Governance: Economic and Financial Issues*, Oxford: Oxford University Press, pp. 103–21.

Conyon, Martin, Simon Peck and Graham Sadler (2009), 'Compensation consultants and executive pay: Evidence from the United States and the United Kingdom', *Academy of Management* **23**: 43–55.

Conyon, Martin and Graham Sadler (2010), 'Shareholding voting and directors' remuneration report legislation: Say on pay in the UK', *Corporate Governance: An International Review* **18**: 296–312.

Conyon, Martin and Graham Sadler (2001), 'Executive pay, tournaments and corporate performance in UK firms', *International Journal of Management Reviews* **3**: 141–68.

Corbett, Angus and Stephen Bottomley (2004), 'Regulating corporate governance', in Christine Parker, Colin Scott, Nicola Lacey and John Braithwaite (eds), *Regulating Law*, Oxford: Oxford University Press, pp. 60–81.

Core, John, Wayne Guay and David F Larcker (2003), 'Executive equity compensation and incentives: A survey', *Federal Reserve Bank of New York Economic Policy Review* **9**: 27–50.

Cornell, Andrew (2008), 'The winning ways of a corporate nagger', *The Weekend Australian Financial Review* (Sydney), 27–28 September, p. 31.

Corporations and Markets Advisory Committee (CAMAC) (2011), *Executive Remuneration*, Sydney: CAMAC.

Cragg, Michael and Alexander Dyck (2003), 'Privatisation and management incentives: Evidence from the United Kingdom', *Journal of Law, Economics and Organisation* **19**: 176–217.

Craig, Susanne and Deborah Solomon (2009), 'Bailed banks paid $40bn in bonuses', *The Weekend Australian* (Sydney), 1–2 August, p. 30.

Crotty, James (2009), 'Structural causes of the global financial crisis: A critical assessment of the "new financial architecture"' *Cambridge Journal of Economics* **33**: 563–80.

Cziraki, Peter, Luc Renneboog and Peter Szilagyi (2010), 'Shareholder activism through proxy proposals: The European perspective', *European Financial Management* **16**: 738–77.

Daines, Robert, Ian Gow and David Larcker (2010), 'Rating the ratings: How good are commercial governance ratings?', *Journal of Financial Economics* **98**: 439–61.

Dalton, Dan and Catherine Dalton (2008), 'Corporate governance in the post Sarbanes–Oxley period: Compensation disclosure and analysis (CD&A)', *Business Horizons* **51**: 85–92.

Davies, Paul (2008), *Gower and Davies' Principles of Modern Company Law*, 8th edition, London: Sweet & Maxwell Ltd.

Defina, Andrew, Thomas Harris and Ian Ramsay (1994), 'What is reasonable remuneration for corporate officers? An empirical investigation into the relationship between pay and performance in the largest Australian companies', *Company and Securities Law Journal* **12**: 341–56.

Deloitte & Touche LLP (2007), *Executive Directors' Remuneration: Your Guide*, London: Deloitte & Touche LLP.

Deloitte & Touche LLP (2006), *Executive Directors' Remuneration: Your Guide*, London: Deloitte & Touche LLP.

Deloitte & Touche LLP (2005), *Executive Directors' Remuneration: Your Guide*, London: Deloitte & Touche LLP.

Deloitte & Touche LLP (2004), *Executive Directors' Remuneration*, London: Deloitte & Touche LLP.

Deloitte & Touche LLP (2003), *Executive Directors' Remuneration*, London: Deloitte & Touche LLP.

Department for Business Innovation and Skills (2011a), *Executive Remuneration, Discussion Paper*, URN 11/1287, London: Department for Business Innovation and Skills.

Department for Business Innovation and Skills (2011b), *The Future of Narrative Reporting, Consulting on a New Reporting Framework*, URN 11/945, London: Department for Business Innovation and Skills.

Department for Business Innovation and Skills (2010a), *A Long-Term Focus for Corporate Britain*, URN 10/1225, London: BIS.

Department for Business Innovation and Skills (2010b), *The Future of Narrative Reporting – A Consultation. Summary of Responses*, URN 10/1318, London: BIS.

Department of Trade and Industry (2003), *Rewards for Failure. Directors' Remuneration – Contracts, Performance and Severance. A Consultative Document*, London: Department of Trade and Industry.

Department of Trade and Industry (2001a), *Directors' Remuneration: A Consultative Document*, URN 01/1400, London: Department of Trade and Industry.

Department of Trade and Industry (2001b), *Directors' Remuneration Report Regulations 2002 and Companies (Summary Financial Statement) Amendment Regulations 2002, Regulatory Impact Statement*, London: Department of Trade and Industry.

Department of Trade and Industry (2001c), *Modern Company Law for a Competitive Economy: Final Report*, URN 01/943, London: Department of Trade and Industry.

Department of Trade and Industry (2001d), *Responses to the Consultation Document 'Completing the Structure'*, London: Department of Trade and Industry.

Department of Trade and Industry (2000a), *Modern Company Law for a Competitive Economy: Developing the Framework*, URN 00/656, London: Department of Trade and Industry.

Department of Trade and Industry (2000b), *Modern Company Law for a Competitive Economy: Completing the Structure,* URN 00/1335, London: Department of Trade and Industry.

Department of Trade and Industry (1999a), *Directors' Remuneration: A Consultative Document,* URN 99/923, London: Department of Trade and Industry.

Department of Trade and Industry (1999b), *Modern Company Law for a Competitive Economy: The Strategic Framework*, URN99: 654, London: Department of Trade and Industry.

Department of Trade and Industry (1999c), *Modern Company Law for a Competitive Economy: Company General Meetings and Shareholder Communications*, URN 99/1144, London: Department of Trade and Industry.

Department of Trade and Industry (1998), *Modern Company Law for a Competitive Economy*, London: Department of Trade and Industry.

Department of Treasury, Commonwealth of Australia (2010), *The Clawback of Executive Remuneration Where Financial Statements are Materially Misstated*, Discussion Paper, Canberra: Commonwealth of Australia.

Department of Treasury, Commonwealth of Australia (2002), *Corporate Disclosure: Strengthening the Framework*, Canberra: Commonwealth of Australia.

Department of Treasury, Commonwealth of Australia (2001), *Towards Higher Retirement Incomes for Australians: A History of the Australian Retirement Income System*, available at http://www.treasury.gov.au/documents/110.html (accessed 30 August 2009).

Dew-Becker, Ian (2009), 'How much sunlight does it take to disinfect a boardroom? A short history of executive compensation regulation in America', *CESifo Economic Studies* **55**: 434–57.

Dewartripont, Mathias, Ian Jewitt and Jean Tirole (1999), 'The economics of career concerns part I: Comparing information structures', *Review of Economic Studies* **66**: 183–98.

Diamond, Douglas and Robert Verrechia (1982), 'Optimal managerial contracts and equilibrium security prices', *Journal of Finance* **37**: 275–87.

Dickson, Martin (2000), 'Vodafone rings the wrong numbers on executive pay', *The Financial Times* (London), 29 July, p. 15.

Dickson, Martin (1995), 'Financial fat cats or tigers – executive pay', *The Financial Times* (London), 28 January, p. 6.

Dine, Janet (2006), 'Executive pay and corporate governance in the UK: Slimming the fat-cats?', *European Company Law* **3**: 75–85.

Donovan, Patrick and Sarah Whitebloom (1997), 'Fury over Glaxo "Fat Cats"', *The Guardian* (Manchester), 23 March, p. 38.

Duran, Paulina (2010), 'War of words proved ultimately enlightening', *The Australian Financial Review* (Sydney), 15 April, Special Report, p. 3.

Durkin, Patrick (2011), 'Fowler case puts spotlight on options', *The Australian Financial Review* (Sydney), 8 February, p. 3.

Durkin, Patrick (2010), 'Dispute over executive pay inflation', *The Australian Financial Review* (Sydney), 10 September, p. 5.

Durkin, Patrick and John Stensholt (2011), 'Cash bonuses deliver for top CEOs', *The Australian Financial Review* (Sydney), 23 November, pp. S1–S2.

Easterbrook , Frank and Daniel Fishel (1984), 'Mandatory disclosure and the protection of investors', *Virginia Law Review* **70**: 669–715.

Eisenberg, Michael (1999), 'Corporate law and social norms', *Columbia Law Review* **99**: 1253–92.

Eisenberg, Michael (1989), 'The structure of corporate law', *Columbia Law Review* **89**: 1461–1525.

Elliott, Larry (1998), 'Ending the boardroom bonanzas', *The Guardian* (Manchester), 31 January, p. 12.

Enderle, G and L Tavis (1998), 'A balanced concept of the firm and the measurement of its long-term performance', *Journal of Business Ethics* **17**: 1129–44.

Enriques, Luca, Henry Hansmann and Reinier Kraakman (2009), 'The basic governance structure: The interests of shareholders as a class', in Reiner Kraakman et al (eds), *The Anatomy of Corporate Law: A Comparative and Functional Approach*, 2nd edition, Oxford: Oxford University Press, pp. 55–87.

Ertimur, Yonca, Fabrizio Ferri and Volkan Muslu (2010), 'Shareholder activism and CEO pay', *The Review of Financial Studies* **24**: 535–92.

Ertimur, Yonca, Fabrizio Ferri and Stephen Stubben (2010), 'Board of directors' responsiveness to shareholders: Evidence from shareholder proposals', *Journal of Corporate Finance* **16**: 53–72.

Evans, J and F Hefner (2009), 'Business ethics and the decision to adopt golden parachute contracts: Empirical evidence of concern for all stakeholders', *Journal of Business Ethics* **86**: 65–79.

Evans, Robert and John Evans (2005), 'The influence of non-executive director control and rewards on CEO remuneration: Australian evidence', Working paper, available at http://ssrn.com/abstract=263050 (accessed 8 March 2012).

Ezzamel, Mahmoud and Robert Watson (2002), 'Pay comparability across and within UK boards: An empirical analysis of the cash pay awards to CEOs and other board members', *Journal of Management Studies* **39**: 207–32.

F&C Management Limited (2008), *Corporate Governance: Operational Guidelines*, London: F&C Management Limited.

Farrar, John (2008), *Corporate Governance: Theories, Principles and Practices*, 3rd edition, South Melbourne: Oxford University Press.

Fattorusso, Jay, Rodion Skovoroda, Trevor Buck and Alistair Bruce (2007), 'UK executive bonuses and transparency – a research note', *British Journal of Industrial Relations* **45**: 518–36.

Faulkender, Michael (2010), 'Inside the black box: The role and composition of compensation peer groups', *Journal of Financial Economics* **96**: 257–70.

Fee, C Edward and Charles J Hadlock (2003), 'Raids, rewards and reputations in the market for managerial talent', *The Review of Financial Studies* **16**: 1315–57.

Ferran, E (2001), 'Corporate law, codes and social norms – finding the right regulatory combination and institutional structure', *Journal of Corporate Law Studies* **1**: 381–409.

Ferri, Fabrizio and David Maber (2009), 'Say on pay vote and CEO compensation: Evidence from the UK', Working Paper, Harvard Business School.

Ferris, Kenneth and James Wallace (2009), 'IRC section 162(m) and the law of unintended consequences', *Advances in Accounting* **25**: 147–55.

Filatotchev, Igor, Gregory Jackson, Howard Gospel and Deborah Allcock (2006), *Key Drivers of 'Good' Corporate Governance and the Appropriateness of UK Policy Responses*, Report prepared for the Department of Trade and Industry, UK, London: King's College London, University of London.

Financial Reporting Council (FRC) (2009), *Louder Than Words: Principles and Actions for Making Corporate Reports Less Complex and More Relevant*, London: FRC.

Financial Services Authority (2009), *The Turner Review – A Regulatory Response to the Global Banking Crisis*, 003289, London: Financial Services Authority.

Financial Stability Board (formerly Financial Stability Forum) (2009), *Principles of Sound Compensation Practices*, London: Financial Stability Board.

Finkelstein, F and D Hambrick (1988), 'Chief executive compensation: A synthesis and reconciliation', *Strategic Management Journal* **9**: 543–58.

Fleming, Grant and George Stellios (2002), 'CEO remuneration, managerial agency and boards of directors in Australia', *Accounting Research Journal* **15**: 126–45.

Fung, Archon, Mary Graham and David Weil (2007), *Full Disclosure: The Perils and Promise of Transparency*, New York: Cambridge University Press.

Garbaix, Xavier and Augustin Landier (2008), 'Why has CEO pay increased so much?', *Quarterly Journal of Economics* **123**: 49–100.

Garvey, Gerald and Todd Milbourn (2006), 'Asymmetric benchmarking in compensation: Executives are rewarded for good luck but not penalised for bad', *Journal of Financial Economics* **82**: 197–226.

Gay, Keith (2001), 'A boardroom revolution? The impact of the Cadbury nexus on the work of non-executive directors of FTSE 350 companies', *Corporate Governance: An International Review* **9**: 152–64.

Gilshan, Deborah and PIRC Limited (2009), *Say on Pay Six Years On:*

Lessons from the UK Experience, London: Railpen Investments and PIRC Limited.

Gluyas, Richard (1997a), 'Governance bombshell – only 1 in 10 up to scratch', *The Australian* (Sydney), 17 April, p. 17.

Gluyas, Richard (1997b), 'Above board', *The Australian* (Sydney), 22 August, p. 36.

Gold, Martin (2006), 'Corporate governance reform in Australia: The intersection of investment fiduciaries and issuers', in Paul Ali and Greg Gregoriou (eds), *International Corporate Governance After Sarbanes–Oxley*, Hoboken, NJ: John Wiley & Sons Inc, pp. 137–59.

Gopalan, Sandeep (2007a) 'Shame sanctions and excessive CEO pay', *Delaware Journal of Corporate Law* **32**: 757–97.

Gopalan, Sandeep (2007b), 'Changing social norms and CEO pay: the role of norms entrepreneurs', *Rutgers Law Journal* **39**: 1–57.

Gordon, Jeffrey N (2009), '"Say on pay": Cautionary notes on the UK experience and the case for shareholder opt-in', *Harvard Journal on Legislation* **46**: 323–67.

Grant, Julia, Garen Markarian and Antonio Parbonetti (2009), 'CEO risk-related incentives and income smoothing', *Contemporary Accounting Research* **26**: 1029–65.

Gregg, Paul, Sarah Jewell and Ian Tonks (2005), 'Executive pay and performance in the UK, 1994–2002', Working Paper, 05/122, Centre for Market and Public Organisation, University of Bristol.

Gregory-Smith, Ian (2011), 'Chief executive pay and remuneration committee independence', *Oxford Bulletin of Economics and Statistics*, early on line – DOI: 10.1111/j.1468-0084.2011.00660.x.

Grigg, Angus (2011), 'Bonus a big carrot, but also a big stick', *The Australian Financial Review* (Sydney), 23 November, pp. S2–3.

Gunningham, Neil and Peter Grabosky (1998), *Smart Regulation: Designing Environmental Policy*, Oxford: Oxford University Press.

Halliwell Consulting (UK) (2004), *Executive Pay in the Pharmaceuticals and Bio-Tech Sector*, London: Halliwell Consulting.

Hamori, Monica (2006), 'Executive career advancement in career moves across employers: The role of organisational-level predictors', *International Journal of Human Resource Management* **17**: 1129–51.

Hancher, Leigh and Michael Moran (1989), 'Organising regulatory space', in Leigh Hancher and Michael Moran (eds), *Capitalism, Culture and Economic Regulation*, Oxford: Clarendon Press, pp. 271–99.

Harris, Jared (2009), 'What's wrong with executive compensation?', *Journal of Business Ethics* **85**: 147–56.

Harris, Jared (2006), 'How much is too much? A theoretical analysis of executive compensation from the standpoint of distributive justice', in

Robert W Kolb (ed), *The Ethics of Executive Compensation*, Oxford: Blackwell Publishing Ltd, pp. 67–86.

Hartley, Robert (2008), 'Goodman takes $70m hit to outflank short sellers', *The Australian Financial Review* (Melbourne), 27 March, pp. 1, 59.

Hawley, James P (1995), 'Political voice, fiduciary activism and the institutional ownership of U.S. corporations: The role of public and non-corporate pension funds', *Sociological Perspectives* **38**: 415–35.

Hawley, James P and Andrew T Williams (2000), *The Rise of Fiduciary Capitalism: How Institutional Investors Can Make Corporate America More Democratic*, Philadelphia, PA: University of Pennsylvania Press.

Hebb, Tessa (2006), 'The economic inefficiency of secrecy: Pension fund investors' corporate transparency concerns', *Journal of Business Ethics* **63**: 385–405.

Henderson, Ian (1998), 'Howard backtracks on corporate law', *The Australian* (Sydney), 16 July, p. 21.

Hendry, John, Paul Sanderson, Richard Barker and John Roberts (2006), 'Owners or traders? Conceptualizations of institutional investors and their relationship with corporate managers', *Human Relations* **59**: 1101–32.

Hepworth, Annabel and Damon Kitney (2010), 'Labor law is forcing up executive pay, bosses warn', *The Australian* online (Sydney), 5 September, available at http://www.theaustralian.com.au/business/labor-law-cracking-down-on-executive-pay-bosses-warn/story-e6frg8zx-1225914509287 (accessed 8 March 2012).

Hepworth, Annabel and Damon Kitney (2008), 'Angry shareholders turn up the heat on directors', *The Australian Financial Review* (Melbourne), 1 December, p. 1.

Hermanson, Dana, James Tompkins, Rajaram Veliyath and Zhongxia Ye (2011), 'The compensation committee process', *Contemporary Accounting Research*, early online, DOI: 10.1111/j.1911-3846.2011.01118.x.

Hertig, Gerard, Reinier Kraakman and Edward Rock (2004), 'Issuers and investor protection', in Reinier Kraakman et al (eds), *The Anatomy of Corporate Law: A Comparative and Functional Approach*, Oxford: Oxford University Press, pp. 193–214.

Herzberg, Frederick, Bernard Mausner and Barbara Bloch Snyderman (1957), *The Motivation to Work*, New York: Wiley.

High Pay Commission (2011), *Cheques with Balances: Why Tackling High Pay is in the National Interest*, Final Report of the High Pay Commission, London: High Pay Commission.

Hill, Jennifer (2006), 'Regulating executive remuneration: International developments in the post-scandal era', *European Company Law* **3**: 64–74.

Hill, Jennifer (1996), '"What reward have ye?" Disclosure of director and executive remuneration in Australia', *Company and Securities Law Journal* **14**: 232–47.

Hirschman, Albert (1970), *Exit, Voice and Loyalty*, Boston: Harvard University Press.

HM Treasury (2010), *Budget 2010: Securing the Recovery*, HC 451, London: The Stationery Office.

HM Treasury (2009), *Budget 2009: Building Britain's Future*, HC 407, London: The Stationery Office.

Holmström, Bengt (1999), 'Managerial incentive problems: A dynamic perspective', *Review of Economic Studies* **66**: 169–82.

Holmström, Bengt (1982), 'Moral hazard in teams', *Bell Journal of Economics* **13**: 324–40.

Holmström, Bengt (1981), 'Contractual models of the labor market', *American Economic Review* **71**: 308–13.

Holmström, Bengt (1979), 'Moral hazard and observability', *Bell Journal of Economics* **10**: 74–91.

House of Commons Treasury Committee (2009), *Banking Crisis: Reforming Corporate Governance and Pay in the City*, HC 519, 15 May, London: The Stationery Office Limited.

Hu, Henry and Bernard Black (2006), 'The new vote buying: empty voting and (hidden) morphable ownership', *Southern California Law Review* **79**: 811–908.

Hudson, Phillip and Helen Shield (1998), 'Rethink on pay-packet law', *The Age* (Melbourne), 16 July, p. 1.

Hughes, Anthony (2009), 'Outrage fails to put a stop to excessive incentives', *The Australian Financial Review* (Sydney), 19 November, p. S13.

Huse, Morton (2005), 'Accountability and creating accountability: A framework for exploring behavioural perspectives of corporate governance', *British Journal of Management* **16**: S65–S79.

IBISWorld Pty Ltd (2005), *Funds Management (Except Superannuation Funds) in Australia*, K7514, Sydney: IBISWorld.

Ingley, CG and NT van der Walt (2004), 'Corporate governance, institutional investors and conflicts of interest', *Corporate Governance: An International Review* **12**: 534–51.

Insight Investment (2007), *Corporate Governance and Corporate Responsibility: Statement of Policy*, London: Insight Investment Management Limited.

Institute of Chartered Secretaries and Administrators (ICSA) (2003), *Principles of Executive Service Contracts,* ICSA Guidance Note 030407, London: ICSA Limited.

Institute of International Finance (2009), *Compensation in Financial Services: Industry Progress and the Agenda for Change,* Washington, DC: Institute of International Finance.

Institutional Shareholders' Committee (ISC) (2002), *The Responsibilities of Institutional Shareholders and Agents – Statement of Principles,* London: ISC.

Investment and Financial Services Association Limited (IFSA) (2009), *Corporate Governance: A Guide for Fund Managers and Corporations,* IFSA Guidance Note 2.00, Sydney: IFSA Ltd.

Investment and Financial Services Association Limited (IFSA) (2007a), *Executive Equity Pay Guidelines,* IFSA Guidance Note No. 12, Sydney: IFSA Ltd.

Investment and Financial Services Association Limited (IFSA) (2007b), *Code of Ethics and Code of Conduct,* IFSA Standard No. 1, Sydney: IFSA Ltd.

Investment and Financial Services Association (IFSA) and KPMG (2003), *Shareholder Activism Among Fund Managers: Policy and Practice, Industry Overview Conclusion and Recommendations,* Sydney: IFSA Ltd.

Investment Management Association (IMA) (2009), *Survey of Fund Managers' Engagement with Companies for the Two Years Ended 30 June 2008,* London: Investment Management Association.

Izan, HY, Baljit Sidhu and Stephen Taylor (1998), 'Does CEO pay reflect performance? Some Australian evidence', *Corporate Governance: An International Review* **6**: 39–47.

Jackson, Calvin, Brian Main, John Pymm and Vicky Wright (2006), 'The remuneration committee process: Some questions regarding remuneration committee decision-making', Paper Presented in the Corporate Governance at the LSE seminar series, 12 October.

Jackson, Tony (1998a), 'The fat cats keep getting fatter', *The Financial Times* (London), 1 August, p. 9.

Jackson, Tony (1998b), 'Riches for the few – directors' pay seems to be rising irrespective of company performance', *The Financial Times* (London), 14 August, p. 20.

Jasso, Guillermina and Eva Meyersonn Milgrom (2008), 'Distributive justice and CEO compensation', *Acta Sociologica* **51**: 123–43.

Jensen, Michael (2001), 'Value maximisation, stakeholder theory and the corporate objective function', *Journal of Applied Corporate Finance*, **14**: 8–31.

Jensen, Michael and William Meckling (1976), 'Theory of the firm:

Managerial behavior, agency costs and ownership structure', *Journal of Financial Economics* **3**: 305–60.

Joint Committee on Corporations and Financial Services (2008), *Better Shareholders, Better Company*, Canberra: Commonwealth of Australia.

Joint Committee on Corporations and Financial Services (2005), *Report on Australia Accounting Standards Tabled in Compliance with the Corporations Act 2001 on 30 August and 16 November 2004*, Canberra: Commonwealth of Australia.

Joint Committee on Corporations and Financial Services (2004), *CLERP (Audit Reform and Corporate Disclosure) Bill 2003, Part 1: Enforcement, Executive Remuneration, Continuous Disclosure, Shareholder Participation and Related Matters*, Canberra: Commonwealth of Australia.

Joint Committee on Corporations and Securities (1999), *Report on Matters Arising from the Company Law Review Act 1998*, Canberra: Commonwealth of Australia.

JP Morgan Asset Management (UK) Limited (2007), *Corporate Governance Principles and Voting Guidelines*, London: JP Morgan Asset Management (UK) Limited.

Jupiter Asset Management Limited (2008), *Corporate Governance and Voting Policy*, London: Jupiter Asset Management Limited.

Kandel, Eugene (2009), 'In search of reasonable executive compensation', *CESifo Economic Studies* **55**: 405–33.

Kaplan, Robert and David Norton (1996), *The Balanced Scorecard: Translating Strategy into Action*, Cambridge, MA: Harvard University Press.

Keay, Andrew (2007), 'Company directors behaving poorly: Disciplinary options for shareholders', *Journal of Business Law* **9**: 656–82.

King, Roger (2007), *The Regulatory State in an Age of Governance: Soft Words and Big Sticks*, Houndmills: Palgrave Macmillan.

Kirkbride, James and Steve Letza (2004), 'Regulation, governance and regulatory colibration: Achieving a "holistic" approach', *Corporate Governance: An International Review* **12**: 85–92.

Korporaal, Glenda and Kevin Meade (2008), 'Flash suit, but Eddie's been stripped', *The Weekend Australian* (Sydney), 8–9 March, p. 1.

Labour Party (1996), *Vision For Growth*, London: Labour Party.

Lamming, Richard, Roderick Martin, Tahir Nisar and Peter Casson (2004), *The Effects of Financial Institutions and Investor Behaviour on Management Practice*, a report for the Department of Trade and Industry, Southampton: School of Management, University of Southampton.

Latham, G and EA Locke (1979), 'Goal setting – a motivational technique that works', *Organisational Dynamics* **8**: 68–80.

Latham, Mark (2003), 'Democracy and infomediaries', *Corporate Governance: An International Review* **11**: 91–101.

Laurance, Ben (1997), 'Cats who want cream should study the options', *The Observer* (London), 6 July, p. 9.

Law Commission, The and Scottish Law Commission (1998), *Company Directors: Regulating Conflicts of Interests and Formulating a Statement of Duties*, A Joint Consultation Paper, Law Commission Consultation Paper No. 153, Scottish Law Commission, Consultation Paper No. 105.

Lawrence, Jeffrey and Geof Stapledon (1999), 'Is board composition important? A study of listed Australian companies', Working Paper, Centre for Corporate Law and Securities Regulation, The University of Melbourne.

Lazear, Edward and Sherwin Rosen (1981), 'Rank order tournaments as optimum labor contracts', *Journal of Political Economy* **89**: 841–64.

Lee, Tracey (2005), 'A lovely set of golden handcuffs, *The Australian Financial Review* (Melbourne), 16 November, p. 4.

Lewis, William (1996), 'Fat cats get more cream', *The Financial Times* (London), 6 July, p. 7.

Lines, James (1978), *The Role of the Chief Executive*, London: Random House Business Books.

Liu, Lisa Shifei and Andrew Stark (2009), 'Relative performance evaluation in board cash compensation: UK empirical evidence', *The British Accounting Review* **41**: 21–30.

Lucier, Chuck, Rob Schuyt and Junichi Handa (2004), 'CEO succession 2003: The perils of "good" governance', *Strategy + Business* **35**: 1–20.

McAdams, R (1997), 'The original, development and regulation of norms', *Michigan Law Review* **96**: 338–433.

McBarnet, Doreen and Christopher Whelan (1991), 'The elusive spirit of the law: Formalism and the struggle for legal control', *Modern Law Review* **54**: 848–73.

McClelland, D (1975), *Power – the Inner Experience*, New York: Irvington Publishers.

McConvill, James and John Bingham (2004), 'Comply or comply: The illusion of voluntary corporate governance in Australia', *Company and Securities Law Journal* **22**: 208–17.

McLaughlin, David J (1991), 'The rise of a strategic approach to executive compensation', in Fred K Foulkes (ed), *Executive Compensation: A Strategic Guide for the 1990s*, Boston, MA: Harvard Business School Press, pp. 5–26.

MacNeil, Ian and Li Xiao (2006), '"Comply or explain": Market discipline and non-compliance with the Combined Code', *Corporate Governance: An International Review* **14**: 486–96.

Main, Brian, Calvin Jackson, John Pymm and Vicky Wright (2008), 'The remuneration committee and strategic human resource management', *Corporate Governance: An International Review* **16**: 225–38.

Main, Brian and James Johnston (1992), 'The remuneration committee as an instrument of corporate governance', Working Paper, The David Hume Institute, Edinburgh.

Maitlis, Sally (2004), 'Taking it from the top: How CEOS influence (and fail to influence) their boards', *Organization Studies* **24**: 1275–311.

Manne, Geoffrey (2007), 'The hydraulic theory of disclosure regulation and other costs of disclosure', *Alabama Law Review* **58**: 473–511.

Manning, Chris and Victoria Sherwood (2008), *Booz & Company CEO Turnover Study in 2007: The Performance Paradox*, Sydney: Booz & Co.

Matsumura, Ella Mae and Jae Yong Shin (2005), 'Corporate governance reform and CEO compensation: Intended and unintended consequences', *Journal of Business Ethics* **62**: 101–13.

Meidinger, Errol (1987), 'Regulatory culture: A theoretical outline', *Law and Policy* **9**: 355–86.

Messner, Martin (2009), 'The limits of accountability', *Accounting, Organizations and Society* **34**: 918–38.

Mitchell, Richard, Anne O'Donnell and Ian Ramsay (2005), 'Shareholder value and employee interests: Intersections between corporate governance, corporate law and labor law', *Wisconsin International Law Journal* **23**: 417–76.

Moore, John (1985), 'Optimal labor contracts when workers have a variety of privately observed reservation wages', *Review of Economic Studies* **52**: 37–68.

Morgan, Angela, Annette Poulsen and Jack Wolf (2006), 'The evolution of shareholder voting for executive compensation schemes', *Journal of Corporate Finance* **12**: 715–37.

Moriarty, J (2009), 'How much compensation can CEOs permissibly accept?', *Business Ethics Quarterly* **19**: 235–50.

Murphy, Kevin (1995), 'Politics, economics and executive compensation', *University of Cincinnati Law Review* **63**: 713–48.

Murphy, Kevin and Tatiana Sandino (2010), 'Executive pay and "independent" compensation consultants', *Journal of Accounting and Economics* **49**: 247–62.

Murphy, Kevin and Ján Zábojník (2007), 'Managerial capital and the market for CEOs', Working Paper, available at http://ssrn.com/abstract=984376 (accessed 8 March 2012).

Murphy, Megan (2012), 'Profit fears behind bonus cuts at bank', *Financial Times*, USA, 2nd edition, 25 February, p. 11.

Myners, Paul (2004), *Review of the Impediments to Voting UK Shares*, Report by Paul Myners to the Shareholder Voting Working Group, London: Shareholder Voting Working Group.

Myners, Paul (1995), *Developing a Winning Partnership: How Institutional Investors and Business Can Work Together*, London: Joint City/Industry Working Group.

Myners Review of Institutional Investment for HM Treasury (2001), *Institutional Investment in the United Kingdom: A Review*, London: HM Treasury.

National Association of Pension Funds (NAPF) (2009), *Corporate Governance Policy and Voting Guidelines*, London: NAPF.

National Association of Pension Funds (NAPF) (2008), *Annual Report and Accounts 2007*.

National Association of Pension Funds (NAPF) (2005), *Voting Guidelines and Statements of Good Practice for the 2004 NAPF Corporate Governance Policy*, London: NAPF.

National Association of Pension Funds (NAPF) (2004), *2004 Corporate Governance Policy*, London: NAPF.

National Association of Pension Funds (NAPF) (2003), *2004 Corporate Governance Policy and Voting Guidelines*, London: NAPF.

National Association of Pension Funds (NAPF) (1999), *Committee of Inquiry Into Vote Execution* (the Newbold Inquiry), London: NAPF.

Nelson, Dean, Jonathan Calvert and Marie Woolf (1995), 'Lapping up more gold-top cream', *The Observer* (London), 17 December, p. 16.

Newtown Asset Management (2008), *Responsible Investment: Guidelines and Procedures*, London: Newtown Investment Management Limited.

Nisar, T (2005), *Investors and Management Practice: A Literature Review*, Report prepared for the Department of Trade and Industry, Southampton: School of Management, University of Southampton.

North, Gillian (2008), 'Closed and private company briefings: Justifiable or unfair?', *Company & Securities Law Journal* **26**: 501–16.

Northern Rock plc (2003), *Directors' Reports and Accounts 2002*.

O'Connell, Vincent (2011), 'The impact of customer satisfaction on CEO bonuses', *Journal of the Academy of Marketing Science* **39**: 828–45.

Ogden, Stuart and Robert Watson (2011), 'Remuneration committees, pay consultants and the determinants of executive directors' pay', *British Journal of Management*, early online, DOI: 10.1111/j.1467-8551.2011.00779.x.

Ogden, Stuart and Robert Watson (2008), 'Executive pay and the search for legitimacy: An investigation into how UK remuneration committees use corporate performance comparisons in long-term incentive pay decisions', *Human Relations* **61**: 711–39.

Ogus, Anthony (2006), *Costs and Cautionary Tales: Economic Insights for the Law*, London: Hart Publishing.

O'Neill, Graham (2007), 'A priori conceptions, methodological dogmatism and theory versus practice: Three reasons why CEO pay research lacks convergence', *Corporate Governance: An International Review* **15**: 692–700.

O'Reilly III, Charles and Brian Main (2010), 'Economic and psychological perspectives on CEO compensation: A review and synthesis', *Industrial and Corporate Change* **19**: 675–712.

O'Reilly III, Charles and Brian Main (2007), 'Setting the CEO's pay: It's more than simple economics', *Organizational Dynamics* **36**: 1–12.

O'Reilly III, Charles and Brian Main (2005), 'Setting the CEO's pay: Economic and psychological perspectives', Research Paper Series, Stanford Graduate School of Business.

Organisation for Economic Cooperation and Development (2011a), *The Role of Institutional Investors in Promoting Good Corporate Governance*, Paris: OECD Publishing.

Organisation for Economic Cooperation and Development (2011b), *Regulatory Policy and Governance: Supporting Economic Growth and Serving the Public Interest*, Paris: OECD Publishing.

Organisation for Economic Cooperation and Development (2009a), *Corporate Governance Lessons from the Financial Crisis*, Paris: OECD Publishing.

Organisation for Economic Cooperation and Development (2009b), *Corporate Governance and the Financial Crisis: Key Findings and Main Messages*, Paris: OECD Publishing.

Owen, The Hon. Justice (2003), *The Failure of HIH Insurance: Volume 1: A Corporate Collapse and Its Lessons*, Sydney: Commonwealth of Australia.

Oxera (2006), *A Framework for Assessing the Benefits of Financial Regulation: A Report Prepared for the Financial Services Authority*, Oxford: Oxera Consulting Limited.

Oyer, Paul (2004), 'Why do firms use incentives that have no incentive effects?', *Journal of Finance* **59**: 1619–49.

Palmer, Philip (2008), 'Disclosure of the impacts of adopting Australian equivalents of International Financial Reporting Standards', *Accounting & Finance* **48**: 847–70.

Panel on Takeovers and Mergers (2009), *Practice Statement 26: Shareholder Activism*, London: Panel on Takeovers and Mergers.

Parker, Christine (2002), *The Open Corporation: Effective Self-regulation and Democracy*, Cambridge and New York: Cambridge University Press.

Parker, George (1998), 'Brown warns utilities after Yorkshire Water bonuses', *The Financial Times* (London), 29 June, p. 22.

Patten, Sally (2011), 'Super-sized tax bill tops $400m', *The Australian Financial Review* (Sydney), 10 June, p. 3.

Pennings, Johannes M (2000), 'Executive compensation systems: Drivers or results from strategic choices?', in Lance A Berger and Dorothy R Berger (eds), *The Compensation Handbook*, 4th edition, New York: McGraw-Hill, pp. 373–89.

Perkins, SJ and C Hendry (2005), 'Ordering top pay: interpreting the signals', *Journal of Management Studies* **42**: 1443–68.

Perry, Todd and Marc Zenner (2001), 'Pay for performance? Government regulation and the structure of compensation contracts', *Journal of Financial Economics* **62**: 453–88.

Petel, M (2003), 'An ethical perspective on CEO compensation', *Journal of Business Ethics* **48**: 381–91.

Pettigrew, Andrew (1992), 'On studying managerial elites', *Strategic Management Journal* **13**: SE163–82.

PricewaterhouseCoopers and the Department of Trade and Industry (1999), *Monitoring of Corporate Governance Aspects of Directors' Remuneration*, London: Department of Trade and Industry.

Productivity Commission of Australia (2011), *Identifying and Evaluating Regulatory Reforms*, Melbourne: Commonwealth of Australia.

Productivity Commission of Australia (2009), *Executive Remuneration*, Inquiry Report No. 49, Melbourne: Commonwealth of Australia.

Psaros, Jim (2007), 'Do principles-based accounting standards lead to biased financial reporting? An Australian experiment', *Accounting and Finance* **47**: 527–50.

Ramsay, Ian (2001), *Independence of Australian Company Auditors: Review of Current Australian Requirements and Proposals for Reform*, Canberra: Commonwealth of Australia.

Ramsay, Ian M and Richard Hoad (1997), 'Disclosure of corporate governance practices by Australian companies', *Company and Securities Law Journal* **15**: 454–70.

Raz, Joseph (1972), 'Legal principles and the limits of the law', *Yale Law Journal* **81**: 823–54.

Reed, Rupert (2006), 'Company directors: Collective or functional responsibility?', *Company Lawyer* **27**: 170–78.

Regnan Governance Research & Engagement Limited (2009), *Regnan Remuneration Reform Proposal*, Sydney: Regnan Governance Research & Engagement Pty Limited.

Remuneration Consultants Group (2011a), *Consultation on the Code of Conduct*, London: Remuneration Consultants Group.

Remuneration Consultants Group (2011b), *Voluntary Code of Conduct in Relation to Executive Remuneration Consulting in the United Kingdom*, London: Remuneration Consultants Group.

Remuneration Consultants Group (2009), *Voluntary Code of Conduct in Relation to Executive Remuneration Consulting in the United Kingdom*, London: Remuneration Consultants Group.

Renneboog, Luc and Peter Szilagyi (2011), 'The role of shareholder proposals in corporate governance', *Journal of Corporate Finance* **17**: 167–88.

RiskMetrics (Australia) Pty Ltd (2008), *Assessing Remuneration Reports for ASX Listed Companies*, Melbourne: RiskMetrics (Australia) Pty Ltd.

RiskMetrics Australia and Australian Council of Superannuation Investors Inc (ACSI) (2009), A War for Talent? Evidence from Top 60 Australian Companies on the Competition for Executive Talent, Melbourne: ACSI.

Roberts, John (2009), 'No one is perfect: The limits of transparency and an ethic for "intelligent" accountability', *Accounting, Organizations and Society* **34**: 957–70.

Roberts, John, Terry McNulty and Philip Stiles (2005), 'Beyond agency conceptions of the work of the non-executive director: Creating accountability in the boardroom', *British Journal of Management* **16**: S5–S26.

Roberts, John, Paul Sanderson, Richard Barker and John Hendry (2006), 'In the mirror of the market: The disciplinary effects of company/fund manager meetings', *Accounting, Organizations and Society* **31**: 277–94.

Roberts, John and Philip Stiles (1999), 'The relationship between chairmen and chief executives: Competitive or complementary roles?', *Long Range Planning* **32**: 36–48.

Rodgers, Waymond and Susana Gago (2003), 'A model capturing ethics and executive compensation', *Journal of Business Ethics* **48**: 189–202.

Romano, Roberta (2001), 'Less is more: Making institutional investor activism a valuable mechanism of corporate governance', *Yale Journal on Regulation* **18**: 174–252.

Rudd, Kevin (2008), 'Global financial crisis', Address to the National Press Club, Canberra, 15 October.

Scott, Colin (2001), 'Analysing regulatory space: Fragmented resources and institutional design', *Public Law*, Summer: 329–53.

Scott, Robert (2002), 'The limits of behavioural theories of law and social norms', *Virginia Law Review* **86**: 1603–47.

Seidl, David (2007), 'Standard setting and following in corporate governance', *Organisation* **14**: 705–27.

Selvaggi, Mariano and James Upton (2008), 'Governance and performance in corporate Britain: Evidence from the IVIS© colour-coding system', ABI Research Paper 7, Association of British Insurers, London.

Semple, Craig and David Friedlander (2010), 'Small fry most at risk from proxy advisers', *The Australian Financial Review* (Sydney), 16 April, p. 67.

Shavell, Steven (1979), 'Risk sharing and incentives in the principal and agent relationship', *Bell Journal of Economics* **10**: 55–73.

Shaw, William (2006), 'Justice, incentives and executive compensation', in Robert W. Kolb (ed.), *The Ethics of Executive Compensation*, Oxford: Blackwell Publishing Ltd, pp. 87–100.

Sheehan, Kym (2012), 'Say on pay and the outrage constraint', in Jennifer Hill and Randall Thomas (eds), *Research Handbook on Executive Compensation*, Cheltenham: Edward Elgar Publishing, pp. 520–75.

Sheehan, Kym (2011), 'Great expectations: institutional investors, executive remuneration, and "say on pay"', in James P Hawley, Shyam J Kamath and Andrew T Williams (eds), *Corporate Governance Failures: The Role of Institutional Investors in the Global Financial Crisis*, Philadelphia, PA: University of Pennsylvania Press, pp. 115–43.

Sheehan, Kym (2009), 'The regulatory framework for executive remuneration in Australia', *Sydney Law Review* **31**: 273–308.

Sheehan, Kym (2007), 'Is the outrage constraint an effective constraint on executive remuneration? Evidence from the first three years in the UK and a preliminary look at Australia', available at http://ssrn.com/abstract_id=974965 (accessed 30 January 2012).

Sheehan, Kym (2006), 'Outrage + camouflage: The utility of the managerial power thesis in explaining executive remuneration', *Company & Securities Law Journal* **24**: 24–40.

Sheehan, Kym and Colin Fenwick (2008), 'Seven: The *Corporations Act 2001* (Cth), corporate governance and termination payments to senior employees', *Melbourne University Law Review* **32**: 199–241.

Shields, John, Michael O'Donnell and Michael O'Brien (2003), *The Buck Stops Here: Private Sector Executive Remuneration in Australia*, Report prepared for the Labor Council of New South Wales, Sydney: Labor Council of New South Wales.

Shivdsani, Anil and David Yermack (1999), 'CEO involvement in the selection of new board members: An empirical analysis', *Journal of Finance* **54**: 1829–53.

Short, Helen and Kevin Keasey (1997), 'Institutional shareholders and corporate governance in the United Kingdom', in Kevin Keasey, Steve

Thompson and Mike Wright (eds), *Corporate Governance: Economics and Financial Issues*, Oxford: Oxford University Press, pp. 18–53.

Solomon, Jill and Aris Solomon (2004), *Corporate Governance and Accountability*, New York: John Wiley.

Sonnenfeld, Jeffrey and Andrew Ward (2007), *Firing Back: How Great Leaders Rebound After Career Disasters*, Cambridge, MA: Harvard Business School Press.

Stapledon, Geof (2005), 'Termination benefits for executives of Australian companies', *Sydney Law Review* **27**: 683–714.

Stapledon, GP (2004), 'The pay for performance dilemma', *Griffith Law Review* **13**: 57–73.

Stapledon, Geof (1996), *Institutional Shareholders and Corporate Governance*, Oxford: Oxford University Press.

Stapledon, Geof, Ian Ramsay and Sandy Easterbrook (1999), *Proxy Voting in Australia's Largest Companies*, Research Report, Centre for Corporate Law and Securities Regulation, The University of Melbourne.

Statewide Superannuation Trust (2008), *Environmental, Social and Governance (ESG) Investment Policy*, Melbourne: Statewide Superannuation Trust.

Stensholt, John and Patrick Durkin (2010), 'Resources chiefs lead the way', *The Australian Financial Review* (Sydney), 17 November, pp. S2–3.

Stigler, George J (1975), 'Regulation: The confusion of means and ends', in George J Stigler, *The Citizen and the State: Essays on Regulation*, Chicago: Chicago University Press, pp. 167–77.

Study Group on Directors' Remuneration (1995), *Directors' Remuneration: Report of a Study Group chaired by Sir Richard Greenbury, London*: Gee and Co Ltd.

Sunstein, Cass (1996), 'Social norms and social roles', *Columbia Law Review* **96**: 903–68.

Super System Review (2010), *Final Report, Part I: Overview and Recommendations*, Canberra: Department of Treasury.

Swanson, Diane and Marc Orlitzky (2006), 'Executive preferences for compensation structure and normative myopia: A business and society research project', in Robert W Kolb (ed), *The Ethics of Executive Compensation*, Oxford: Blackwell Publishing Ltd, pp. 13–31.

Sweeney, John (1995), 'Does he just love being in control – Cedric Brown', *The Observer* (London), 30 April, p. 30.

Thomas, Randall and James Cotter (2007), 'Shareholder proposals in the new millennium: Shareholder support, board response and market reaction', *Journal of Corporate Finance* **13**: 368–91.

Thomas, Randall and Kenneth Martin (1999), 'The effect of shareholder proposals on executive compensation', *University of Cincinnati Law Review* **67**: 1021–81.

Thompson, Steve (2005), 'The impact of corporate governance reforms in the remuneration of executives in the UK', *Corporate Governance: An International Review* **13**: 19–25.

Tirole, Jean (2006), *The Theory of Corporate Finance*, Princeton, NJ and Oxford: Princeton University Press.

Trade and Industry Committee, House of Commons (2003), *The White Paper on Modernising Company Law*, Sixth Report of Session 2002–03 (HC439), London: The Stationery Office Limited.

Trades Union Congress (TUC) (2006), *TUC Fund Manager Voting Survey 2006*, London: TUC.

Treasury Committee, House of Commons (2009), *Reforming Corporate Governance and Pay in the City*, HC 519, London: The Stationery Office Limited.

United Nations Environment Programme Finance Initiative (UNEPFI) (2009), *Fiduciary Responsibility: Legal and Practical Aspects of Integrating Social, Environmental and Governance Issues into Institutional Investment*, Geneva: UNEPFI.

United Nations Environment Programme Finance Initiative (UNEPFI) (2006), *United Nations Principles for Responsible Investment*, Geneva: UNEPFI.

United Nations Environment Programme Finance Initiative (UNEPFI) (2005), *Fiduciary Responsibility: Legal and Practical Aspects of Integrating Social, Environmental and Governance Issues into Institutional Investment*, London: Freshfields Bruckhaus Deringer.

United States House of Representatives Committee on Oversight and Government Reform, Majority Staff (2007), *Executive Pay: Conflicts of Interest Among Compensation Consultants*, Washington, DC: Committee on Oversight and Government Reform.

Unknown (1997a), 'Boardroom salaries – appeal falls short of specific curbs on pay', *The Financial Times* (London), 26 November 1997, p. 10.

Unknown (1997b), 'Governance practices far below world best – AIMA', *The Australian* (Sydney), 25 July, p. 29.

Unknown (1996), 'Fund chiefs on perilous ground', *The Guardian* (Manchester), 27 September, p. 20.

Urban, Rebecca (2010), 'Proxy advisers are looking for love in all the right places', *The Australian* online (Sydney), 23 January, available at http://www.theaustralian.com.au/business/proxy-advisers-are-looking-for-love-in-all-the-right-places/story-e6frg8zx-1225822686383 (accessed 8 March 2012).

UTS Centre for Corporate Governance (2003), Submission from UTS Centre for Corporate Governance to Commonwealth Parliamentary Joint Committee on Corporations and Financial Services in respect of Exposure Draft – CLERP (Audit Reform and Disclosure) Bill 2003, 17 November, Sydney University of Technology, Sydney.

Villiers, Charlotte (2006), *Corporate Reporting and Company Law*, Cambridge and New York: Cambridge University Press.

Voulgaris, Georgis, Konstantinos Stathopoulos and Martin Walker (2010), 'Compensation consultants and CEO pay: UK evidence', *Corporate Governance: An International Review* **18**: 511–26.

Vroom, Victor (1964), *Work and Motivation,* New York: Wiley.

Wade, James, Joseph Porac, Timothy Pollack and Scott Graffin (2006), 'The burden of celebrity: The impact of CEO certification contests on CEO pay and performance', *Academy of Management Journal* **49**: 643–60.

Walker, David (2009), *A Review of Corporate Governance in UK Banks and Other Financial Industry Entities*, London: HM Treasury.

Walsh, Katie (2011a), 'Court upholds caps breach', *The Australian Financial Review* (Sydney), 9 August, p. 8.

Walsh, Katie (2011b), 'Clarity on relief for super tax penalties', *The Australian Financial Review* online, 22 December, available at http://afr.com/p/national/clarity_on_relief_for_super_tax_HvbIxOLobKp8Z rPSt2lfQI (accessed 8 March 2012).

Wen, S (2009), 'Institutional investor activism on socially responsible investment: Effects and expectations', *Business Ethics: A European Review* **18**: 308–33.

Working Group on Corporate Practices and Conduct (1995), *Corporate Practices and Conduct*, 3rd edition, Melbourne: F T Pitman.

Working Group on Corporate Practices and Conduct (1992), *Corporate Practices and Conduct*, 2nd edition, Melbourne: Information Australia.

Working Group on Corporate Practices and Conduct (1991), *Corporate Practices and Conduct*, Melbourne: Information Australia.

Yermack, David (2010), 'Shareholder voting and corporate governance', *Annual Review of Financial Economics* **2**: 103–25.

Index